Calendar Girl

Tricia Stewart is a director of a medical educational software company, which she runs with her husband Ian. She also teaches yoga and is training to teach Pilates. Along with the other calendar girls, she continues to raise money for the Leukaemia Research Fund. She has two children, Lizzi and Micky.

To Pam,

Merry Christmas,

TRICIA STEWART

Calendar Girl

In Which a Lady of Rylstone Reveals All

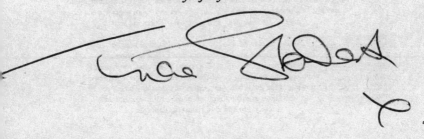

PAN BOOKS

First published 2001 by Sidgwick & Jackson

This edition published 2002 by Pan Books
an imprint of Pan Macmillan Ltd
Pan Macmillan, 20 New Wharf Road, London N1 9RR
Basingstoke and Oxford
Associated companies throughout the world
www.panmacmillan.com

ISBN 0 330 48994 1

The prayer on p. 23 is from *The William Barclay Prayer Book*,
edited by Ronald Barclay, reprinted with kind permission from
The William Barclay Estate and HarperCollins Publishers.

Picture credits
All photographs are from the author's private collection, unless otherwise stated.
Copyright © Northeast Press Limited, *Sunderland Echo*: page 1 – wedding photo.
Copyright © Terry Logan: page 1 – Micky, Angela and John; pages 3 and 4 (all);
page 6 – Angela; page 7 (all); page 8 – Tricia and Ian.

5 7 9 8 6 4

A CIP catalogue record for this book is available from
the British Library.

Typeset by SetSystems Ltd, Saffron Walden, Essex
Printed and bound in Great Britain by
Mackays of Chatham plc, Chatham, Kent

What an inspiration to be part of this experience. We had no idea it would bring new experiences, new friends and the rediscovery of old ones. The spirit and inspiration behind the calendar is John Baker. This book, which began as a diary of my letters to my daughter Lizzi, is the true story of an amazing reaction to our way of remembering a special, courageous man, with a great sense of humour. He will be enjoying every aspect of this calendar, alongside my Mam in heaven, or wherever we go.

To Ian, Lizzi, Micks, George; to everyone I have laughed with especially my friends at the Sheep Pens, all those mornings when ideas evolved into reality.

Contents

Acknowledgements

I am trying not to sound like the Baftas, but I understand why they have to do it!

My life has been full of wonderful people, family (especially my sisters who have patiently listened and advised on the lot!) and friends. I never thought I would be telling these special people in a book, written by me, how much I have enjoyed their love and friendship and encouragement.

Firstly, a big thank you to my friends from school for the humorous way they dealt with my mobile phone at the start of the media furore on the reunion weekend. We have laughed together for years.

I must say a heartfelt thank you to my original yoga group, inspired by Barbara, six brilliant joyous women, sharing experiences along with exercise. Now when we meet we share more experiences (mine lately) than exercise. I have appreciated all their sound advice and support.

The calendar – what can I say but a massive thank you to all who helped us: Graham Kennedy of Jennings Brewery for the launch and shipping out of 50,000 calendars; Nick Magoolagan for setting us on the path; Terry Fletcher and Carol Green for their advice as journalists; all our sponsors; Chris and Natalie Gregson of the Devonshire Arms Cracoe; Rylstone & District

WI for their patience and support; local businesses who sold calendars FOC for us; WI Head Office for allowing us to use the 'WI' name; the LRF team for their marvellous support; the calendar team – the eleven brave girls who took their clothes off for such a worthwhile cause; Terry Logan, our photographer for making us look so good that over 300,000 people wanted the calendar on their walls.

What can I say about the new friends I have made through the calendar? It has been a privilege meeting them, especially Preethi, the wise one; Amanda with her angels; Diana who made this book happen; Ene Riisna from the US *20/20* show who found us an agent and took the calendar to America; Agnes and the *60 Minutes* crew; Workman Publishing in New York; Kim and Ellen Morgenstern whom we love; Sean Stowell from BBC who made the best documentary; my publishers, Pan Macmillan; my own editor Catherine Hurley (fancy!); Bryn, Saks, hairdresser to the Calendar Girls; the men behind the calendar girls for their patience, support and dedication to shifting calendars; 'Mr September' John Clancy for cleverly coming up with 'Baker's Half Dozen'; cheers to the Baker's half-dozen girls for having the courage to continue fundraising in the nude. What a team!

Finally, to my friend Sheila who told me to get on and write a book.

To: Lizzi Stewart, Flat 51, Bayview Waters, Piermont, Sydney, Australia

22 July 1998

Dear Lizzi

I'm writing this after one of the hardest phone conversations I've ever had. I simply didn't know how to tell you that John had died. I never thought this would happen. I was so sure he would survive — even in the last few hours I believed he would improve. I'm sure that John believed he would beat it, too, although he had spoken about how he had deteriorated in the last week. Last night he developed a chest infection that they couldn't control. They gave him massive antibiotics, he was drifting in and out of sleep, still smiling when he woke up. Later it developed into pneumonia. Ange couldn't bear for him to have any more discomfort. She asked him if he had had enough and he said yes. She kissed him and told him she loved him, and the last thing he said was that he loved her. They sat with him and talked about family holidays, all they'd done over the years, laughed and cried. His time in the hospital in Leeds has been tortuous for the whole family. There could have been a chance and he wanted to take it, he had coped so well with the chemo although he was weak.

Throughout it all he has been so brave and strong, never complained, just loved Ange and worried about her. People say she has become strong, but we know she has always been strong. She has supported and cherished John, been terrified, seen problems and pushed for a solution, given him injections and looked after him so well. I can't understand why they lost in the end and I don't think I ever will. Rachel and Matthew have been wonderful, supported her and looked after their dad in a totally unselfish way. They are so with her now, but their lives will never be the same. What a loss he is. I am sure they expected him to be here for ever, like a rock for them all.

Lynda and I saw John last night. Ange asked us to come and say goodbye. We stayed a while, then left so they could settle down for the night. On the way out we looked up at John's window from the car park but couldn't see anyone. John must have died then, and they were beside him, all held hands and said a prayer. The nurses went into the room, they were crying too.

It was terrible to hear you sound devastated on the phone. I am sorry I led you to believe this wouldn't happen, I was so sure. I am really pleased you are coming home, it will be wonderful to see you. You are right, why would you want to be out there when this has happened.

Night night my angel, see you soon.

    Lots of love,

    Mum xxxxx

*

John Baker's death hit our little community hard. You don't know until you lose someone just how important a part of your life they have been. He and his wife Angela were my great friends and, as in small, close-knit communities everywhere, we all instantly rallied round Ange. We could only begin to imagine how we'd miss our friend when his death really began to sink in, but for now we needed to help Angela through this terrible time.

At least Lizzi was coming home, thank you God for that. Lizzi, my twenty-one-year-old daughter, had set off for Thailand in November 1997, with plans to travel to Australia and New Zealand and stay away at least a year. When I told Lizzi of John's death her instant reaction was to get home to us as quickly as possible.

'Home' was the village of Cracoe in North Yorkshire. It is a typical Dales village, full of traditional stone houses, overlooked by the Fell, the fields split by drystone walls. We are so lucky to live in Cracoe, looking straight out of our window on to the hills, in every direction in the village is a walk. A stream runs through the croft behind our garden, where George, our Labrador, plays when there are no sheep. The people here are diverse: farmers, National Park employees, businessmen, teachers, lawyers, artists and nurses. About 200 people in all. There is a farm shop, a café and a pub – all anyone could need. Lots goes on, the pub, the Devonshire (the Dev) is the hub of the village. During the period of my story it was run by Chris and Natalie Gregson, who have taken the village to their hearts and vice versa. They are about the same ages as Lizzi and Micky, who have both worked there and become good friends.

We have lived here for fifteen years, but would still be called 'offcumdens' by locals – in a friendly, caring way, I hope. I was born in Sunderland, proud of my roots and my accent, but love the Dales, although I do miss the seaside. We found a difference in Yorkshire folk when we first moved to Skipton, not as up front friendly as in the North East, where you invite everyone who comes to your door in and force them to have a cup of tea. We stood on a few doorsteps at first but now have loads of good friends. I had a wonderful childhood in Sunderland, the youngest of five children and a twin. Two brothers and two sisters, the perfect mix – Peter, Ibber, Marg and John. My mam was forty-six when she had the twins – John and me. She was wonderful, loved us all and never seemed older than any of our friends'

mams. She always said there was 'worse things than bairns' –
usually when she heard someone was pregnant! My mam died ten
years ago but she's still very much alive in my heart. I think about
her every day. I had the same kind of close relationship with her
as Lizzi and I do, although not so candid on sex. (My mam used
to say 'your father took care of all that', which is probably why
there were five of us.) Lizzi and I are very close. We're near
enough the same size and since she was about sixteen, we've been
fortunate enough to be able to share each other's clothes – except
shoes. She has been lucky not to be six foot with size 10 feet. Ian
is 6 ft 2 in, I am 5 ft 10 in with size 8 feet (7 on a good day)
and Lizzi is 5 ft 9 in and takes size 6. I have always been gutted I
couldn't wear her shoes.

Ian and I met as student radiographers at Sunderland Royal
Infirmary, not love at first sight (although it did cross my mind
that I would marry him but I have never told him that). He was
very handsome and cool – a lot like Micky is now. He said he
was attracted by my freckles and spectacular legs, he can still
remember what I was wearing – we could have gone on *Mr &
Mrs*. He was in the year behind me so benefited from having all
my books free and studying at my house instead of a freezing flat.
Student life was just hilarious on Cherry Bs and cheap cider. We
married in 1971 and two years later, in 1973, we moved to
Skipton when Ian left radiography to work for Ilford X-Ray. Five
years after that we moved out to Cracoe, when we bought the
house of friends moving from the village. By then, Ian had left
Ilford X-Ray and set up his own business selling medical software.
I ran the office for him, doing all the admin while he went and
saw the customers.

For Ian and me the first twenty-six years were good but we
lost something after that. Perhaps it was the fact that Lizzi and
Micky were leaving the nest and we had to adjust to being 'us'
again. We seemed to have lost sight of each other, or maybe it's
truer to say that I felt Ian had lost sight of me. We argued a lot,

usually because I wanted to do stuff like cycling, walking and swimming. Ian didn't, he preferred to go to the pub and relax. I wanted him to be fitter but though he was always buying new exercise gadgets which ended up gathering dust, he never wanted to join in the things that I liked doing. Before we had the kids we had a speedboat and used to go to Windermere every weekend to water-ski. Once Lizzi was born we sold it because I was scared I would be drowned and not be there to look after her. Ian and Micky had motorbikes when Micky was eight and rode around the Dales, but they are long gone, although Ian still dreams of a Harley Davidson. We had totally focused on the kids together and been at one and now that was slipping away. Perhaps also careerwise Ian was not happy. Our business was reasonably successful but it was becoming more and more difficult to live and work together. Ian might have been happier if his work life had been more distant from our home life.

Most of my mornings began with walking George up Fell Lane to a spot we'd christened the Sheep Pens, the collecting place for the sheep off the Fell. For a long time now Ros and her cocker spaniel, Polly came along and, on fine days, my neighbour Angela also joined us for the walk. Ros and I had had a go at jogging around the village to get fit, but we never quite took to it and were soon back to walking to the Sheep Pens. Each morning, before work Ange and I met Ros at the corner of Fell Lane and, totally ignoring the dogs, we just talked all the way up. We'd stop there and do two complete yoga breaths, three corkscrews (a Pilates exercise for the neck and shoulders), then back down, still talking. Everything – husbands, children, dieting – was discussed and usually resolved. Then I usually had my breakfast at Angela's, John had got into the habit of setting a place for me and he would have it ready when we returned. Ian would already have left for work.

Angela was one of the first neighbours to call when we moved to Cracoe from Skipton. She introduced herself and her family:

her husband John and her children, Matthew who was twelve and Rachel, fifteen. Lizzi and Micky were eight and six respectively. She asked me if I would like to join WI. I was thirty-five then and admitted it hadn't been on my list of priorities. Ange told me that people would think I was funny if I didn't join. Luckily I became a member, taken to my first meeting by Ange, and in due course I would save her from a few nervous breakdowns over WI flower arrangements. Before I knew her, she had volunteered for a 'show theme' arrangement, chosen *Chess*, so a black and white arrangement. Her flowers were four foot long when she started. When John came home from work, they were about three inches and she was in tears. He stuck them in her chosen receptacle and, with red eyes hidden by sunglasses, disguised in a headscarf, she deposited her entry in the 'Bulb Show' at Skipton Town Hall and rushed out. She got 8 out of 20. Not worth a nervous breakdown. He told her never to enter a competition again.

We were 'neighbourly' friends at first, but became closer when I was recovering from a thyroid operation in 1987. Ange herself had a terrible five years with illness from 1993 to 1998, and had lots of operations. Matthew played cricket with Micky, Rachel babysat, even though Micky was wild (in an appealing way). I loved to go to Ange's house, there was always yummy stuff to eat, served nicely, without the chaos of our house. Their door was always open and they were so welcoming. The kids would play in their garden, being mindful of John's lawn! Then, we had a black Labrador called Digger, who Ange and John looked after when we were away, and always took on their walks. He loved them too, as George did.

Ros Fawcett owned the Cracoe Café when we first came to Cracoe. She has two children James and Helen, the same ages as Lizzi and Micky. They all played out together, in the safety of village lanes, a stream, straw to make dens, trees to climb, riding bikes and roller-skating. Micky especially loved Ros, wanted her to be his replacement mum if ever he needed one, and not just because he loved the strawberry ice-cream at the café. Ros had always avoided Angela's invitations to join WI because having run a café all day, she didn't want to make suppers for WI. When I was ill after my thyroid operation, Ros came around every day, like Little Red Riding Hood, after a hard day's work at her café with a big basket of freshly cooked food for us all. My mam, who visited from Sunderland regularly, also loved Ros, said she was so 'bonny' with wonderful kind eyes. If you sliced her like a stick of rock, I know kindness would be written all through. She has a brilliant sense of humour, very dry and clever. She worked so hard, with two little children, but always had time for people. She sold the café and, for the last five years, has run a dress agency in Skipton, where all my clothes come from. She is my true friend.

Ange more successfully recruited Lynda Logan to WI. My first recollection of Lynda is striding through Skipton in hat and cowboy boots (fully dressed), looking very superior. She owned the wool shop and my mam and I often went in there. I didn't know her as a friend until she moved to Cracoe to the house next door to Ange and John, then really got to know her when she joined WI. Ange knocked on her door and asked if she would like to come to WI with us and Lynda laughed (in a superior way!) and said she didn't really think it was her scene. However we persisted and got her there as a guest, she won £50 in the raffle and joined! Our friendship developed from then, living so near. She has two grandchildren, Edward and Helena, who is also Angela's granddaughter. (Ange's son Matthew married Lynda's daughter Georgina.)

Lynda paints in oils (her husband Terry Logan is also an artist) and had done a couple of paintings of Lizzi. About a year before John became ill I'd had an idea for Lynda to paint some of us girls in the nude, in a group, before we got much older and deteriorated, discreetly covering each other, then we could all hang it over our mantelpieces. A kind of celebration of our friendship. She brought a sketch of Ros, Angela, me and Lynda and our other friends Moyra, Sandra and Mary (who is Ros's business partner at the dress shop) to WI one night and had us all discussing where and how to take a photo for Lynda to paint. We decided on a little wood/copse dressed in bin bags, which we would whip off when the photographer was set up. We chuckled over that but that's about all.

Lynda and Terry's dog Brady was in unrequited love with our then dog Digger – both boys, but we are free spirited in the Dales. Lynda helped us with our new puppy, George, coming in every day to let him out and feed him. Digger had grown old and we had bought the golden Labrador puppy so the kids wouldn't be so upset when Digger went to the big kennel in the sky. Unfortunately he lived another year and I would come home from work each night to two children, two dogs, piles of puppy poo covered with newspaper, because it made them sick to clear it up. I, of course, relished it. Lynda and Terry now have a collie called Sky who likes to watch television. It's a shame *That's Life* isn't on any more, she could be on!

Sandra Sayers, who lived across the road in Cracoe with her husband Philip, would often drop by in the evenings and walk George with me. Sandra and I had known each other before I moved to Cracoe. She and her sister Leni had a wonderful Interior Design shop in Skipton, where I'd first met them. She and I joined the WI about the same time.

All of these friends came to a yoga class I'd set up at the village hall. I'd done yoga for years, since before Lizzi was born. I'd started at a local class in Skipton where my teacher was a lady called Barbara Goodman. Meeting Barbara all those years ago changed my life. She made me realize the true value of things, appreciate the outdoors, walking, cycling, and that less was more. She was definitely a woman before her time, especially on green issues. She would often babysit for us and then Ian and I were free to go out without worry, and no time limit to return. She would sleep over and walk our dog the next day before we got up! My mam loved her, I have wonderful memories of all the times we had together, forcing me to drive and not be a wimp, mending our bikes, all sorts of things, she was a true soulmate. We'd kept that yoga group going for years and still met up once a month or as often as we could manage, not so much for exercise now as support and counselling. The group would listen to the events of my life unfold like a penny novel, as my mam would have said.

One night, washing up after our WI meeting, someone started talking about a yoga class in Grassington, a village three miles down the road. Barbara had often said that I could teach it and when one of the group, Moyra suggested that I start a class in the village hall, I thought why not, even though I was scared stiff. I did a plan and made Lizzi work through it to time it and give me confidence. Lizzi has always said, whatever I want to do, 'you can do it Mum'. On my first night, about ten neighbours and friends turned up and it settled into a usual class of ten or twelve. I was grateful to Moyra for making me do it. Moyra Livesey had moved to the nearby village of Rylstone some time after we moved to Cracoe and she joined our circle of friends and, naturally, WI. Very confident and capable, she was instrumental in organizing WI and social activities.

I tried to get Ian to come along to the yoga class because by this point he was overweight and smoking a lot and I wanted him to be fit. But he preferred to meet us in the pub afterwards. That emphasized the differences between us and seemed to symbolize the difficulties that had set into our relationship. I tried, unsuccessfully, to make him exercise more. His mam had died at fifty-six of heart disease and I worried a lot about him having a heart attack. Lizzi worried and nagged with me, while Micky had a more 'live and let live' attitude, but they both knew that it caused tension between us. After many arguments, I made a conscious decision not to nag any more, just to do my own thing with exercise, especially my yoga group, which had developed into a great combination of 'students'. This switch-off made our relationship deteriorate even more.

The yoga class was in Cracoe Memorial Hall, known to locals as the 'Hut'. A wooden building, draughty, basic, but wonderful. The Hall was rebuilt with Millennium and Lottery grants in 2000, and we now have a superb village hall, but I still have a great fondness for our original 'Hut'. Our yoga classes took place there on a Friday night. The heating would be on, but not really warm. I would light candles all around, Enya playing and a joss-stick or two. I wanted everything to combine to give that relaxed feeling of letting go of the outside world, especially on a Friday night after a week at work.

After a chat, we'd lie down, legs up the wall and start with gentle stretches, some Pilates, some Alexander Technique, then on to stronger exercises. No competition, everyone letting their bodies tell them what to do. After an hour came relaxation, the best time of all! Warmth is needed to relax properly, especially in a chilly hut, so cosy clothes and socks on and either in sleeping bags or under a blanket. There was a huge sigh of relief from the whole class. John would settle down immediately to go to sleep. Before total relaxation, I liked them to chill with alternate nostril breathing, candlegazing or sometimes 'om'. John refused to do any of it, just lay flat. He was waiting for the 'bedtime story', some words of wisdom which I read after I had talked them through total relaxation. He told me once not to rush those words, but to say them slowly and meaningfully. I tried to heed his words and slow down.

That year, after Lizzi left to go to Australia, we had our Christmas yoga class, with mince pies and sherry as usual. Cucumber on the eyes (in slices) and legs up the wall, a very relaxing evening. If only we all did this each day, there would be a lot less stress, especially with Ian, things could improve. The class always looked so funny with the cucumber on their eyes, but so relaxed! One night I spoke and ten heads with cucumber on the eyes all turned towards me, it made me chuckle. The group was good together, full of positive energies. I had decided to give an award for the most improved pupil of 1997. A homemade award, of course, made from an old rosette, on which I wrote 'most improved pupil'. I know yoga is not competitive, but John had improved so much, especially after having his hip replacement, that the award had to be his. During sherry and mince pies, I announced the winner. For his valour, courage and sheer strength of spirit in returning to yoga a 'new hip' man (and even though he'd never do the alternate nostril breathing), I gave John his badge. He was overcome, but not as much as Ros, who'd thought the award was hers. John turned to Ros and said, 'Well, you've something to strive for next year.'

The yoga group and the WI formed the basis of our social life in Cracoe. If you weren't doing the Cat, you'd probably be baking a cake or knitting a cardigan for the monthly meeting. It was a supportive and friendly community and we had some wonderful times.

I remember one magical night especially. It started in Lynda and Terry's garden, then ours, following the sun until we were in the field behind Lynda and Terry's house, which we called 'Far back of Terry's' (that is how old farmers named their fields). We sat on the grass: Sandra and Philip, me and Ian, Ange and John, Lynda and Terry, Philip and Ian played guitars, Sandra, Lynda and Angela sang. We were all very drunk. Ange usually watched what John drank but, hidden by Ian, he was drinking whisky in secret. On big nights out he would sit between Ros and Mary, fellow whisky drinkers, and they would fill his glass secretly! We laughed and joked, and kept running back to our houses for more drink and food.

Whatever we were doing, we always laughed. I discovered early in our friendship, for example, that I could really make John

Baker laugh. John had quite a stern exterior but he had a great sense of humour. Angela would say that he was good for at least one belly laugh a day. The first time we went on holiday together, to Tolon in Greece, it was a revelation for John. On their previous holidays, Angela hadn't been allowed to have a sun-lounger, umbrella or a coffee on the beach – John was careful. He used to tell her to go in the sea if she was hot. In complete contrast, the Stewart family always hit the shops immediately, new lilos, snorkel, masks, flippers and umbrella, kitted out in seconds. Trying out new cafés, hiring sunloungers, water skiing and windsurfing, the Bakers were soon in the swing, Angela and me popping off for drinks all day. They had never had such a hectic holiday, it was brilliant.

Once we all went together to Opera in the Dales, *Carmen* at Burnsall Village Hall. An experience to say the least, John and I laughed a lot, in fact I felt an uncontrollable wave of hysteria at one point and John was in tears of laughter, especially after the hot punch in the interval. The passion of the love scene just didn't seem to grip us, on that little stage in the village hall, looking at the Captain's white socks, thrashing about on a narrow bed.

*

It felt a bit like I was going through the motions that first Christmas without Lizzi. I've always loved Christmas and in Cracoe it is wonderful. My son Micky would be home for Christmas. He was away at University in Liverpool but he was always popping in and out, hanging around, concerned about how I was managing without Lizzi, always rushing back from Uni to see me. Sometimes I wish he would just be like normal sons and ignore me! If only. He was nineteen then, bit of a free spirit, never really committed to the educational system. From his birth he could break my heart with a look or a careless word and still can. But Christmas wouldn't really be the same without

Lizzi, in fact wasn't really the same without little children. Christmas for the Stewarts had always been such a family time. Marg and Ralph, Steve and Helen (my sister, her husband, son and daughter) always came for a country Christmas in Yorkshire and the house was full. When we did the Sainsbury Christmas shop we couldn't fit another morsel in the car, and drove home surrounded by French sticks. We had brilliant times, all up at 4 a.m., no one allowed downstairs until we were all awake – setting up Scalextric and train sets, eating selection boxes and feeling bilious by breakfast time. Steve and Helen were grown up now with their own homes to celebrate in, which is wonderful and how it should be. Marg and Ralph would be visiting them. I would be putting the tree up on my own this year.

And of course, Christmas wouldn't be Christmas without the WI dinner. The WI is at the centre of so much that we do, all year round, really. It sometimes feels like there's more than twelve meetings a year, like periods. The Women's Institute originated in Canada, then came to Britain in the early 1900s. The WI nationally offers women the opportunity of friendship, sharing and learning – not just in traditional interests such as arts and crafts, but in the latest developments in IT, health, fitness and science. Those values are still vital, but also WI campaigns on high-profile topics such as human rights, women's health, sustainable development of the environment, AIDS awareness, pensions, justice and support for rape victims, and can comment on a wide range of issues.

Locally, each month we meet at the village hall, have a business meeting, a speaker (who range in topics from Tiller girls to conservationists), then supper. The suppers are on a rota system, three members each month, so for eleven months you relax, one month a year you make supper. Rylstone & District WI are well known for their yummy suppers. There is a raffle and a competition each month. The competition points are added up over the year and a rose bowl is awarded at the Christmas dinner to the winner. The annual spring show is called the Bulb Show. These are competitive shows, organized by the different WI groups. Entries include flower arrangements, produce, various handicrafts, such as needlework and knitting. My first exhibit was a child's cardigan, which I sat up nearly all night to finish and the judge's comment was 'would have been better if buttons had fitted the buttonholes'. I never knitted another!

The first Thursday of every month was WI and we, that is Angela, Lynda and I, would often grumble on WI nights after a busy week at work, but after the speaker, the chat and supper, which was always very good, I'd come home glad to have gone after all. We were some of the younger members, so it was often us who volunteered for whatever was going on. That year we had our Christmas dinner at the Dev, they always looked after us. It was a laugh and, as I wrote to Lizzi, I was lucky this year not to get yet another freezer bag clip out of the present basket (a girl can only use so many!).

There was the annual WI carol service at the Catholic church in Threshfield which I always love even though I'm tone deaf. Angela did a reading. I thought about it, but I didn't dare. Hell, I get palpitations giving the vote of thanks at our WI meetings and I know everyone there. We lit a candle for Lizzi in Oz, and everyone had a good sing while I had a good mime. Then mince pies and a cup of tea. Ian and I went on to the village quiz afterwards at the Dev, and played with Lynda and Terry, did OK, but not good enough to win. Not even the raffle, which made Ian cross. He wasn't the only one who seemed to believe that winning the quiz was life or death. There were some nasty moments when the winners were announced, it was very competitive. The fun is in winning not in taking part!

Ian and I were rubbing along, arguing over vital issues like whether to have turkey breast or the whole works. During one of our frequent rows, he spat out that he'd been planning to send me on a surprise trip to see Lizzi in Australia, but thought perhaps he wouldn't now. He'd spoken to Lizzi about it and she wrote him this letter which explains at lot, I think.

Letter from Lizzi to Ian, written on 7 December 1997:

Haad Rin Beach, Ko Pha-Ngan, Thailand

Dear Dad,

Thank you for the fax, it was lovely to hear from you. I am absolutely fine and Thailand is fantastic. We are in Ko Pha-Ngan at the minute before moving to Krala tomorrow, then maybe Phuket. We have very few days left really as we have to be in Kuala Lumpur by the 14th or 15th December.

I think the ticket for Mum is a wonderful idea. I will have to talk to you once I get to Aussie, though, around the 21st/22nd of December. I have to be very honest here and say that I am planning on coming home around the end of February/beginning of March because I know I won't be able to stay away from Adrian for that long. I think three months away will be plenty. So it would be a good plan for Mum and I to come home together and maybe stop in Fiji or somewhere for a few days. I think it's a brilliant idea. BUT DON'T TELL HER! I know how easy it is when you've got such an exciting secret to let it slip, but you have to be strong. Over the phone I will also tell her not to bother booking anything because I want to come home around then. Even if she is being shitty with you, don't turn round and say 'well, I won't bother booking your surprise trip to Australia'. PROMISE!!

I hope you two are sorting things out back there. Things were looking pretty dire when I left. You know the only thing you have to do, don't you? Exercise. That's it. I know Mum is really worried about you, especially about a stroke. Dad, it is so important to look after yourself. There are men out here 50+ with young babies up doing yoga every morning looking really young and fit. You just have to make it a way of life. And, the most important thing is that you are doing it for yourself. That *you* make a conscious decision to change your life and just do it. Don't get anyone else involved, you don't need to. If you do want any advice ring Adrian, because he knows loads. Please don't be an old-looking, middle-aged man sneaking behind rugby stands for cigarettes and sneaking glasses of whisky. Stand in front of a mirror and say 'is this who and what I really want to be at 50?' And I think you'll find the answer is probably 'no'. Come on Dad, you know how it feels to lose a parent, the most important person in your life. Please, please Dad, don't put me and Micky through that. There's so many simple things you can do to prevent it. OK? Have you taken all this in? All right, that's the lecture over, I hope you have taken some of it in, because I really mean it. I could not stand to lose you, so make a promise right now. Make today the first day of the rest of your life.

Guess there is not much more to say here. I miss you lots and I love you so much. Love to Mum.

All my love,

Liz xx

Well, Ian and I blew the surprise bit of it, but I still planned to go and see Lizzi and Australia. I hummed and hawed about the expense of the trip but when a £500 Nordic Track arrived for Ian to put his clothes on – his latest exercise toy – I sent it back and booked a ticket.

What a brilliant decision. I had a wonderful time in Sydney with Lizzi, a city with beaches. Such a healthy outdoor life in the sunshine – how heavenly to go to the beach after work. The people looked good, happy, chilled and the restaurants were great. My forty-ninth birthday was ace. I wondered how I could possibly top it for my fiftieth. I'd been staying in Lizzi's flat, which she shared with six friends, near the beach in Sydney. It was marvellous. On my birthday morning we had cards, pressies and balloons in the flat. I bought a February 11th *Sydney Herald* as a souvenir. We had brunch at Studio 4, the café down the road from the flat, next to the news studio. Sunbathed, swam, showered and off to Toni and Guy's, Sydney for haircuts. My stylist was lovely, I felt totally relaxed after my head massage, just let him do what he wanted (with my hair). Lizzi's was French and came up to her waist. We bought a crate of Fosters and a couple of bottles of Shiraz for the boys and girls at the flat for that night. Lunch, then home to shower and into black frocks and high heels for the opera. Drinks on the balcony and took the bus to the Harbour and the Opera House. It was a lovely warm night with loads going on. We sat a little impatiently through the opera – the usual plot – attraction, lust, love, jealousy, betrayal, murder and suicide. We had good seats, and we could see the English subtitles, which enhanced the plot for us. The couple in front made a point of not looking at them. Surrounding us were what were obviously Americans on a whistlestop tour of Oz. Halfway through the third act, the American lady next to me said to lean across her so we could see the Southern Cross. I thought she meant in the sky, but realized it was on stage left. I leaned across her (she smelt of moth balls), then she made Lizzi look as well, so it was a long lean for her. When she sat back, her seat had gone up and she slithered to the floor. We were overcome with hysteria, as she struggled back up. The non-subtitle couple in front told us to be quiet, and an usherette was on her way, so we had to contain ourselves until the next interval. Lizzi thought it was a bonus that we were let out between Acts. We had a glass of wine, sat on the steps of Sydney Opera House, ate a box of Maltesers and looked across the Harbour at the lights on the water. We walked back, called in at a bar called the Rocks for a Southern Comfort, then home. Ian had sent wonderful exotic flowers for my real birthday (in Oz it was a day early). I was quite touched, but wondered how much it had cost to send flowers in Australia.

If somebody had said stay another month I would have done,

but even so, I was looking forward to being home and seeing everyone. It was hard leaving Lizzi, trying not to cry. We'd had such a joyful time together. After a long, dull flight, Ian picked me up from the airport with the news that John Baker had had a CT scan because they suspected a tumour. This was out of the blue – John had seemed fine when I left. Angela had had more than her share of health scares over the last five years, but John had seemed so fit and healthy. What a shock.

2

As soon as I got home I went round to Angela's. She seemed stunned by the news. She told me that John was having an operation the next day to remove a tumour from his colon, the diagnosis was non-Hodgkin's lymphoma. I just couldn't believe it. All this while I had been away, Lizzi and I had been completely unaware of this dreadful news. He would need six months of chemotherapy after the operation. They were both sat on the settee in the lounge. Ange was shocked by the suddenness of the diagnosis. John calmly said it would be OK, that he would be fine. He was so positive and brave, calm and philosophical, in control like always that I felt sure he would be OK. I didn't really feel afraid for him.

I was so glad to be back home to help them. John, who had encouraged Lizzi to travel when she'd wavered, telling her not to miss a wonderful opportunity, didn't want Lizzi to come home when he'd got ill and Angela agreed. It was so hard to tell Lizzi. I knew she would want to come straight back but I managed to convince her to stay and John was adamant he would see her at the end of her trip. Over the last couple of years Lizzi and John had become really close. He had helped her with her dissertation, encouraging her to study, giving her deadlines.

What followed was horrendous. John came out of hospital

after about three weeks to recover at home from the operation and get ready for his chemo. Angela seemed to be coping really well. We were all devastated, really, but rallying round for Angela and her children Rachel and Matthew. Like lots of people who come up against the serious illness of a friend, we decided to raise some money for the ward where John was treated. I had baked cakes for coffee mornings and helped at school functions but never really fund raised for a particular cause.

We decided to walk the Three Peaks to raise money – about thirty of us (Ian opted out – no surprise there). When we spoke to John about it, he wasn't keen to begin with. As Assistant National Parks Officer, he'd seen the damage done through erosion and these now common fund-raising walks had caused their share of damage. But in the end he gave us his blessing. We began a training programme organized by David Livesey, who we now called Red Leader.

At this time Ian's and my office was on the Business Park at Broughton Hall, a stately home whose estate has been converted to offices. To celebrate the 400th anniversary of the Tempest family, there was a mega 'do' on the estate in a massive marquee for 900 people. Roger Tempest had formed a band, made up of business people on the estate. Ian was lead vocals and harmonica. The evening was fantastic, the band was a huge success, I felt really proud of Ian, so did Lizzi. Sandra and Philip, Adrian and Lizzi and I ended up skinny-dipping (secretly) in the Hall's private pool. The 'Broughton Blues Band' continued to practise and play together. Ian suggested they play again to raise funds for John. He was doing his bit, instead of walking. I think the men were particularly shocked by John's illness, but it seemed easier for us women to physically help, so the walk was a great way for them to be involved, like the band was for Ian.

Some days John was well enough to sit out in the sun in their garden, but other days he was really bad. I kept popping in, trying to help Angela, who was coping amazingly, though she was petrified most of the time. She said she wanted to run away, for it all to be a dream, but she was and is so brave. Sometimes I'd stay over because the nights could be long and frightening. One night, John was so ill, we rushed him to emergency, he was nearly in renal failure. Lynda was at the house too and came in the car to the hospital. John was worried that Ange wasn't eating so had made Lynda cook home-made broth under his instruction, to build her up!

The staff on the ward were on full alert for us and I think it was then that we began to realize just how serious this was. The next day John started his chemotherapy and was in and out of the hospital every few days. He would be OK, then his temperature would rise, and he would have to go back into hospital immediately in case it was due to an infection.

One weekend when John was feeling good, he gardened and cooked and it was almost like old times. Georgina, his daughter-in-law, brought him a packet of sunflower seeds because she'd noticed that lots of his get well cards had sunflowers on them. She suggested he pot them up, then give the plants out to all his friends and family, to grow for him, because when they bloomed, he'd be in remission. He seemed almost calm, quite spiritual about his illness. We could still make him laugh, especially when we talked about the next idea we'd had for fund-raising. The Alternative WI Calendar. Following on from the idea of our nude friends painting, I'd come up with another idea. At one WI meeting, when our president asked if we had any photos to submit for the WI calendar, which traditionally comprises countryside scenes, village greens, sheep and postboxes, I just thought we could do an alternative in the nude, featuring the crafts of the WI – in the tasteful style of the Pirelli calendar. I told Ange, who just laughed. Over supper I shared the idea with a few more girls, who also laughed. John did too as we described the different poses, in the garden, behind a fence or a garden seat, all nude. We said that John could be the token man, that he could watch us while he was getting better. I could just picture him sitting in a chair, in his dressing gown. He said we would never do it, that we were all talk. It was a bit of a joke that made us all, and especially John, laugh.

He was determined to get to a rugby match, to watch Wharfedale play, despite having been rushed into hospital with a high temperature the day before. Matthew and Angela took him to the game. He stayed in the Land Rover, all warm and cosy and thoroughly enjoyed the match. What a star! From seeming steady that day, we'd watch him go downhill again the next week, after his next chemo.

All we could do was carry on and hope. One night, we did the annual Fashion Show for Vogue (Ros's dress agency) in Skipton to raise funds for WI. As usual, we all modelled the clothes and sold tickets to other WIs. It was in the Hut and Ian had recorded some upbeat catwalk music for us to sashay to, but unfortunately we had to turn it off, because it was too loud and the audience couldn't hear the commentary. It was amusing, I had to model a flowery frock with big sleeves and a belted waist, I looked like Heidi skipping down the mountains. John insisted Angela come and model, even though he was still in hospital, on antibiotics again for a high temperature.

Throughout his illness John never complained or seemed scared. One night when I was away, Ros stayed with them. John was dreadfully sick during the night and they called an ambulance. Ros said he sat in bed and told Angela he wouldn't travel in the ambulance without something in his stomach; he wanted a Weetabix. Ange refused to get him anything because he would surely be sick in the ambulance. They argued and Ange turned to Ros and asked her what to do – she said 'give him a bloody Weetabix'. He ate every bit and wasn't sick in the ambulance! He could be so stubborn, especially about food. He took great comfort in his faith and the fact that people were praying for him. Ros said that terrible night, after the Weetabix, he read a prayer whilst waiting for the ambulance. She had never seen anyone do this before, it seemed such a private moment and it really touched her.

> O God help me to live one day at a time
> Not to be thinking of what might have been,
> Not to be worrying about what may be,
> Help me to accept the fact that I cannot undo the past and
>   I cannot foresee the future,
> Help me to remember that I will be never tried beyond what
>   I can bear,
> That a Father's hand will never cause his child a needless tear,
> That I can never drift beyond your love and care.

Each morning, his friends from their Methodist Chapel met there to say prayers for John. Even though he was clearly very ill, he was still looking out for Angela. They had always been a close, supportive couple, really enjoyed each other's company, we all dreaded the thought of Angela on her own. When she would ask me if I thought John would die, I always answered no, because I couldn't imagine her surviving without him. I was so positive he would get better, I think I made other people believe it too. Ironically, the thing that worried me most was that my sunflower, which John had given me to grow, was dying. I couldn't bear to think of it as an omen.

Saturday, 27 June, the morning of our twenty-six mile Three Peaks Walk dawned. What a day, torrential rain and we could hardly see a hand in front. The first peak, Pen-y-Ghent was shrouded in mist, very Bronte-ish. Unfortunately no sign of a Heathcliffe. Nearly thirty of us met in the car park at the village of Horton, all wrapped up, trying to be positive about the weather. At least we weren't lonely, there were 450 Heart Foundation walkers with us too. It was a struggle up the steep rocky face then nothing but bleakness down the other side. We couldn't see any scenery for the rain. The second 'peak' was Great

Whernside. After a change of clothes at the checkpoint (where Ian was positioned with coffee, sarnies and dry clothes) the rain stopped and the sun shone. The third peak, Ingleborough looked like Mont Blanc; we decided not to look ahead but take one step at a time. We eventually reached the top and it was a wonderful feeling. We rang Angela and John from there to say we had done it. He was in Airedale Hospital, so proud of us all.

It took us about ten hours in all and we arrived back at the car park at seven-ish, all lying about, chilling. Home for a long soak, then Chris and Natalie put on a Three Peaks supper for us all, with a meat and potato pie featuring three peaks on the top. It felt so good to have completed the walk. There was a great atmosphere in the pub. We had taken lots of photos to show John that we'd actually done it.

The lift that we got from the walk was soon dispelled by the awful reality that John didn't seem to be improving. Angela and Matthew had lobbied hard to get John a place on the Lymphoma Unit at Leeds where he was due to have stem-cell treatment – an awful procedure but John wanted to go through with it. But it was here that John died in the early hours of Wednesday 22 July 1998, after three weeks' treatment in Leeds General Infirmary and only five months after being diagnosed with cancer.

The night before, Angela asked me to come and say goodbye and I had driven over with Lynda, still believing despite all that John would recover. Even after I left John so ill that night, I'd been half-expecting a call from Matthew the next morning to say that John had rallied round. I think Angela knew better. When I got home from the hospital, the house was empty because Ian was away on business. I phoned Lizzi in Australia to tell her that it didn't look like John was going to make it. She said she'd come home straight away even though she knew she might not see John. Why would I want to be on the other side of the world when this is happening to all of you over there? she said.

I went to bed and slept until the phone rang at seven the next morning. It was Matthew to say that his dad had died not long after we left. I was devastated.

Angela had gone home with Matthew and Georgina. The next day Ange, Matthew and Georgina went to the unit to collect John's gear and a girl called Frances was already in his room. Angela felt no bitterness that it wasn't John, she was so pleased someone else would have a chance.

I cried when I told Lizzi, then again when I spoke to Ian, but after that I managed not to. No time for blubbing, I knew that I'd have to be strong. Angela came back to Cracoe from Georgina and Matthew's Wednesday teatime. I bought massive sunflowers and left them at the back door to welcome them home. Later I went for my tea (for a change), then Lynda and Terry and Rachel called later on, then David and Moyra came. We had a wonderful night in spite of the great sadness, laughing and crying, saying how much John would have enjoyed the evening. He loved people to be at his house, discussing, debating and laughing at jokes. He loved my 'Geordie' jokes – like the whippet one. A Geordie walking along the beach with his whippet meets a friend, who says 'How man, I haven't seen you for ages.' To which he replies that he has been made redundant from the pit and with his redundancy he has bought the whippet which now goes everywhere with him. His friend, feeling sorry for him invites him to the club for a pint. But Geordie doesn't want to leave his whippet, so his friend says bring it and say it was his guide dog. On arrival at the club, he tries to get in with the dog. The booncer says there are no dogs allowed, to which he replies, 'I'm blind, man, this is me guide dog.' The booncer looks at the whippet and says 'They nomally give you Alsatians or Labradors as guide dogs.' Geordie reaches down to touch the dog and says 'What've they given us, like?' No matter how many times we told it, John always laughed.

It was so hard for Ange coming back and no John for ever now. She would miss him so much. There would be such lonely times for her, but she had all us friends and family and church. Emma and Harry would fill her life and maybe there would be more grandchildren in the future.

John had planned his funeral down to the last detail, and Matthew and Georgina stayed with Angela to help her sort things out. Cynthia, their great friend from church and the choir, came and they practised the hymns, with Angela singing them. It was brilliant listening. If you have to die, Cracoe is a good place.

I looked forward to my children coming home, too. Micky was due and Lizzi would be here soon. I was so proud of my bairns – I had wanted them to care and they did. Lizzi's boyfriend Adrian went to collect Lizzi from the airport and drove her up. It was wonderful to see her after nine months away. She looked good, suntanned and fit. Ange was relieved to see her. We were all having a meal at our house when they arrived. The young ones went to the pub after dinner, then I went to stay with Ange. Lizzi came around after. We all needed to talk about John, it would be a while before what had happened really sank in for Lizzi. She hadn't been here through John's illness. The last time she'd seen him he was fit and well, drinking slivovitz and encouraging her to discover the world. Strange times. Ange and I drank tea and refilled our hot water bottles throughout the night. I felt numb.

Ian and I met Ange at the Chapel of Rest, where John was – an odd experience but I was glad to have done it. Angela went in with her daughter Rachel and came out saying that John looked much better than he'd done at hospital. Frank, Angela's dad, leaned over and said 'eeh lad they have done a lovely job on you,' and they had. He looked lovely, as if he was lying back in his chair in the garden and smiling. Ian and I chatted to him as if he was alive and asked him if he could use a bit of divine intervention and go to Cracoe and tell Dennis and Steph, John's cousins, how to start the lawnmower because they were struggling when we left. When we got back home they were still working away in Angela's garden and the lawnmower had started and the grass looked wonderful. We knew John would sort it.

On the Sunday before John's funeral I went to Grass Woods with George. He would miss his walks with John. Often on a weekend, they would collect him. Later we played a game of intervillage rounders, calling ourselves the JB (John Baker) Allstars. We were out to win and we did, thanks to Lizzi's skills. Eeh John. We just need the cricketers to do it now for the double crown. We had a little celebration in the Dev afterwards.

Everyone gathered at our house the night before the funeral and though it was lovely it was so strange to be gathered together for this reason. We decided to walk to the War Memorial (which locals called the Pinnacle) at the top of the Fell, the next morning before the funeral and put sunflowers on it for John. They would be there looking over Cracoe for us all. He loved the Fell, and the walk up to the top.

We woke to mist and rain, but still packed up for the walk. Angela didn't want us to go in case something happened to us. We said we would just go to the Sheep Pens and put the sunflowers on the Fellgate, then come back down. So Marg, Lizzi, Ros, Micky, Matthew and I set off in the rain. We got to the gate and decided to have our snacks there if we weren't going on. Ros was with us and we were just tucking in when Red Leader came round the corner and asked what were we doing, he never let us stop for snacks so early and why weren't we up the Fell. We explained our worries and he told us he would 'lead' us, that he knew the Fell like the back of his hand. We were all game and put the coffee back in the flask and Ros went back to tell Ange that we were off. It was brilliant and the mist lifted a bit. The walk was wonderful, we seemed to do an easier route with Red Leader, or perhaps he made it seem easy. Marg and Matthew carried the sunflowers up. The weather was still iffy, but we were confident of Red Leader's powers. At the top it was lashing and it was tricky attaching the sunflowers, but the men did it valiantly. We had our snacks and read a couple of verses of a poem called 'Success', one I used to read during yoga relaxation. It was particularly relevant for John. He had achieved so much success in his life – you could truly say that he had left 'the world a bit better'.

We rang Ange from the top to reassure her and set off down. Halfway down, the mist cleared and it looked so spooky as the view just opened up in front of us. We were back home by 9.30, thanked Red Leader and went home for a bath. I was thrilled we had done it and we could almost see the Pinnacle from the garden.

John's coffin was due through Cracoe at 12.30. We stood at the front door and watched the car go by, then followed to the church. There were quite a few people at the church already and we waited until John went in. The church looked lovely with sunflowers. Sandra brought two terracotta urns for the flowers and arranged them, as only she can. The church filled up steadily, then the school room, then they shut the doors and started the service. Ange was at the front with Rachel and Neil, Matthew and Georgina, Frank and Joyce, beside John. They were so brave, smiling at people, finding seats.

John's funeral was a wonderful experience, truly a celebration of his life, all he had achieved and people there who loved and respected him. I know now what my mam meant about a 'lovely funeral'.

Keith Hopper, the vicar who Ian and I had known since university days, led the service, Lizzi and I walked to the front together. I read 'Death is nothing at all' by Henry Scott Holland, remembering how John told me to read the sayings at yoga slower, and took my time – it was easy to do. Lizzi managed the prayer so well, with just a tremor and she looked at Ange and at John all the time. She said a prayer, which began 'I said a prayer for you today, I know God must have heard . . .' It meant a lot to Ange. Lizzi just finished before starting to cry.

The Eulogy was good. There was a PA system and lots of people were outside, there were so many people there, it was incredible. When we came out the sun was shining and everyone stayed at the front of the church talking, some crying, some laughing. We could look at the fells all around and there was such a good feeling of John. I am sure he approved of his day. Ange talked to so many people, she was marvellous.

Hélène, a French lady who practised shiatsu and had become a friend, was outside the church, having arrived late. She had missed my reading but what was uncanny was that she had trans-lated the same reading from French and written it out on card for Angela. Hélène had read it at her mum's funeral. She was so lovely, said she could feel the energy coming from the church like a giant sunflower.

Eventually we moved on to the Dev and sat outside. The food was in the dining room and everyone mingled around, but most stayed outside in the sun. Emma and Harry, the grandchildren, ran around. It was a real celebration, very party-like and John would have loved it.

Ange was so strong at the funeral – she smiled and sorted seats out for folk and John was in front of us all the time. Rachel and Matthew were so brave. It is such a loss for them all. The first time Ange suggested John could die, I just thought he can't do, they can't be without him, not Ange, and if we were all positive enough, he would live. To think how many lives John touched is amazing – there cannot be many people, living in a large or small community, who cause such an effect and make friends, relations and colleagues turn up like they did for him. His life was a success, but could have gone on to be more and that is what I can't accept. I do not have that faith – I believe in an afterlife, and am sure I will meet my mam, John, Digger and lots of people again – but I don't actually believe in a God as an entity. Lots of fun and joy has gone out of our lives. I won't be able to make John laugh until he cries again – perhaps in another world!

The sun continued to shine all afternoon. Everyone sat outside at the pub, remembering and laughing. As Emma left she said she had really enjoyed Grandad's party.

I think we all did.

The days after John's funeral, I felt totally bereft. There was a huge hole that felt almost like a physical pain. God alone knew how Angela must have been feeling. I felt so sorry for her imagining the emptiness. I sometimes felt that bleakness and it was not my husband who had died.

It was good though to have Lizzi home, popping about, organizing us. Mostly we sat and talked and drank cup after cup of tea and spent ages reading all the letters and cards Angela received every day. Ange tried to pick up the threads of her life and when we resumed our yoga classes she came along. The last time she'd come to a class was the night we'd been laughing and joking about John's 'award'. I went back to work, Angela did too and Lizzi agonized over whether to rejoin her friends in New Zealand.

We had a dinner for Lizzi for her birthday. What a contrast it was to her twenty-first, which was a riotous weekend affair, with lots of family and friends. We just had a meal in the Dev and it was a bit miserable because Ian and Lizzi were at loggerheads again. She seemed to bring out the worst in him, he couldn't do or say anything right for her. The evening was peppered with little nasty comments to each other or exasperated looks. Lizzi's being away hadn't improved their relationship.

Angela came along but she was so sad, though she tried so hard to be positive.

The night after Lizzi's birthday I met Angela at the Chapel of Rest to collect John's ashes. I'd got all the arrangements mixed up and I arrived early. I sat looking through into the chapel at another coffin which had lots of pink satin. I don't want pink, I thought, I wonder if they do black, I'd look better in black. I thought about what flowers I'd like, as you do. Angela arrived and we went in together to collect the casket. For some reason, they were insistent that Angela not open it but she arranged to have letters and cards that she and Rachel had written placed in the box. It was heavier than I expected and I wondered what John would think to going up the Dale in a box on my knee in the car. She did open it at home, I knew she would, just to check and put some more letters in.

John's ashes were buried the next day in a heartrending service in the graveyard, close to Angela and Cracoe and beneath the hills. The words of his favourite psalm were on the stone – 'I will lift up mine eyes unto the hills, from whence cometh my strength'. I hadn't really known how strong John's faith was, he'd never rammed it down your throat but just quietly believed for himself. That was his way.

Angela went on holiday to Portugal with Matthew and Georgina shortly after that and I missed her. It was a strange feeling, with her away it felt as if John was still alive and just away on holiday. When she came back Angela returned to her job as Registrar of Births and Deaths in Skipton, which she'd done for fifteen years. She found this very difficult, witnessing others' grief and joy on an almost daily basis. She decided she needed a new job, something completely different. She applied and got a job as a Parks Information Officer at Grassington. This had been John's territory and he'd have laughed at the idea of Ange there now. It was quite a change from being Registrar, but then this was a time of changes.

The autumn can be a melancholy time and this year it felt even more so. Maybe that's why we were even more determined to cheer ourselves up. One morning Lynda and I walked to the Sheep Pens and she asked if we were going to get on with this calendar. Even if it didn't come to anything, at least it would be something for Ange to do through the winter. I agreed. I talked to Lizzi about it and in her usual encouraging way she thought we should go for it. What better place to start the ball rolling than at our first WI meeting since the summer? All our prospective 'models' would be there. From our chats about the nude friends painting I thought we could count on Sandra and Moyra.

Sandra had been in on the idea of the calendar since the start and initially we'd thought about shooting it in her garden, which is very secluded, and for her husband, Philip, to take the photos. We had often been to the Turkish baths in Harrogate together, as had Ange and Lynda, so there was no embarrassment about nudity between us.

Moyra Livesey had also been in on the idea from the beginning. She was a bit less comfortable with nudity than some of us and wasn't happy with a man taking the photos, but she loved the idea of the calendar.

We also thought we'd ask Rita Turner, a WI stalwart. Shortly after she'd moved to Rylstone she joined the WI and was an active member from the start. She served as Vice President and was our choreographer for the VE day show in 1995 which, before the calendar, was one of the biggest hits for us girls. The four villages, Cracoe, Rylstone, Hetton and Flasby, which make up Rylstone and District, did a wonderful day of entertainment, sports in the school field, a tea in the car park, all in the dress of the day. There were land girls, soldiers, GIs, RAF, Naval Officers, everyone looked fantastic. I was a nurse. On the evening we had a slot in the 'show'. Secretly (shades of the calendar), we had been rehearsing for weeks in the Cracoe Café for a Marlene Dietrich type show. Lynda was on stage first in the mac and beret, under a lamp built by her husband Terry. She sang 'Lili Marlene', then for the last chorus she flung off the beret, slipped of her mac to reveal suspenders and fishnet stockings, and then another eight Marlenes walked on the stage as we appeared from behind the stage to loud applause and laughter. We 'sang' two more numbers, including a dance routine (taught by Rita). It was fantastic. And a foretaste of things to come.

The night of our first autumn WI I enlisted a few more 'months'. First, I sounded out Christine Clancy who lived in Cracoe and was a long-time member of WI. We always chatted and laughed at meetings, sharing hilarious times on steward duty at Bulb Shows. Judges had to each be accompanied by a steward, one year Chris's duty extended into the next day. She was accompanying the person who was judging the cooperative tables (a joint effort on a 'theme' from each institute, each entry comprising more than one item to be judged). It took so long and was so intense! She knew about the idea of the calendar from joky conversations at meetings, usually over supper. She was nervous about it because she was quite shy but she was willing to do it for John and Angela. It took real guts for her to agree but I thought she'd look wonderful.

Next was Lynn Knowles, who had only recently moved to Cracoe. She and her husband had bought Lynda and Terry's house (they'd moved three miles up the Dale to a wonderful old house, Park Grange), next door to Angela. Angela invited her to join WI, which is where we all met her. Soon after she came John's illness was diagnosed, so she'd been through that with us. I explained all about the 'alternative WI calendar' as we were now calling it and our reasons for doing it. She agreed too which was extremely brave not having known us very long. We'd never even been to the gym or the Turkish baths together. Maybe that was the next step – a trip to the Turkish baths. It was ages since we'd last been, it is so relaxing.

Our next 'candidate' was Beryl Bamforth. Beryl had been a

WI member for thirty-four years, serving as President and secretary. Like Christine, I mostly knew her through WI and I'd
always admired her, for her sense of humour, personality and
have-a-go-at-anything attitude. She'd been a friend of Angela and
John's since they moved to Cracoe and joined Grassington
Players, an amateur dramatics group. Beryl's husband, Terry was
headmaster at Cracoe school and conducted the church choir in
which Ange and John sang. They are both involved in amateur
dramatics and musical societies. She produced and directed us in
two comedy plays for WI, a hilarious experience. Beryl said 'yes'
to the calendar immediately. Terry was in bed when she got
home, and she told him she had agreed to be in a nude calendar,
he said 'oh' and went back to sleep.

Just talking about the calendar seemed to cheer us up. We
were moving on. On the forty-ninth day after John's death,
(although we didn't realize it was that night) which our friend
Hélène had explained is the time, in Eastern philosophy, when
his physical presence will leave and he will go on to the next
level, Angela and I took a walk after work into Rylstone to place
some flowers on John's grave. It was sad, especially of course for
Ange, but my heart felt less heavy.

Angela came back to ours for tea and decided to walk home
alone in the dark, feeling she had to do it sometime. I hummed
and hawed about following her and when Lizzi said just go if I
wanted to, I followed her round. She was pleased to see me. We
drank more tea then Ange went upstairs for the hot water bottles
and she screamed. I rushed up after her and saw there was a bird
on the bathroom curtain. She was standing looking at it. It was
not distressed in the least. I went in and closed the door. When I
opened the window wide – it had been on a narrow tilt – I saw
it was a little bluetit. It flew backwards and forwards between
Ange and me, not at all frightened of us. Then it landed on my
head. I felt it and panicking said to Ange 'it's on my head' but it
was so calm, it was amazing. Ange was nearly hysterical with

laughter by now. I told her to put her hand out and the bird flew straight on to it. I am sure it was John, his spirit was in the bird, especially on the night it was. The bird was not frightened at all and no mess, no flapping wings. We watched it go backwards and forwards from the window to the shower rail, then on to the light pull. We must have been in there twenty minutes. Eventually Ange said 'come on John that's enough now, we need to go to bed' and seconds after it flew on to the top of the window, looked at her and then flew out. We had such a laugh over it and I felt a lot better about everything, John was pleased I was there with Ange, I was sure. What an incredible thing to happen.

*

Lynda and I decided we needed a meeting to get the calendar moving. We met in the pub and I took my clipboard to look official. It was Friday 18 September 1998, two months since John's death. Present were, Angela, Sandra, Lynda, Moyra and me. We made a list of crafts and months, to see who could do whichever craft they liked. Lynda decided on painting, perhaps with a beret on, I could picture it. I visualized Ange's like the *Monty Python* sketch, nude with tailcoat on, playing the piano. She could play Jerusalem, the WI anthem. I could do papier mâché, with a bit of paper stuck on my cheek. We laughed so much, everyone was so very enthusiastic. We were sort of keeping it secret but Chris and Natalie, who run the Dev wondered what we were laughing about. We told them our idea and they thought it was great. Chris came over to us later, with a cucumber stuck down his trousers, saying could he be in the calendar too.

We discussed who would do the photos, some girls did not really want a man taking their photos. We thought perhaps Lynda's daughter Georgina or Lynda herself. Terry could do hers and show her how. We decided to do it at Lynda's house, Park Grange, which was perfect for it – all aga and beams, very country-like. Lynda and Terry had moved out of Cracoe itself a few years ago to a beautiful house a few miles away. When we'd first talked about it I'd imagined the photos out of doors but it was a bit chilly for that now.

Ros was in the pub, having her tea, and we asked her if she would do it. She said she couldn't possibly take her clothes off but when we said it was in John's memory and to raise money for Leukaemia Research, she went home as Miss November, to be photographed knitting a scarf. More scary for Ros than the thought of taking her clothes off was that she would now have to join WI. She'd avoided the suppers all these years but had helped us out in plays when we'd been short, a bit like the guy who isn't really gay, just helps them out when they are short.

Things were taking shape. We had models for every month except April, so we made a date for the first 'shoot', which I was quickly learning to call it. We needed another girl. We discussed who to ask. It wasn't just about being in WI, but about the friends of John and Angela. I asked Sandra if she thought her sister Leni would do it. She agreed and, aged forty-five, became the youngest calendar girl. Leni was a long-time member of WI, but of a different branch, so she joined Rylstone and District to do the calendar. We now had a full complement of 'calendar girls':

> January – Beryl Bamforth
> February – Angela Baker
> March – Lynn Knowles
> April – Leni Pickles
> May – Moyra Livesey
> June – Sandra Sayers
> July – Lynda Logan
> August – Rita Turner
> September – Christine Clancy
> October – Tricia Stewart
> November – Ros Fawcett

The night of the first photo shoot – 27 September – was magic, better than I'd imagined and hard to do justice to in words.

Seven p.m. was the appointed time and in the afternoon I rang round to tell Ros, Ange and Lynda to loosen their bras so they would have no marks. Ange and I arrived to the sight of women in dressing-gowns. They were getting changed in the kitchen and it was buzzing. Terry had all the camera gear out, plus Ange's halogen light from their cine days twenty-five years ago! The plan was for Terry and Lynda to set up the shot and Terry leave and we strip off. The lounge looked like a film set, with sunflowers in a terracota pot. They had worked so hard, I hadn't realized the planning involved. I had just thought 'right let's get on with it' but had no idea of how to carry it out.

Terry set up the first shot, Moyra behind a vase of flowers, looking like she was waiting for the colonel to return from war. She was first because she was most nervous and didn't want to lose her nerve. He left and she disrobed and Lynda tried to do the shots under Terry's shouted instruction from the other side of a solid oak door. But this was a bit of a farce, Terry couldn't see where the light was or how the shot looked. The slightest movement changed the whole perspective. Lynda found it hard to interpret his instructions. It was ridiculous – we all realized this wouldn't work. Practicality overcame modesty and all of a sudden Terry became the official photographer and it just rolled along swimmingly! We were hidden behind our props anyway and it wasn't as if we were walking about in the nude. We all watched each other's shots in our dressing gowns. Terry was marvellous and handled it so professionally (I hadn't realized until then that his background was art direction). It was Moyra's idea to wear the pearls, which along with twinsets are the traditional garb of WI. She had brought some and Lynda found another set – we had to share them and one set of earrings.

The next shot was Angela – she just doffed off and started playing the piano in the nude, she was brilliant and looked so good. She said 'If we are doing it we are doing it right.' John would have loved it, but I am sure he was with us all night. She had come with no make-up on at all, so I made her up before her shot. It must have taken some guts for her to even be there but I'd always known she had guts.

The next shot was Sandra in the potting shed. We all wandered around outside in dressing gowns and trainers drinking wine and having a wonderful time. What a good thing their house is secluded, otherwise it would have looked very dodgy, the potting shed all lit up and Terry taking photographs. We kept peeking in and it looked so good. Terry had obviously thought this all through so thoroughly and with Lynda as Art Director, things were running smoothly.

I was next with a cider press and apples and wine bottles. It is quite a large article, fortunately no trouble for Terry to lift about. You know what they say: 'the bigger the girl, the bigger the prop'. Terry had built, actually built this cider press, when they lived in Canada. Lynda had wondered for years what its purpose was, why they had brought it back and now she knew. They had collected windfall apples from the orchard, all arranged in front of the cider press, along with empty wine bottles. I must admit I felt apprehensive momentarily in the nude, breathing in and trying to look unwrinkled. Lynda and Terry instructed from the front and I just did what I was told. Didn't even comb my hair, just reapplied lipstick. After all, I couldn't make a fuss, this is what I'd wanted for ages.

Rita jam-making by the Aga was the next shot. It was tricky because it was very hot, and difficult to cover up in front of an Aga. The jam pan was large, but unfortunately had to be on the stove so not in front of the body much. We used a tea towel, but worried that it might look a bit contrived. We would have to see.

Ros was dreading her photos. She was crocheting Brady's (Terry's old dog, now dead) patchwork rug, and was wrapped in it with her jeans rolled up to her knees. We all remembered that knitted blanket of Lynda's. When Brady was poorly he used to be covered up with it and we always knew when Lynda was feeling down, she used to be lying on the settee under it. More of a natural remedy than Prozac. We couldn't get Ros to take her jeans off and they must have been cutting the circulation off to her thighs. We had to keep remembering to position the sun-flower, because we wanted the sunflower theme all through the calendar. She looked nervous, but so lovely.

Lynda's was next and we all strolled up to the studio. Terry set her up at her easel and she put a rag over her leg to hide a vein. He took a lot of photos, Lynda looked brilliant all white and smooth and very sexy. She posed holding her pallette. Our first idea was for her to wear a beret, but Terry dispensed with that straight away.

It was magic, we were all so chilled by now and draped about in our dressing-gowns. I never imagined it would all go so well, but still there was more to come. We all came downstairs to more wine and nibbles and I don't know who suggested the idea, at the end of the evening, perhaps me, but it could have been Lynda. As it had all started with the vision of a nude painting of us friends, we decided to do our 'friends' photo. No one was embarrassed now and all just doffed off and positioned ourselves on Lynda's settee. Lynda stood behind and Ange and Ros on the settee, the rest in front. Still very discreet, not showing any front bottoms, which was the rule, nothing tacky, we wanted this to be sophisticated, with humour and poignancy. What a shot. We adjourned to the kitchen for snacks and more drinks still in our dressing-gowns and Lynda took photos of us all again.

We eventually got dressed, all hiding from Terry now the photos were done! Lynda said that Terry was still smiling the next day and couldn't believe that we had done it, and so easily. When I got home Ian's comment was Terry's got a good job. All the husbands knew vaguely what we were doing, but hadn't realized, as we hadn't, that Terry would take the photos. If there were any mutterings from the men, they didn't filter back to us. We knew how professional it had all been. Nonetheless Terry was relieved he didn't receive any abusive phone calls from an aggrieved spouse.

I couldn't wait to see the results. What a night. As we pulled the car out of Lynda's drive, Lynda 'flashed' in the headlights. John must have been chuckling from Heaven.

The next night, a few of us went to Leeds to the Brotherton Wing, the ward where John was treated, to give the cheque for £5,000 from the Three Peaks Walk. It was very hard for Angela and Matthew to go back when not so long ago John had been so ill here. It was the first time Lizzi and Ian had been there.

All the staff were pleased to see us. We chatted in the staff room. The ward is always full and they work so hard. Sister Rosie showed us the machine they will buy with the money. It will have a plaque with John's name on. Ange talked to them for a long time. We told them about the calendar, but I am not sure they believed us. Perhaps looked at us and thought 'oh dear'. They laughed, but I thought 'we'll do this you know and we'll raise money for you'.

Three days after the first shoot the photos came back and we went up to Lynda and Terry's to see them. The seven of us sat around Lynda's kitchen table. It was quite scary. Terry had sorted what he thought were the six best ones of each shot and we each had to decide on the final one. The sepia effect looked so good, I was thrilled with mine, they all looked so professional. Seeing those photographs, how Terry made us look so good, was brilliant. Rita's shot hadn't worked, it was too exposed by the Aga, so she decided on a retake. Lynda didn't like the light on hers, Terry said it needed to be done in daylight, perhaps the next morning, which was easy for them to do. Moyra's was just like a black and white film, perfectly posed behind her flowers. Angela was showing too much bottom, although the picture worked well. Terry persuaded Ros that she needed to show some leg, and the jeans would have to come off. She reluctantly agreed. The potting shed shot of Sandra was good, but Terry thought she should try a shot with 'legs', perhaps embroidery on the settee. I realized then that we could really do this. I think we all felt that way though I know that some of the husbands, David Livesey in particular, were still very sceptical. Mind you, they hadn't seen the photographs. Ian was very scathing about it but that just made me more determined.

We set up another shoot. It was even funnier than our first time. Lynda was terribly ill at the time with what turned out to be shingles of the inner ear, yet she struggled through our shenanigans. That night we shot Chris playing darts, not a lot to hide behind. We knew we might have to rethink this one. She was very brave and apparently had wrung her hands together all the way there. She had loosened her bra when I rang her, so she had no marks. We took Angela's again, this time with a bit less bottom. And decided to dispense with crocheting for Ros and made her knit a scarf instead. We made her take her jeans off, though she was still well covered with the scarf. Lynda found her knitting needles but then there was no wool. Lynda appeared with a ball of string.

Next was the picture that I'd imagined from the first moment I'd thought of the calendar idea – the WI meeting. Originally I saw it in the old Hut, with Beryl sat on the stage, back to that big mirror, naked of course. All of us facing her in chairs, seen in the mirror making notes, naked and perhaps with hats, taken from the back (so to speak). But traipsing over to the Hut and doffing off was just a bit too complicated so we set the shot up in their living room. Terry did it the opposite way around, taken from in front of Beryl and our backs. Lynda, by this time had rushed down to the doctor's for some antibiotics. We missed her direction, forgetting to move any pictures off the wall, all those details she had sorted, and we had to redo the shot. After an hour, she was back and we tried to be quiet because she was in agony. But it was hard to maintain silence. It was a great night again and it was all coming together.

Finally we did the December shot which we'd originally planned wearing Santa outfits but instead decided on Santa hats. There were nine of us there for it, Rita and Lynda were missing but we didn't think anyone would notice. We trimmed up for Christmas: baubles, tinsel, greenery around the inglenook, the lot. There were only five hats, so I had tinsel around my neck. Three were sat on Lynda's coffee table, she would need to wipe that over well with Dettol. Trying to hide nipples and bits on nine girls was tricky. Terry had to keep shouting out who had to cover up and what. We sang carols and laughed a lot. Lynda had mince pies and cold tea for sherry, very nicely arranged on the coffee table. When we finished we ate the mince pies.

I couldn't quite believe it. Terry collected the next lot of photographs and we'd arranged a meeting to look at them and decide where to go next. Terry opened the meeting by displaying the photographs and the enlargements for the mock-up of the calendar. The enlargements looked brilliant. I could envisage the calendar now. Once again he had chosen six of the best of each set and each of us chose our final one. They were all great although Christine wasn't keen on hers. She thought she looked like her mother! We thought we'd redo Chris, perhaps with a teapot, which truly epitomizes the WI. Then we discussed raising sponsorship money. We would need a few thousand to cover repro and printing, also the cost of the photographs. Perhaps two thousand pounds, which sounded a lot, but if we printed and sold a thousand we thought we could cover it. But the enormity of what we didn't know about selling calendars set in and we decided we needed some advice.

We thought a lot about who to ask for advice, deciding on business and media people: Tom, who is a journalist and came to our yoga class, Nick who had been in advertising and now ran a successful holiday homes company, and had surprised us with his generous offer to help us in any way he could, and Carol, also a journalist who lectures in media studies at the local college.

Another meeting (before these my only meetings had been WI) and what a bizarre night. We all sat around the table and asked our advisers whether they thought it would work. We needed someone outside of ourselves to give us an honest opinion. I was surprised and thrilled at their enthusiastic response to the whole concept. They were convinced it would work. (We discovered much later that Nick had been totally gobsmacked by the photographs, but he didn't let on that night. He was completely cool and professional about it all.)

We asked about how to go about reaching newspapers and magazines; how on earth would we get publicity? Nick said to go for no cost advertising and try local newsagents. Which sounded fine except if I was going to be walking into newsagents trying to flog naked pictures of myself I thought I'd rather do it where they didn't know me! All the time we were discussing 'the calendar', the nude photos were all over the table, including the 'friends' photo. Angela kept trying to sly her photo away and under her note pad to hide it. But someone always wanted another look, and she had to display it again. Tom thought March (Lynn Knowles's shot) would be most popular and said the problem would not be getting the publicity, but handling it all afterwards. Nick offered to sort printers out and pay for repro. He said we could store the calendars at his company's warehouse. He had offered to help ages ago, when he first heard us brainstorming in the pub. They finally convinced me that there wasn't time to launch it for 1999. I knew they were right, really. It was already October and calendars were normally launched the spring or summer before. No way could we organize the printing in two months. But I was so eager to get the calendar out. We'd just have to keep it quiet a bit longer. In any case, a millennium calendar would be much more effective. Lynda made a yummy supper and we all went home to plan how to get sponsorship.

It is amazing how life changes and we adapt. Ian and I were

trying to carry on our business, though I have to admit my attention was seriously diverted. We travelled up to the Annual British Ultrasound Conference where we normally do a lot of business. I usually enjoy conferences – I prefer being out and about with people to sitting in an office with the phone – but I wasn't really looking forward to this one. Apart from anything else, Ian was starting to get frustrated with all the calendar talk and with how it was keeping me from business. I think by now he'd starting referring to it as that 'fucking' calendar. Things between us were not great.

He groused about the position of the stand, but there was nothing we could do at that stage. We were next door to a geriatric American 'couple' – he had orthopaedic shoes and she seemed deadly. The other side of our stand was Basil Fawlty – unfortunately not as amusing – with hormone replacement drugs. I was just anticipating a joyful week, when in walked a couple of very Sloaney girls and I thought – here we are legs, bosoms and lipstick all week. Ian rushed over to help build their stand, not at all chewed now, surprisingly enough. However I misjudged them, we got on well. They were brill and while I went to the loo, Ian gave them a complete résumé of my interests. On my return we were into yoga, reading palms, Pilates and nude calendars. After all, our four days turned out not so badly. I knew that Amanda and I would stay in touch, we were already firm friends.

We arrived back to Cracoe in time for Bonfire Night and headed down to the Dev, where we normally watched the fireworks. I saw Ange first at Lynda's and caught up with the news. She was OK, just. She didn't want to go to the pub. It was so hard for her without John. Thank goodness we had got the calendar.

The next night we did the final photoshoot. I was the only one not to be retaken, which just meant I am easily pleased, not gorgeous. Lynda was still in a lot of pain but feeling much better than last time. It was so lucky her retake was done before she

became so ill. The main one to do was Christine. As more had
been photographed, they were becoming more daring – a good
job then that this was the last, otherwise we could go too far!

Terry and Lynda set up Christine with teapot and milk jug –
very exposed, but discreet still. She looked wonderful – much
better than with darts. Lynda popped out to the shop for iced
fairy cakes, very WI. Then she stuck cherries on from her
Christmas cake supply. After the photos, she put them back –
I'm sure we later ate them in her Christmas cake. The positioning
of the milk jug was crucial, not to mention the spout on the
teapot, Chris was marvellous, never flinched, just kept pouring
tea under instruction from Terry.

Terry had designed a back cover for the calendar that included
a picture of John and a sunflower. Angela and I worked all of one
night trying to write the dedication. We wanted it to be just
right. I took it home for Ian to read, and he thought it was good.
Then, Angela's son, Matthew added some final bits. When we
saw the mock-up of the back cover, Lynda and Angela cried. I
was so proud to read the line Concept by Tricia Stewart. The
dedication read:

John Richard Baker, Assistant National Park Officer for the
Yorkshire Dales National Park, died in July 1998 aged 54.

During his illness John's friends raised money for leukaemia and lymphoma research. John's wife Angela and her
friends are members of the local WI, and the idea of the
'Alternative WI Calendar' was born. This idea provided much
mirth and entertainment for John throughout this difficult
time. After his death, they were determined to continue.

John grew sunflowers from the onset of his illness and
gave them to friends and family in the hope that he would
be recovered by the time they flowered. Unfortunately, this
was not the case, but the sunflower lives on as a reminder of
John's life and has now become an unofficial symbol for all

fund-raising for leukeamia and lymphoma research by John's friends and family.

John died before the completion of the calendar and it is dedicated to him.

Next was to add captions to each month and once more, we set off up to Terry and Lynda's. Angela, Terry, Lynda, Tom and I sat around the table and awaited inspiration. There were some underlying ideas because at our previous meetings we had brainstormed on captions such as, for March – let's sift again like we did last summer; July – if a picture paints a thousand words; August – if you're ever in a jam; February – if music be the food of love. We laughed so much, looking through an old Home and Country, full of women cooking and hoovering, in frocks and high-heeled shoes, looking after their man after a hard day at the office. I wanted to be 'Seasons of mists and mellow fruitfulness', but they made me be 'fruity and full-bodied'. By the time we got to December, quite easily and with much hilarity, Tom came up with 'Happy nude year'. To press . . .

When we saw the first proof, we were all pretty amazed. Lynda saw it first with Terry, she cried again! Ange and I went straight to their house after work, what a moment, it was so impressive. All the other girls came later and the enthusiasm was unanimous. Until then, I don't think any of us had quite realized just how hard Terry had worked on the calendar. When I looked at it, I knew the calendar would be a success and cause a stir.

While Terry was organizing the printing, we all got busy on sponsorship. It was strange telling people what we'd done. On the one hand we were proud of the calendar and wanted people to support it and make lots of money, but on the other, we wanted it to be low key. After a while, we began to forget that what we were talking about was nude pictures of ourselves. Ros did so well with all the businesses around 'Vogue Fashion Emporium'. We all sponsored the calendar ourselves either through businesses or personally. I'd been chasing Jennings, the local brewery, and finally we were put in touch with a man called Graham Kennedy, their PR guy. Lynda and I arranged to meet him at the Dev for lunch. I don't know what he expected, but what he got was two middle-aged women clutching a nude calendar. We discreetly showed him the proof. He seemed completely unfazed, instead he was encouraging and positive. He offered to help us with press releases and a launch, as well as offering us the use of mail order facilities through the brewery.

It was all very exciting and, getting caught up in the spirit of it, we decided to spring a little surprise on Terry for his sixtieth birthday on Christmas Eve. Off with the clothes again! This time Sandra's husband Philip did the honours. We kept our knickers on this time and had cardboard cut out letters spelling out 'Happy 60th Birthday' to hide our bits. Ros grabbed the biggest letter first and held on to it for dear life. Lynda had to tell Terry it was a WI night, so she came out with her basket. On Christmas eve, Lynda sent Terry to the pub with Simon and Matthew. He had no idea that Lynda had organized a surprise party. And I think he liked his card best of all.

With the Christmas holidays over, we turned our attention back to the calendar and were delighted that all our efforts at fund-raising had earned nearly £4,000 worth of sponsorship. The next hurdle was getting the blessing of the WI, which we felt the calendar could not really do without. We went to our local headquarters in Ripon, the North Yorkshire West Federation; Lynda, Angela, Moyra and me. It was our first visit, so it was after a little tour that we got the calendar out. It seemed bizarre showing other middle-aged WI ladies photographs of us in the nude. There was a worrying silence while they studied the photos. Then one of the ladies said she wanted one for her husband for Christmas. What a relief, they liked it. I next wrote to head-quarters in London explaining about the calendar and was delighted to receive a response shortly after Christmas that sounded positive. They took up our offer to travel down to London to show them. By then we had also decided that, as we wanted to donate any money raised from the calendar to the Leukaemia Research Fund, we needed to show them, too. Their headquarters is in London so we decided to combine this with our visit to WI House, the headquarters of the WI.

Four of us, Moyra, Sandra, Angela and me, set off for London to show them the proof of the calendar. I had never been to WI headquarters before. They must have wondered what was coming from Rylstone and District WI now, our President having complained about the rise in subscriptions on our behalf several times. We drove down with Ian, then in on the tube, the Northern line, which is a bit tatty. We witnessed an argument between a boy with a ghetto blaster and a gentleman who didn't want to listen to the music. Quite frightening but we just watched like everyone else in the carriage and didn't get involved. We took a taxi to the hallowed offices of WI House and had our photo taken outside. A very impressive grand old building, lots of offices, much bigger than we had expected. We were shown into a room by a PR girl, who looked very young – more like you'd expect at *Marie Claire* than WI. The whole operation seemed very professional. I don't know what exactly we'd been expecting, tea and cakes perhaps (of which there was not a sign). But it was a bit scary sitting waiting with the calendar. After all, we were about to show these women photos of ourselves in the altogether. Eventually the vice chairman came to meet us. She had raised funds with a cookery book in Wales – our proposal was a little different! A group of us sat in the room and we showed them the calendar proof. We obviously looked different clothed as they didn't recognize any of us. But they seemed to like it – what a relief – and were keen to do all they could to support it.

We discussed the implications of the calendar. WI is a charity and therefore could not itself support another charity. We didn't expect them to promote the calendar, but we wanted and needed their support and at the very least they needed to be aware of its proposed existence. We left a copy of the proof for them to take to their next committee meeting. It will make a change on the agenda, a nude calendar featuring their members, so to speak.

We went on to the meeting with the Leukaemia Research Fund. They were lovely and very enthusiastic about the calendar as a fund-raiser for LRF. We had cakes and tea there, such a good positive, amusing meeting. They would help us all they can, with the press launch and their PR man, Andrew Trehearne, agreed to work with Jennings to ensure maximum publicity.

These meetings made us realize that we had to decide how and when we were going to launch the calendar. We deliberated over the launch date. Terry was worried that it would leak out and someone would copy the idea and go before us and steal our thunder. After much discussion and soul searching, Monday 12 April was chosen. Tom had advised us to go on a Monday to get the best reaction, not lose it over a weekend. We would have loved to go first with our local paper – the *Craven Herald*, which comes out on a Friday. Angela and I had already met with the editor, Ian Lockwood, initially when we told him all about the calendar. He had kept the secret, so we felt really bad that they wouldn't be the first. Tom's advice was sound, he knew the 'business'. We reached a compromise and agreed with Ian to a teaser in the *Craven Herald* the Friday before the launch. We hoped he wouldn't be upset and take his bat home. A big factor in the decision was the Leukaemia Research Fund's annual conference in Leeds on 17 April. We thought that would be one of our biggest selling days with over 200 people there. Graham Kennedy of Jennings totally supported the plan to tie it in with the LRF conference. One difficulty with this date, however, was that Sandra was going away on the 13th, but if we waited for her to come back, we would miss the best timing. She would miss the immediate response (if there was any), but we couldn't risk waiting and it being leaked. There was Easter before that, so it would be perfect timing afterwards. All journalistic advice was against Bank Holidays, because of no newspapers being printed. It was a hard decision, but it seemed right.

Terry, Lynda, Angela, Ros and I met Graham Kennedy for lunch in the Dev. The decision had been taken to go on the 12th at the Dev, only seven months from our first 'meeting' there. Chris and Natalie would do food and wine supplied by Jennings. They'd been so helpful, listening to all the discussions, but maintaining the secrecy. We'd set up a table in the dining room with Jennings display boards behind and 3ft by 2ft blow-ups of three of the photos, sunflowers in the urns, nibbles and drinks. Graham suggested that I do the opening speech (horror) but no one else offered. I'd introduce the girls then open it up for questions and photos. He would send out the press releases to get radio and TV there. He suggested music – perhaps Neil Sedaka's 'Calendar Girl', and then we would make an entrance together and sit behind a table in front of the cameras, if there were any there! I couldn't believe it was going to happen, after all the planning and talking, the discussions, deliberations and soul-searching we'd been through.

We talked about outfits for the launch, knowing we needed to look like a team, yet be classy and striking. We decided to all wear black with a small sunflower on our lapels. The sunflower had become the unofficial symbol for the calendar and we wanted to emphasize its importance. The next decision was who to invite on the day. All our sponsors had to be there because without them we would have struggled. I had suggested that Angela invite everyone that she wanted – her friends, family, John's old colleagues. Ian had designed an invitation in the form of a page of a calendar, the April page, with a sunflower on and the 12th highlighted. They were so good. We delivered them all by hand and worried that we would have to eat all the nibbles ourselves.

The next hard decision was when the press releases should be sent out. Graham thought before Easter, but we were worried that it was too long for them to sit on a desk and perhaps be leaked or ignored. We'd decided to use Sandra's photo with each release. She was going to be away straight after the launch day, but at least her photo would be be seen everywhere on the day. I sent thirty off to Jennings – it seemed strange posting all those naked photos of her. Terry and I persuaded Graham to wait before sending out the press releases, to go for the Tuesday after Easter and avoid April Fool's Day. If they landed on desks on 1 April, it could be mistaken for a joke.

We also had to decide how many calendars to print. We wanted a thousand, but the printer said it wasn't worth switching on for less than 3,000. God only knew how we would get rid of this many calendars – we'd be mulching them down for briquettes in winter. But 3,000 calendars would mean £15,000 for LRF, which would be fantastic. I'd ask Lizzi to tote them round a few newsagents with me if I had to.

February 11th and my fiftieth birthday had rolled round. I remembered how last year in Sydney I thought I'd had the best birthday ever and wondered how I'd better it this year. Well, now I knew. It was such a great night. I arranged for loads of us to go to a Greek restaurant in Colne. Marg and Ralph came with Helen and Keith. Lizzi, Micky, Adrian and about twenty others got on our coach from Cracoe to Colne. We had a brilliant night with loads of laughter and a wonderful atmosphere, just missing John. After the meal came the only true surprise of my life, I honestly had no idea, and was gobsmacked. Even when Terry gave me the envelope, I didn't imagine that inside was a nude card done by seven of the men. Mr March, Mr May, Mr June, Mr July, Mr September, Mr October and Mr November, all posed like the Village People. Apart from their boots all they had to cover themselves was assorted hats which they held over their vitals. In their other hand they held up a 'Happy Birthday' banner in big letters. I couldn't believe it – what a shock and what a picture. All my scathing remarks about how the men would never take their clothes off, and all that time Terry had organized it. They took the photographs at Terry's house with, apparently not a lot of embarrassment. Lynda told them to go into her lounge and take everything off and they did as she said, but then we know she can be very bossy. Everyone in the restaurant was in hysterics. What a surprise, I loved my card. I shall never forget my fiftieth birthday. With the imminent launch of the Alternative WI Calendar, it seemed that perhaps fifty was the age to strip off!

In the midst of all this, I had to make 'my favourite room in a shoe box', yes really, for the WI Bulb Show. I chose my yoga room, with cushions and elephants, very ethnic, but rushed and badly made, true to form as usual. I thought I'd only get about 4 out of 20, but in the end they gave me 13, and the advice that the cushions would have been better not stuck down. How would I have kept them in position, I asked myself. A valuable contribution to Rylstone and District WI's chances of winning the show, which we didn't.

All Fools' Day and Lizzi and I couldn't resist a little 'calendar' prank. The year before we'd sent my sister Marg a letter asking her to stand in for Betty Boothroyd as Speaker, during her holidays, because they had heard she could speak loudly. It is always much funnier sending April Fools than receiving them. We sent all the calendar girls letters inviting them to do a centrefold for *Penthouse*. We found it absolutely hysterical but it was probably not that amusing to them. I wrote that I had heard they had done a nude calendar and offered a lot of money for them to pose. It read:

Dear
    I understand that you have posed naked on a WI calendar (my source is discreet and this information is for me alone). I am sure there will be massive publicity surrounding the

launch of this calendar and whatever your reply to my proposal, I will not go public before the launch date.

I offer you 'centrefold' in the May edition of *Penthouse* Magazine. The timing is perfect for this edition following your recent exposure. My brief with *Penthouse* is to celebrate the glory of the older woman and this calendar which you and your friends have produced is nectar to my soul. The centrefold will be tastefully photographed. If you have not actually seen a Penthouse Pet (Heaven forbid), I will forward you a copy immediately to demonstrate the sheer beauty of the exposure.

Please consider my proposal carefully, payment will be generous and think what you will achieve for womanhood in full bloom.

I will contact you at the weekend, or if you want to speak to me sooner my extension is 7680.

I look forward to hearing from you very soon.

Yours truly

  Petronella Sapcote

   Promotional Editor.

I don't suppose it got anyone for long. Angela guessed it was me but I got her for a second. But Lizzi and I loved it, and got quite carried away making up letterheads and a website.

Two weeks before the launch we had a WI Fashion Show at the Chapel in Hetton, featuring Vogue Fashions from Ros's shop and Beryl brought interesting news. Her son knew a journalist from the *Guardian*, who would like to talk to us about the calendar, with a view to an article. Fancy the *Guardian*! I felt very excited about appearing on the 'Woman's page' but we were worried about talking to her before the 12th.

We drove up to Terry's for a first view of the poster. I have to admit that for the first time throughout all of this I was a little disconcerted looking at a 3ft by 2ft poster of myself, seeing things you can't see on the smaller version – namely my left nipple. It looked large. I must have looked worried for Lynda said 'well you wanted it, now you've got it', which was true. I had wanted it and now it was happening I couldn't have any doubts, mega nipple or not.

Five days before the launch we had a bit of a tense pre-launch meeting at Park Grange, Lynda's house – very animated. A major discussion ensued about whether names, age or details should be divulged. Mine had gone out with the press releases but apart from mine there were to be no calendar girls' names on the calendar. It would say copyright Logan Studios and the printers' name on the back cover. Some of the girls were insistent their names weren't to be shown, which was fair enough. Their choice.

We still had not got a calendar, the printers were struggling to fulfil the order. It was very close to the deadline now and it looked like we would be lucky to have 100 for the launch.

Press releases arrived at all kinds of places – regional papers, nationals, local TV, BBC, ITV, Channel 5 – on Wednesday 7 April and immediately my phone started ringing. I hadn't anticipated this response and all I said was that I couldn't talk about anything until the launch on Monday.

Clive White from the local *Telegraph & Argus* wanted us to do a photoshoot at Terry and Lynda's. He needed to do it then so that it could be ready for the Monday edition and he promised not to use it before then. We said yes, we knew nothing and just had to trust. Clive's daughter Phoebe worked at the Dev and so she'd known about the calendar and he couldn't believe that she'd kept it a secret from him. We all met at Lynda's in our launch black for photos in the garden with a very bossy photographer. We just did as we were told, smiled, laughed, stuck our arms out in a gesture of joyfulness. Could this be the first of many shoots. Who knows?

We'd agreed to go ahead with the *Guardian* interview and I rang the journalist and we chatted a bit. She seemed really nice and reassuring when I confided our fears about talking to her before the launch (but she would I suppose). She arranged to come up to see us in Cracoe and I told her she'd have a brilliant time. I'd never expected the *Guardian* to be interested and it was very exciting. I had to remember, though, that we owed lots of local people an awful lot for their support and we were all terribly keen not to offend our friends and sponsors.

We were at such a pitch of excitement now and it was all beginning to seem a bit unreal. I wondered whether anyone was having second thoughts but it was too late now, we couldn't go down that road. I talked to Lesley Gililan from the *Guardian* again and she'd decided to do telephone interviews rather than come up. They too wanted to run the article on Monday and thus we'd be breaking our own embargo (we hadn't even known what an embargo meant before and now we bandied it about constantly). I discussed with Terry and Angela what to do. We felt we might miss the chance if we didn't just let them run with it. What if no one else was interested and I had turned this down. As Tom said, if the Queen Mother died on Sunday night no one would turn up, so we must get what we can. We had to go with it, shit or bust.

We still didn't have a calendar and it was beginning to feel desperate. The Friday before the launch Terry called at the office first thing with a calendar not even bound, he had rushed to the printers to collect it. It was the first time I had seen a copy of the real thing and it was so wonderful. But there was no time to linger over it. Local and national newspaper editors were clamouring not only for copies of the calendar, but wanting us to ISDN photos down the line for them to reproduce. What a learning curve. Terry had left the office and gone to the Tempest pub, in between collecting calendars, but I needed him now to find me an ISDN line. I rang the pub and described him, and they found him immediately, which totally impressed me, until I discovered he was the only one in the bar. He came back to the office, rang round a few places and finally we were in business.

Off went March, June and October, down the line (as they say) to appear in the papers Monday morning. It was all very scary. Tom had warned us about the press reaction and we were now beginning to think we should have taken the warning a bit more seriously.

We celebrated our move into this new media world at Lynda's. She sat at her table, looked at us all, and asked who was going to want naked pictures of us lot on a calendar. Three thousand people, I hoped. We wondered about Monday, who would come and had last-minute discussions on which black clothes to wear, pearls, no hats. Some of the girls had bought new frocks especially, I hoped it would be worth it. What would the husbands think about the photographs? They had sort of known what we were up to but still none of them had seen a single shot. Well actually, Miss March's (Lynn Knowles) husband had seen a quick flick. He would only donate sponsorship money if we agreed to let him see the calendar. His only reaction, on seeing Lynn behind her sieve was, 'Where did you get those pearls?' What if the husbands were embarrassed by the photos? Too late now. I think we were scared.

That weekend it was my school reunion in Aberdeen with the girls, what a weekend to be away. We have been friends since infant school, four of us, the other four since junior school. How would I explain the calendar to them? I met Pamela at Doncaster station and caught the train to York and met up with Alwyn and Wendy, who were on the Newcastle train. Suzanne and Angela came from King's Cross to York. The arrangements worked perfectly, it was brilliant to see them and we all travelled to Aberdeen together, talking and laughing the whole time, or at least when I wasn't on the phone. Talk of the calendar reminded us of our time in Girl Guides and TPON. Soon the whole train knew about TPON. The Pool of Nakedness. When we were in the Girl Guides we used to go to camp each summer in a big furniture van, to a barn on a farm. We slept on straw and dug toilets in the wood. No wonder we are back to nature kind of gels. In the middle of the woods there was a largish pond, and we would tramp off through the woods in outdoor gear (not Berghaus then, more Woolworth), then take all our clothes off and swim in this pond. We would be about twelve, I suppose. The nakedness started early.

This was the weekend of the mobile phone, I had taken Ian's phone with me. I could barely work it, but I learnt fast. It started on the train to Doncaster to meet Pamela. Radio Leeds really liked Sandra's photo and wanted to interview her live on radio on Monday at the launch. It would be good before she went away. I rang her to arrange that.

I talked to Andrew from LRF in the loo on the train swaying about, only to stop irritating everyone else in the carriage with constant calls. He was having loads of interest. I didn't anticipate it would start this soon, but I knew nothing really. Constant calls, I kept having to ring Terry to make decisions on who to talk to. The *Daily Mail* had contacted him and wanted us to go with them Monday morning, we didn't know what to do. Terry didn't want to upset anyone, but I felt we should go for our best shot. Even if no one else was interested we had the *Guardian* Woman's Page and the *Daily Mail*. The *Mail* is a female paper and we wanted them. I gave an interview to the *Mail* guy on the edge of a stream outside a restaurant near Norma's, in a little Scottish village. They were all sick of my mobile, they'd hardly known anything of the calendar before, but they felt they were living it now. Next the guy from the picture desk rang me for photographs. Terry took over and back to his printer friend's to ISDN more photos to the *Mail*. That was it now, we couldn't go with anyone else. Although, we'd already done the *Telegraph & Argus* for Clive. Local first!

All weekend I kept running through my launch speech in my head. It was so scary, I was sure my voice would go. But I had my Triple A. Last time I had my shiatsu, Hélène told me about this homeopathic combination which calms you down, stops the panic, so you can concentrate on what you are doing. I'd always hated public speaking. I used to stop off school when it was my turn to read in Assembly and I still got palpitations giving the vote of thanks at WI. I hoped it would work. I'd soon know.

I 'performed' my launch speech for the girls. They were very supportive and not at all surprised at what was happening. We had a brill weekend at Norma's, everyone was fine, we did lots, talked lots, drank lots and laughed. We really needed longer together to catch up. Nothing changes.

We caught the train back from Stonehaven on the Sunday. It was a long journey. Fewer phone calls today, sad saying bye to everyone. They would be buying the *Guardian* and *Mail* the next day and I hoped we wouldn't be disappointed. Perhaps nothing would be in.

Back home eleven-ish and Ian met me at the station. He'd been taking calls from the media as well so he knew what was going on. He was looking forward to finally seeing the photos. He'd tried and tried to get me to show him before, but we'd all agreed not to and had stuck to it. Terry had managed to get a hundred calendars which should be enough for the week, probably the month!

Angela's lights were still on so we called in. She was nervous for tomorrow, it would be very emotional for her. We were both scared but there was no stopping it now. Would we be in the papers tomorrow? I felt awful leaving her. We said goodnight, but I couldn't help feeling that we should be staying together tonight. Tonight of all nights was a terrible night for Angela to be alone.

4

What a weekend, what a week, and then what a day. Launch day dawned, 12 April 1999, and I awoke at 7 a.m. Ian went for the papers. I felt like an actress looking at her reviews. Lizzi was up, too, waiting for them – no doubt we all were. I could hardly open them, but the articles were brilliant, especially Lesley Gililan in the *Guardian*. The headline was 'From pinnies to pin-ups', using the March and October pictures. She called us Baker and Stewart, very left wing. Headlines in the *Telegraph and Argus* 'Have WI got nudes for you'. Others were 'Wine, women and goosepimples' and 'Revealed: leading figures of the WI'.

I rang Ange, Lynda and Terry, and none of us could quite believe the coverage. We'd all been up early. Terry had heard the calendar mentioned on a TV programme talking about tomorrow's papers. Sarah Kennedy mentioned it on her paper spot and Terry Wogan talked about the ladies who had done a nude calendar. What a result. It was so exciting.

Then the phone started. Thank God that Lizzi was here with me because she and I were answering two phones. I'd borrowed Ian's mobile, which I'd only just come to grips with. A very persistent girl from *This Morning* tried to get us to recreate the shots in the studio, but no way. We hadn't anticipated this kind of request at all. I told the girl definitely not. What I didn't tell her was that we could only be nude in dim light and hidden behind some prop. Never in the bright glare of a TV studio! GMTV wanted to come up to Lynda's and film us. Radio stations from all over the country were ringing and by 9 o'clock I'd already done about six interviews. It seemed to come naturally, I think because I knew everything about the calendar, it was easy to talk about it.

I was due to be over at the Dev to set it up for the launch but it was virtually impossible to get off the phone. Perhaps we should have had more numbers available, if only we'd known it was going to be this busy we might have thought about giving a couple of alternative telephone numbers but then who would have wanted to do it? Micky and his friend Ben arrived; they were collecting the big sunflower Ben had made at college to put in the dining room at the pub. I was meant to be meeting Graham Kennedy and Angela to bring flowers and vases and generally set things up at the Dev. Eventually I managed to leave the land line and took Ian's mobile.

Lizzi and I called round for Ange. It would be a hard day for her, seeing John's photo everywhere, but she seemed OK. When we arrived at the Dev a few of the girls were there already and the atmosphere seemed tense. Perhaps it was nerves what with being there so early. Lizzi looked at me and said 'You know you'll never feel the same way about these women again.' It sounded ominous and I was feeling so up and excited that I didn't give it much thought. We started to arrange the flowers and hang up some photos. The vases of sunflowers looked lovely. Graham Kennedy was there, too and he set up the stand while Terry hung the blow-ups of March, June and me. They looked impressive but my nipple looked the size of an eggcup. Didn't dwell on that.

The room looked good, but I still felt scared about who would show up. We rushed back home to change. All the while, the mobile just rang continually. The Yorkshire TV programme, *Calendar* wanted traditional WI stuff, like knitting and cakes to film with us. Matthew and Georgina had arrived at Angela's, so Matt said he would organize a calendar from our branch President, a chocolate cake from Joyce and a knitted hat from our secretary. The two phones continued to ring, every radio station in the land, including Chicago who wanted an interview organized for that night. Lizzi took over the phones while I showered and did my hair. What a rush. I needed longer than this to be transformed. Finally struggled into my tights while refusing *This Morning* once more.

It was wonderful having Lizzi, like an angel, taking the phone while I threw myself into black, sunflower pinned on, name badge, a bit of gel on my hair. Then it was 11 o'clock, so I grabbed my notes and my Triple A and off we went.

The scene at the pub was complete mayhem. The car park was full of satellite vans, cars and photographers' gear. Angela stood anxiously at the door, wondering where I was. She was so relieved to see me. I had a brief flicker of doubt. Could we handle this reaction? How would we keep the heart of the calendar and not get swept along by the hype. How would everyone handle the publicity and, especially, how would Angela cope? Photographers everywhere, TV cameras, I only just squeezed in the back door. I overheard Miss March (Lynn) refusing some disgruntled photographers' demands for 'different' shots. They seemed cross that the embargo had been broken – that the story had already been in three major papers – but we just acted dumb. How did that happen, we wondered? Eventually we placated them with the promise of something after the launch 'ceremony'.

It was so chaotic that we couldn't gather all the girls together, so all thoughts of our entrance were forgotten. Lizzi now completely took over the phone, she was like my PA, we could never have managed without her. Ten minutes after our scheduled launch time, I led the calendar girls into the dining room of the Dev, to be surrounded by the biggest furry microphones I had ever seen. The room was packed with people standing all around.

I popped two more Triple A to keep my heart out of my throat. We all stood behind the table laden with sunflowers. I stood up – no time to play 'Calendar Girl' now – with a sea of faces looking up at me expectantly, but I did it without faltering. I told them why we'd done it, because John had died and how his death had affected us, inspiring us to make the calendar in memory of him. I said how we'd done it, and that we hadn't imagined such a response as was happening right then. The Triple A worked.

Next Rita Swallow, chairman of North Yorkshire West Federation WI spoke about the calendar and WI's support for us. She was brilliant and it was wonderful. Finally I opened it up for photographs and interviews and total chaos ensued. The tabloid photographers (as we now knew them) wanted their photograph. We felt pushed into it and after all our discussions about keeping the dignity and integrity of the calendar, maybe on reflection we shouldn't have done it, but the pressure was completely overwhelming. It was a difficult decision, but after discussion, Sandra, Miss June agreed to do it. She was off to the Far East the next day and would miss the next week. She refused to pose outside in a binliner, as they suggested, but we went upstairs in one of the bedrooms and she posed (not quite naked) behind her page on the calendar with us all around her. That shot appeared all over the place the next day.

It was still manic in the pub. Someone herded us outside for a line-up, on the other side of the road, waving at lorry drivers, all beeping their horns. Calls came through non-stop for radio interviews or TV appearances and I was trying to organize who would go where. Lizzi was brilliant organizing journalists from *The Times*, *Independent* and *Mail* to be collected from Skipton station and brought to the pub or to Lynda and Terry's house, in the next couple of days. The funniest moment was when she walked through the room, grabbed us, saying which journalist was arriving when, that she had refused the pushy woman from

Richard and Judy for a fourth time, GMTV were calling back about Tuesday morning, and 'had anyone heard of Jimmy Young because he wanted an interview tomorrow'. Girls of twenty-two don't listen to Radio 2. The 'Headline hunt' on Ken Bruce's show had the biggest response ever since the start of the programme. The winner won with 'more me vicar', which was very close to what we'd discarded as Christine's caption, not wanting to offend the church.

Micky was interviewed for *Look North* BBC. He described the calendar as 'awesome'. He looked cool, but said afterwards that he was petrified and couldn't have said another word because his throat 'went'! Moyra's son was also interviewed, he was good too, about his mum liking flower arranging! Some of the husbands were interviewed in the bar. A journalist asked David Livesey what he thought of Miss March: 'She certainly fills a sieve,' he answered. All the husbands were pleasantly surprised and very positive when asked. Ian was interviewed on TV in front of my poster and said he thought it was beautiful. He spoke really nicely about it and I was grateful and a bit relieved. He was very proud. Keith Hopper, our vicar, told the cameras he thought it was wonderful. Funnily enough Terry was left in peace.

Carol, one of our 'advisers', interviewed us for Dales radio. I was struggling deciding who should go to what TV studio, do the radio interviews, and pose for what photographs in the pandemonium that had developed. Carol's advice was that I couldn't attempt to share the media out equally. As a journalist she knew that certain girls would be asked for more than others, especially Angela, and that some would be more adept than others at handling it. I thought that in any case some of us would be keener to do different things than others but I tried to be fair about it all and fair to the spirit of the calendar as well. Yorkshire TV wanted two girls for *Calendar* news, *Look North* a girl and a husband, and *News 24* asked me to go. Angela should really have gone, she has a strength and courage, a heartfelt way of speaking but she had been interviewed all day and was drained by now.

We refused the shows *Vanessa* and *Trish* which we all felt were not for us. The emphasis needed to be on the reason for the calendar and not on defending the nudity, which those kinds of programmes would do. We did British Forces Radio. We decided that Ros and Chris should do BBC *Look North*. Lizzi and I went with them to do BBC Leeds for *News 24*. Sandra and Leni were picked up to be on *Calendar* news. We had covered the whole country in radio stations between us. By 5 o'clock nearly all the press had gone and finally we left the pub. What a day. I would not have believed it if I hadn't been part of it. Angela went home with Matthew and Rachel. She had been so brave. It was very emotional for them all, but what a tribute to John, he would have been proud of her courage.

I had never been to BBC studios before, well not to any TV studios really, so we were very excited and scared too. Ros and Chris were on after us, so we stayed together, as I went straight through to the studio and connected to London. I couldn't see them, just myself and tried really hard not to keep touching my earpiece all the time. There was a problem with the 'iris' on the camera, so the guy in London talked to me and I talked the engineer through it, but all failed. I thought we wouldn't manage until the sports presenter (a girl) came and just fixed it so easily. It was so easy, I loved the interview and didn't want to come off. Lizzi's boyfriend Adrian saw it in Liverpool on *News 24*, fancy! Then it was Ros and Chris's turn to go into the studio with Clare and Harry for *Look North*. This is quite a big programme round here so Chris was nervous, but they did a great interview, talking about John. They looked very cool chatting to Harry and Clare. Clare said it was not the kind of calendar to hang in garages, but should be in an art gallery, then Harry told everyone to go buy it.

We popped to the pub across from the BBC afterwards, then back home to walk the dog and, believe it or not, go down to the pub quiz at the Dev. Terry, Lynda, Angela, Ian and I often played as a team. It was a weekly quiz and most of the calendar girls played. Each team took a turn devising and running the quiz and that night it was our team's turn. Since we had never in a million years anticipated this response we hadn't thought to cancel. I was sure it would all be over in an hour and the quiz would be a good way to avoid an anticlimax.

I got home to loads of messages on my phone and it took ages to call them all back and arrange more coverage. Then it was time to go and do our quiz. I had arranged for Radio Chicago to ring me at the pub, so Angela took over my rounds, while I did the interview. He was a really nice guy, who got the whole picture, why we did it – some people just understood straight away. I'd just finished that one when the James Whale programme rang and I did it live from the Dev, standing outside of the bar to avoid the noise of the pub. I managed to do answers and the snowball, the brief last round. I can't remember who won. I went straight home to bed, completely exhausted. Rachel rang and told us that the TV was on at teatime in their lounge when the BBC coverage of the calendar came on and showed John's photograph. Harry (who was two) ran through to her in the kitchen shouting 'Mummy I have found Grandad'.

The next morning was an early start, 6 a.m., for GMTV, who would be filming up at Terry and Lynda's. We were upstairs when the crew arrived. A very entertaining guy, a bit 'nudge, nudge wink, wink', called Richard McKee, set the scene from Lynda's garden with a view over the Dales, a sleepy dales village where nothing happens, but behind closed doors . . . The first interview was on the sofa in the lounge, he asked good questions, especially to Angela. We were all set for the next bit after the adverts, a line-up of all our legs first. I had to put some tights and a skirt of Lynda's on, because I was in trousers. Then the satellite link went halfway through the next interview. It was snowing by then and perhaps it was down to the weather, but the camera girl said they had already had problems with that camera and it needed replacing. Eamon just talked through it and they cut to something else and we were history. That's TV for you, very fickle. Chatted more with Richard, then all went back home for a rest.

While we were filming this, Ian collected the papers from Grassington. We were in the *Mail*, *The Times*, the *Scotsman*, and the *Yorkshire Post*. Jenni Murray wrote that she would have our calendar on her kitchen wall, the luscious and lovely ladies of Rylstone and District WI, the only role model to which she would aspire. Best of all Mac did a cartoon in the *Mail*: an older couple meeting three typical WI ladies and the man is flashing, opening his coat, and his wife says 'Ignore Donald, he's still a bit miffed that I posed nude for our Women's Institute calendar'. I got a copy from him and sent him a signed calendar.

I received non-stop phone calls from 10.30 a.m. until after the Jimmy Young show at 1.15 p.m. I couldn't get off the floor for over three hours – the calls were constant on two phones. Each time I tried to get up and change, they rang again. Radio interviews, more requests for TV appearances and newspapers, also people wanting calendars. Of course we'd run out almost immediately and we needed more quickly. We'd been promised more by the end of the week.

Jimmy Young was brilliant, he sussed the heart of the calendar immediately and asked such relevant questions. Ange, Terry and Lynda listened to it at Ange's house and cried. Then we went to the café for lunch to escape the phones. After lunch I attempted a few hours in the office to do some work, but the phones just kept ringing, both office lines and the mobile, outside on the wall to get a signal. It was incredible, I needed Lizzi here again to help me. If only I'd realized what an effect this would have, she could have taken the week off. I needed an assistant, a PA.

I did more radio interviews and some newspaper interviews. Fortunately there were no photographs because by now I looked scruffy. Lizzi told me I'd have to look good at all times now that I was famous, but I couldn't manage it that day. Would try tomorrow. I had tea with Angela. We were completely worn out, but ecstatic.

Next morning, Wednesday, off for the papers first thing. Ian was by now getting used to the early-morning visit to the newsagent. We'd made the *Daily Mail* for the third day in a row. Lynda Lee Potter wrote a brilliant article, headed 'Hooray for a fine body of women'. The *Navhind Times*, wherever that is, India I think, quoted Ros saying we drank quite a lot of red wine before we'd stripped off. She will never escape that quote now. Zoe Williams in the *Evening Standard* wrote a carping piece, both about WI and older women stripping off; perhaps she has a hang-up about her body, poor girl. April (Leni) and June (Sandra) featured in the *Daily Sport*, on one of the three pages that seem to make up the entire paper, really you could read it all before you left the shop. I made Lizzi go buy it and she was horrified when she came out of the shop, said it was almost a pornographic paper. Fortunately no one saw her buy it. We didn't understand the headline, well until Lizzi explained it, but I don't want to repeat it! Miss June (Sandra) also featured in a Dutch paper, which had her ten years older at fifty-five, she will get lots of letters asking for her face cream secrets.

We'd arranged to meet a crew from Sky TV who were filming a piece for a German station. After a hectic morning's reading, Angela and I decided to go before work to meet the crew from Sky TV. We sat and chatted with a really nice lady called Pamela while Miss March baked in her kitchen for the cameras. Christine, Ros, Ange and me sat around the table looking slightly gormless. Then they filmed Christine and I walking over the Splash bridge. Looking very natural, or not.

Then back to the office to try again to catch up with some

work, but still mega calls. A *Daily Mail* reporter – Natalie Clarke – wanted to come to do a piece on us. The *Sunday Mirror* wanted to do a shoot, a fashion shoot with us all dolled up on Wednesday night. A very droll guy at the paper, called Ivor, said he would organize make-up girls too. This was all too exciting. I arranged for it to be in the new Village Hall. Our old hut was closed waiting to be removed but unfortunately the new building wasn't completed yet, so I had to ring the builder on his mobile to see if we could get in and whether it was safe to be there. Yorkshire TV rang to arrange delivering blocks for the shoot, the *Sunday Mirror* had arranged to borrow them. I had no idea why they needed blocks but I needed someone to be at the hall when they arrived. Three phone calls later it was organized. Ivor wondered if I could hire everyone ball gowns for the evening which I thought was going beyond the realms of capability especially with the German TV shoot and the *Daily Mail* that afternoon. Told him we would dress up as best we could. Rang all to tell them the news. They thought it was hectic! I organized the meeting in the Dev with Natalie Clarke, tried again to do some work calls. I should have had the week off, if only I had known it would be like this, but then who could have guessed?

Another German film company 'Brissante' arrived late morning. We met them at Yorkshire Dales Radio at 2 p.m. with Chris, to be interviewed by James Wilson live in the studio, which is a small hut in the car park, but very exciting for us. Carol was there, she had organized it. We were a little late but did OK and were filmed by the RTL Germans running in and out of the building, looking very staged and silly. Next stop the pub where we met all the other girls. Natalie was also there from the *Mail*, so in and amongst it all we were interviewed by her one by one, whilst being filmed by the Germans. Natalie wanted the photograph of us in our dressing-gowns taken after the first shoot. Terry sorted it out. She would pay, so all the more for funds.

Lizzi had been for an interview in Leeds for a 'proper' job, then, thank God she came back to the pub and took over the phone. Loads of arrangements were made: Sarah Baxter from the *Sunday Times* would send Cosmo Landesman for Thursday night; Ann Trenaman from the *Independent* to arrive the next morning; Valerie Grove from *The Times* to arrive the next afternoon. I couldn't believe all these proper broadsheets wanted us. I spoke to a researcher from Channel 5 called Katrina who wanted to meet us with a view to possibly doing a documentary. I suggested she stay at the Dev, the nerve centre at the moment. I booked her in and sent directions. She would drive from London which always impressed me, when women just drive.

Eventually we left the pub to collect our frocks from home for the *Sunday Mirror* shoot at the village hall. The blocks were there, obvious now they were for us to sit or stand on, plus two photographers, one quite handsome, plus three make-up girls. It was a wonderful atmosphere, such fun, with a few bottles of wine to liven us up (as if we needed it). We looked so good after professional make-up. The girls looked so gorgeous, with long gloves, best frocks, it was a great night. Ivor promised a £500 donation. Then after all that palaver and fun, the *Mirror* didn't even use the fashion shoot. What a waste of time and money. Still a lesson learnt and I made sure that Ivor was not going to renege on his £500 donation. He promised he would. He sounded so world weary but perhaps that's just the life of a journalist on a tabloid.

Despite the fame and filming, the dog still needed exercise and I managed to walk with George. Ros and Ange came with me and we caught up with all the latest phone calls. Terry Wogan had mentioned us again, told everyone the calendar was sold out, which would create more demand. Like the old farming saying, nothing sells like a shortage. In fact we hadn't sold out but it was proving incredibly hard to keep up with demand. In that first week, we only had the first hundred calendars and Jennings, who were the contact on all the press releases for getting calendars, had none. Requests for the calendar were coming direct to us, letters addressed Rylstone WI, would find their way to me, thanks to Roy the postman. At the beginning we tried to respond to all these ourselves, but as time wore on and the volume increased, we would pass most of the calendar requests on to Jennings.

The following day, Thursday, was the most hectic of the week. When I came home from the office there were thirty-nine messages on the voice mail and twenty-one on my mobile. It took ages to go through them all and reply. The BT guy called at the office to check the lines. He thought there must be a fault because there had been so many complaints but the lines were jammed. I rushed from one interview to another, from one location to another. *The Times* was at Lynda and Terry's, the *Independent* was down at Ros's shop, and so on. I enjoyed them all – most of the interviewers were women and they all got it and were brilliant.

We met Katrina from Channel 5 in the pub. She was lovely, and initially just wanted to chat to us and get a feel of the calendar. I liked her a lot. She drove back to London, with lots of maternal instructions from us, and some ideas for a ten-minute documentary on *Real Lives*. Interspersed with her, we walked over to Gordon's field (the farmer opposite) to have photographs taken for *The Times*. Terry said the photographer was famous, so we did what we were told. Chris held a scruffy lamb, we fed hens and he was up a ladder taking photos. Our WI President was with us and she walked what seemed like miles through the fields without complaint.

We arrived back, with a touch of sheep muck, or lamb muck, especially Chris, and waiting for us in the pub were: a Channel 5 producer, a *Sunday Times* journalist and a photographer from the *Independent*. We shared ourselves amongst them as fairly as possible. The *Sunday Times* man was Cosmo Landesman and the interview with him was very noisy, just like Lizzi hates to see us, fighting to speak. We seemed to get louder and louder. Some of our meetings had been like this, with most of us shouting to be heard – eleven women can make a lot of noise. He wanted to record the lot, so we were fighting for the mike, well it was chaos. I thought he was cleverly trying to draw a confrontational angle from us, to get us to slag off traditional WI, to say they were fuddy-duddy and the calendar would offend other WI members. Angela was sat next to him, and gave him one of her steely looks. 'One thing we were not,' she said, 'was stupid.' He seemed put out that there were other national papers there, the *Independent* photographer especially seemed to bother him. Cosmo Landesman was the first but wasn't to be the last to try and find a negative angle. We would do our damnedest not to let them get it.

Oddly, I had a call from a *News of the World* reporter, asking about my fiftieth birthday card. I had no idea how he could possibly know about that. He offered money, serious money, but I told him no way. That morning the *Mail on Sunday* offered Terry £5,000 for the negatives from my birthday card. How do they know? I couldn't remember anyone talking about it at the launch. When I got home for tea I found a guy loitering outside the house. He introduced himself as the *News of the World* journalist of the earlier phone call. He offered a wad of money, intimating it was in his top pocket, for my birthday card. Lizzi was with me and we just laughed. The joke was the card was on the top of the pine cupboard in the lounge, visible through the window. He asked about negatives but we gave nothing away. I think he might have offered £20,000. Lizzi was gutted, it would have paid her car off and her student loan. I see now how they get people to do it. The card was not part of the calendar and would have destroyed the whole concept. Eventually we thought he got the message and left. However, not a gutter pressman for nothing, he immediately went to Terry's house and told him I had sent him to collect the negatives. Terry declined too. I decided to hide the card and Terry secured the negatives. Though

I think we'd handled him properly, the advent of this slightly negative 'take' was vaguely disconcerting.

A researcher (as I now knew them) called from *Living Room*, Thames TV, about cooking a spotted dick live on their afternoon programme. They wanted me, Lynda and Angela to appear next Tuesday and would send train tickets. At first she asked what was a typical WI pudding, I said 'bread and butter pudding, jam roly poly', but she insisted on spotted dick, then went into hysterics, as if we didn't realize why they had chosen spotted dick. Of course we hadn't baked one for years, or in my and Ange's case, ever. Ange asked her mum how to do it.

By Friday there were only a few pieces in the papers including a lovely piece in the *Craven Herald* (the editor had known John), but I tried to avoid media and do some work. No time for a morning walk, poor old George. I managed a morning in the office first and did a bit of work. What a week it had been. We were all tired now, and not used to spending a week together in such circumstances, in fact not used to spending a week together under any circumstances, let alone in the public eye. We needed a break from each other. Perhaps we should not have done the interview with German TV. We were filmed at Rylstone walking around the duck pond, it was freezing. They needed a few takes so it was a bit fraught and took ages to do. We were all knackered, had had enough and wanted to go home. It was really too much at the end of a hectic week. They were nice people, but it all took too long. This had been our only mistake really this week, and there was a valuable lesson to be learnt: we must not just accept everything that is offered. We had already turned down *This Morning*, *Trish* and *Vanessa* so far and we needed to be discerning. Finally finished eight-ish and went home to bed at last.

During all this incredible publicity we'd managed to get only one hundred calendars. Jennings' phonelines had been jammed all week with nothing to give but promises. Fortunately Terry managed to get 200 calendars for the Leukaemia Research Fund Annual Conference at Leeds University, the reason why we'd chosen this launch date. We knew there would be lots of people there and we thought we would sell lots of calendars. Terry picked Ange, Ros, Chris and me up and on the way we collected lots of copies of newspapers: the *Independent*, *Times*, *Yorkshire Post* and *Daily Mail* on the way. The calendar was in them all. The *Times* article by Valerie Groves was brilliant, with a wonderful photo of Ange. I thought she was a sound woman. I would save them all; I needed some files. The *Independent* article was very amusing. The *Mail* was over three pages, the fourth time that week for the *Mail*. It was wonderful reading them all in the car on the way to Leeds, where Moyra, Rita and Lynn met us.

The conference was good. We had our own stand and sold all the calendars we had. It was hectic because we had to bag each one and stick an LRF sticker to fasten the bag. We met some amazing people, all touched in different ways by leukaemia. The professor responsible for John's treatment came and talked to Angela about John and the treatment and the research they were involved with at present. It meant a lot to her. It was good to see Andrew Trehearne and Jennifer Baxter again and be introduced to Douglas Osborne, the chief executive of LRF. They were completely thrilled with the publicity the calendar was getting and very supportive.

The conference finished about 5 p.m. and back home Ian had cooked us all a meal. He had been very patient. Our business really depended on both of us pulling our weight and I hadn't been at work much this last week. When I was it was all calendar. It would calm down soon. We looked back over the first week of the calendar. We were waiting for another 5,000 from the printers. I felt we would sell thousands now. All our families were thrilled with the success, Ian's dad and step-mum Jenny loved the coverage and were keeping the cuttings for me from the *Northern Echo*.

The next week as the phone calls quietened down and more calendars were printed, we needed to organize ourselves to sort letters – we had absolutely loads – and start sending out calendars. Although Jennings were inundated with requests for the calendar, people were writing to us too, so we needed calendars and soon. Lizzi sorted us into a team. There were so many letters with orders. I had hundreds of phone calls for calendars, it was amazing. We worked all day, fulfilling orders at Angela's. Envelopes were a problem, the calendar was not standard size, we needed extra large cardboard-backed envelopes. I organized them through work from our supplier. No trouble!

We tried to keep ahead of the letters and orders even without the calendars, sticking labels on envelopes ready for when they came in. We kept telling folk they were coming, then they didn't arrive. It was a bit difficult to be honest. Even though the calendar didn't start for another eight months (January 2000) people wanted calendars now. Loads of people had called into the pub especially to buy calendars and there weren't any left.

The *Sunday Times* piece didn't appear which didn't really surprise us since Cosmo had seemed so bothered about the *Independent* photographer. There was a horrid piece in the *Sunday People* with members of their staff recreating our pictures, not good at all.

In the midst of the chaos, a young lad from Leeds Student Radio rang for an interview. He sounded such a nice lad, he rang a couple of times and I don't know why, but I said yes. I persuaded Lynda and Ange to come with me, told them they would enjoy a train trip to Leeds and these boys, Ollie and Wil could be our sons, so we owed it to them to do their interview, because it counted towards their degrees. The subject was the pressures on girls and women to be thin, and there was a guy from a model agency and a teenage magazine on the lines. On arrival at the University we were met by two lads just like Micky. They took us to the studio, a room nearly on the roof of the building, full of brill looking students. It was their first broadcast, they were very nervous so I told them about Triple A and how it had helped us. By then we were standing outside on the roof because it was so squashed inside and, without thinking, I gave them Triple A to calm them down – little white pills to students on a roof. Could have been in trouble. The interview was great, very animated, those two boys will go far, we will look out for them on TV in the future. We strolled back to the station, had a coffee on the way and talked about the reaction to the calendar. We still could not believe what had happened that week.

On the following Tuesday Ange, Lynda and I had a very early start for our spotted dick spot and caught the 6.50 a.m. train to King's Cross direct from Skipton. Terry dropped us off early. It was very exciting, dressed in our black with sunflowers. A few people recognized us, so we tried to get in first class, but failed. Angela had the spotted dick which her mum Joyce had made earlier in a carrier bag, plus a calendar each for the Queen and Queen Mum. Ange thought we could take them one each to the Palace because they are members of Sandringham WI. She assured us we would be able to leave them at the Palace, wasn't sure myself. The journey was good, I love not having to change at Leeds. We arrived at King's Cross with Lynda desperate for the loo because she doesn't like the train toilets. While she was down in the loos, a bomb scare was announced over the tannoy. Angela was looking for the car to take us to the studios. I couldn't find either of them. Eventually Lynda emerged, slightly ruffled, having heard the announcement, then Ange returned having found no car. When I told her, she made us walk miles from the station, although the regular travellers just hung around outside the entrance. She could see the headlines 'calendar girls blown up in London' and she didn't want that kind of media coverage. We ended up in a café from where I rang the car company and shortly a gold Mercedes collected us.

It took us to a very swish building, all glass and steel. The researcher met us, checked on the spotted dick, dissolved into hysterics again, and sent us into make-up and hair. I had expected the works but she didn't bother much with my hair. We looked good though. Then into the green room where we met a young guy from Harrogate who was the youngest person to sign a million-dollar contract at Nashville. He had performed at the Grand Oprey. He autographed CDs for us.

We thought we should make some enquiries about the palace. Ange said you had to arrange to hand stuff over – she had been before with her Girl Guides. I rang the Buck House Press Office and spoke to a press officer who'd never heard of the calendar – obviously read no papers that week, calls himself a press officer. I asked him if he had been in a retreat and very patiently he said he would call me back. A message came to the green room 'a call for Tricia Stewart from Buckingham Palace' – fancy! The Queen's press secretary was away, so this was his deputy, who said we could deliver the calendars to the police box in front of the Palace.

We were taken on to the set. Lynda had her LRF pinny on by now and was looking through the ingredients. A handsome young man wired us up, which meant slipping a microphone up our jumpers. The set looked like a well-equipped kitchen until you opened the cupboards and they were completely bare. Ange had told them what to buy and there were piles of stuff, far too much, dishes of currants and the bread crumbs were bright orange for fish. Ange told them we needed fresh ones and threw the set into panic, looking for a mixer, and a runner went out for half a ton of bread. The real spotted dick was placed in a steamer. The producer positioned us and the interview started. We outlined the background of the calendar, it was so hard for Ange when John's picture came on the small screen above us. I saw her falter then continue to speak. Lynda was very amusing with the ingredients joking about how you need two hands to handle a spotted dick – to tie the greaseproof paper. She loved it – a born actress. There were other interviews in between and the producer told us to look busy, so Ange just cleaned up the whole set while we pretended to cook. It was spotless when she'd finished and she told them to keep it like that. As soon as filming stopped the whole crew descended and ate every bit of the pud even though, as Ange said, it was clap cold and no custard. Off the set, we had a cup of coffee and some cakes and all congratuled us on a great performance. Lynda knew she had been destined for performing.

A different car was waiting to take us to Buck House. The driver knew about the calendar, gave us a fiver and we took his address to send a copy. He dropped us a little walk away on Buckingham Palace Road. Ange was in control now, intent on getting us into the Palace and we knew how determined she could be. On arrival at 'The Gate' we saw two policemen who, fortunately, knew about the calendar. We took their addresses, too, to send copies. Then Ange worked her charm, they rang through to the private detective and within seconds we were walking on the red carpet to the Privy Purse. The private detective welcomed us, sent for the press guy and then bought a calendar. We sat on gold and green chairs, Lynda overwhelmed that she was on the Queen's chairs. The equerry, in gold epaulettes took the Queen and Queen Mum's copies. Ange had written on them 'To a WI member from the Alternative WI Calendar Girls'. She then asked the guy in the epaulettes if the Queen really got the stuff that was left there. He answered, 'Madam, I can assure you she does, the Queen likes to keep abreast (pardon the pun) of everything.' Couldn't say fairer than that. We left the Palace, walked on the red carpet again and said goodbye to our new friends on the gate.

We got a taxi to Marks & Spencer at Marble Arch but by then we were too knackered to shop. We just had a cuppa and a little rest, then on to Elstree studios to record *Backstage* on BBC Digital. A big black car collected us to go to the studios and I went to sleep in the back. Lynda told the driver she was a bit nervous and he said not to worry as no one watched BBC Digital anyway. It was a very different show, in a youth club type setting, with a relaxed, chaotic even, atmosphere. Lynda asked where make-up was and a girl told her there was a mirror in the loo. Julia Cadbury, the presenter, an extremely shy girl, did a great interview, then we sang a song with Leo Sayer, well I mimed. Next it was into another car to King's Cross and home on the last train. As we walked down the platform to our compartment, Lynda said it had been one of her best days. I thought there would be lots more.

I was still doing some work for TKI, our medical software company, but it was difficult. I was in the office the next morning when I got a phone call from *Look North*, who wanted to film an update. Gillian Baxter from the BBC came to the office and filmed me and Ange talking about sales and the media response. She went over to Lynda's art gallery in Ripley to interview Lynda and Georgina and film them packing calendars to be posted out. By this time, only a couple of weeks after the launch, we'd sold 3,000 calendars and we needed more.

We'd actually managed a walk that morning and I was able to update Ros. We discussed so much walking to the Sheep Pens and hardly thought about the dogs. But we needed to update all the girls so we called a calendar meeting at Lynda and Terry's house. We needed to decide how many more calendars to order and just generally debrief. We all sat around that same table where a few weeks before Lynda had wondered who would want to buy our calendar and there we were discussing another 10,000 print run. All read the latest letters, reported in on the phone calls, press calls, etc. We were all a little shell-shocked with the continuing interest. Most of the calls still came through me. If I hadn't been self-employed I would have got the sack. Lynda looked really tired, she was still recovering from shingles. So much had taken place at her house and Terry had been so involved organizing photographs all over the universe, they were exhausted. But everyone still seemed to be finding the success exciting, no one wanted to opt out. And there were still loads of amazing letters each day. We signed loads of copies of the calendar, passing them round the table. We sold the signed calendars for £20 and people think they will be collectors' items in a few years. I must get signed copies for the kids for posterity. We had a joyful evening, basking in our success and wondering what the future held.

A researcher from the *Esther* show rang wanting three of us to appear on her show, the subject to be changing stereotypes. It seemed we'd altered the image of WI for ever and they wanted us to talk about it. It would be recorded next week, so I faxed him our résumés for him to choose the three. It was far better for them to decide and take it out of my hands. He chose March (Lynn had had a lot of exposure in the press), November (Ros) and me (my idea). We were off again! All this in only a fortnight. I was knackered but exhilarated at the same time. I couldn't seem to fit any yoga or relaxation into the schedule.

Then it was Ian's fiftieth birthday on 25 April: amongst all this there had been a party to arrange. We had a great time at the Dev, of course. The band were good, fancy playing at your own fiftieth with your own band. Lots of folk there, great supper. Once again, Chris and Natalie organized all that. It was good to see everyone, Marg and Ralph, Helen and Keith came over. Micks made a classic statement which I overheard while dancing and Ian was singing: he said it was no wonder he was fucked up with a mother who's a nude model and a father who thinks he is a rock star. I hoped the exposure wouldn't damage him! Or us, come to that.

5

Three weeks after the launch and nearly all of us were on or recording for TV. Granada *Breeze* wanted five models for a live show, so Christine, Sandra, Moyra, Rita and Beryl were being collected by car in Skipton and taken to the studio in Manchester. Ros, Lynn and me were off to London to do *Esther*.

We set off on the early direct train and tried to upgrade to First Class, but you can only do that on weekends. So we made friends with the steward/guard whose badge said Frank, who organized breakfast in the restaurant car. I had never eaten on a train before, not properly sat down in the restaurant. Mind, to be a waitress on a train, you'd need Kwells every day. Such a good train journey, it just whizzed by, laughing, and swotting up on WI facts from our WI manual. Ros was still not at one with her mobile, jumping each time it rang and then forgetting to turn it off after a call. Last week I had heard her whole conversation, trying bras on in Marks & Spencer with her sister, Ann.

We arrived at King's Cross and finally, after much discussion, research and costings we bought a Rover ticket and headed by tube to Marks & Spencer. It was as if we had been released from captivity and never been in an M&S shop before. As we walked along I remembered I had arranged an interview with Cleveland Radio re 'the Image of the Older Woman' so I did it in the window of Wallis, trying to get out of the way of the shop music.

We found a pub and rang the number Dermot (the researcher) had given me to order our car to Shepperton Studios. A very nice guy picked us up, and when we arrived we where ushered straight into the green room for snacks where we met Dermot — a brill lad. He had our clothes taken to be 'steamed'. Esther was recording three shows that day and we had no idea when they would be transmitted. There were lots of other guests there, really interesting. The theme was changing stereotypes, so there was an outsize model (smaller than me), a Liverpudlian, an Irish Lord with no dosh, an overweight fitness instructor, female police inspector, and an ex-con, now a probation officer. We all went to the BBC canteen overlooking the *Blue Peter* garden, I actually saw Petra's statue. We tried to spot stars, Ros is so good at recognizing famous faces. We spent our allowance on a sandwich and the chat was great with such different people. Lord Kinsay was a few stereotypes in one, Irish, a pile of stones in Ireland and a bit of a toff. We signed calendars for everyone, sold lots and took orders. Then into make-up, I love that bit, it is so relaxing. Esther walked through make-up and because everyone is always so friendly, Ros just said 'Hello Esther' but she totally blanked her. I'm sure it was unintentional but it made us chuckle.

Then we were given a little room to wait in. I made them relax with their legs up the wall. I took two Triple A, gave Ros just one and it made her so subdued, she was nearly asleep, she was obviously calm enough. The runner came for us. I was a bit nervous now, another Triple A — Hélène hadn't said if there was a maximum dose. I knew we would be up on the stage in 'the chairs', I would have been gutted to be in the audience. They wired us up and Esther came out for a rehearsal. She mispronounced Rylstone, but we daren't tell her. I could have managed a glass of red wine now. It is amazing how many people are involved in a show, I am sure they could cut down. Lizzi could do that job, popping about with a pad and a headset. It looked to be a good show: Lord Kinsay (the Irish Lord) was brilliant and there was definitely a plant, a Mormon woman, who tried to savage Ros, saying she must have been forced to pose nude. Ros spoke up, wagging her finger, saying yes, she had been nervous, but had wanted to do it for John. A young lad stood up and said he thought that after listening to both, there would be more people now wanting to join WI than the Mormon Church. After the recording we had drinks in the green room, got paid our expenses and signed more calendars. A car came to take us to our hotel and it was sad leaving Dermot who had already become like a son. Outside our hotel lots of prepubescent girls had gathered waiting for West Life. We met them in the lift and they looked all of twelve too. We were recognized in the bar by Germans, so perhaps it was worth doing those three German programmes after all. Finally to bed.

We had no Frank on the train back home the next morning. I went straight from Skipton station to a new Jennings pub with Terry to meet the directors. Apparently the phone lines were still jammed at the Brewery and still no calendars yet. They have been so good at Jennings, none of us ever envisaged this kind of reaction. The girls must be sick of irate phone calls. I am. I blame Terry Wogan, he kept saying we were sold out!

At home, there were loads of messages waiting: I'd changed my answer-machine message to a calendar update. Amongst the messages there was good news – more calendars were due. The printers were in Leeds and they delivered the calendars directly to Embsay, Nick's warehouse next to his office buildings. We would then collect them from there, no trouble for all of us forming a human chain, to carry them from warehouse to cars, then from cars to Angela's garage, at first. This changed when we realized how damp Angela's garage was and Ros then stepped in and stored them in her gazebo. It was such hard work, they were so heavy and weighed the cars down. The driver from Jennings would then collect them from us. By about the third week most of the requests were being passed on to Jennings but we were still reading some letters and sending out some calendars ourselves. It was hard to resist some of the requests. Terry had set up a system where all the calendar girls would collect boxes from Ros's place, log it in, and then deliver the money collected to Angela. It was all pretty informal.

Whenever we ran out of stock, there would be a big backlog of letters so we'd try and get ahead by spending an evening, usually round at Ange's, reading the letters, replying when we needed to and pre-addressing the envelopes for when the next delivery of calendars arrived.

It was marvellous how the calendar was selling. We were selling loads of copies ourselves at our various events. People were always ringing us to complain that they couldn't get through. Even Lynda Lee Potter had to wait six weeks for her calendar. Ian, Dave (from the band) and John (Christine's husband) spent all of one day on David Kirkham's (a friend from the village known locally as Frostie because he sold frozen goods) stall in Skipton Market selling calendars. They sold out, all 500 and raised £2,500. It was the May bank holiday weekend and they said it was mayhem, everyone clamouring for calendars. People were queuing down the High Street before the stall was open as they had heard there would be calendars. Ian said all human life passed by that day. Skipton is hectic on a bank holiday. Rachel and Emma helped them. Emma kept telling people it was her Grandad on the calendar. Rachel was brave to be able to do it looking at her dad's photo all day.

Down at the Dev, they'd also been getting lots of messages for us (amazing how easy we were to find) and today, a strange one. It seemed we'd been awarded a 'Rustic Oscar' and they'd left a phone number to call. I thought, 'wonderful, a countryside award'. However, when I called there was sensual music playing and a voice saying 'welcome to the world of erotica', so nothing to do with the country. I spoke to a woman called Tuppy Owen and discovered that it was in fact an erotic Oscar, which we had been awarded for the calendar. We would have to go to the Sex Maniacs' Ball in London to receive the award – a Golden Flying Penis – who has a wide enough mantelpiece for that? When I shared this with Ros, she laughed and said that she had. Almost speechless I told Tuppy I would let her know.

Sometimes Ange and I stayed up late packing calendars after work. I ordered the extra large envelopes which, under Lizzi's instruction, we had pre-addressed ready to pop the calendar in when more stock arrived – no trouble, tape them up, pop them in the car and to the post office. The money was rolling into Ange's tea tin in her cupboard, hundreds of pounds. We had never envisaged this amount of money. We had set up a Calendar Girl bank account and appointed a 'treasurer' to, we thought, just pop a few cheques in the bank now and then when in Skipton. How wrong we were. We were inundated with cash and cheques. It became a mammoth task, sorting out Ange's tea tin full of money.

There was so much happening that our morning walk to the Sheep Pens became twice as aerobic for me as I seemed to talk non-stop updating the others on what was going on. The reactions to the calendar were overwhelming, from so many people, who sent us wonderful letters and donations, lots written on sunflower paper or cards. To continue promoting the calendar, Ros had sent it out to lots of celebrities and we were delighted with the response. People such as Terry Wogan, Jimmy Young, Ken Bruce, Sarah Kennedy, Maureen Lipman, Victoria Wood, Michael Parkinson and Neil Sedaka. Glenda Jackson had written for a copy on House of Commons paper. Ros also received a letter from Jo Brand with a donation. Ros saw her on Clive James's show, when he asked her if she'd heard of the WI calendar, and she mentioned that she had attended the WI AGM at the Albert Hall, where we got a standing ovation from 8,000 women. She suggested she could be Ms December behind a bungalow. We received a lovely reply from Alan Bennett, on a postcard with a self-portrait, and he warned us 'not to be seduced by showbusiness' and that Victoria sponges were much more worthwhile.

Well, I can't really speak for the others but I thought I'd have a damn good flirt. I was relishing all this media attention and was sometimes disappointed when we had to say no to things. For example I received a call from *Eurotrash*, who wanted us to go on the show and I would have loved to do it, I think it is a brilliantly irreverent programme. But we couldn't, it was not for us. Terry wanted to go to see how Lola stood up.

Channel 5 had decided to go ahead with a documentary about us called *Real Lives*, which seemed singularly inappropriate to our story: everything that had happened to us over the calendar felt far from 'real', more surreal. The producers had decided to film the piece at Terry and Lynda's and we met up there one morning. I was hoping it wouldn't take too long as I was still trying to fit work in. I always underestimated how long I would be out of the office, not intentionally but Ian was very sarcastic and cynical. We were all spending a lot of time on the calendar, days off work, nights out. But everyone seemed to be enjoying it, none of the girls complained. Of course, it was easier for the self-employed among us.

Ange and I drove up to Linda's for 9 a.m. Katrina, who we'd met earlier and liked, and Chris her producer, plus a cameraman were already there looking at the rooms with Terry deciding where to shoot. They wanted a quite sexy, sultry beginning to the piece, which worried us at first because the last way we wanted to be portrayed was tacky. However we talked it through and it seemed OK. Ange was filmed painting her nails, letting a white satin slip fall off the chair (not her at all), putting her lipstick on, then adjusting her hat. They filmed all day – Ian was right – couldn't believe how long it all takes.

Lynda arrived later and she did the putting the stocking on bit, she was good. The whole day was very amusing. I recreated my picture (clothed), so Terry had to cart the cider press out again, then to the Spar to buy apples. Katrina interviewed me in that pose, she asked how it all started, the reasons, I told her it all. Then Angela sat at the piano, again fully clothed. She had them all in tears, she was brave to do it, but what she said was so important, she is the heart of the calendar. Later in the afternoon all eleven of us recreated the 'meeting' picture, all trying to find our hats again and sang 'Jerusalem', well I mimed as usual. In the evening we all ate at the Dev on Channel 5's bill. We finished the filming the next day and I thought it was going to be a good true piece.

I think we'd all had a great time doing it and any reservations we might have felt about it were completely dispelled when we watched it when it was shown in June. Our two days' filming was reduced to a six-minute slot but it was brilliant. They had definitely got the heart of the calendar, the reason behind the whole venture. We all got together to watch it, ensconced in my lounge with wine. Angela's interview was so poignant, no wonder they'd been in tears when they filmed her. As it happened, Angela, Lynda and I featured most which I felt created a bit of an atmosphere with some of the girls afterwards. The producer and Katrina had asked specifically for individual interviews with the three of us: with me because it was my idea; Angela obviously as the reason we did the calendar and Lynda as the photographer's wife. The girls' reaction reminded me that early on, in fact on launch day, Carol had warned me that it was going to be difficult to give eleven people equal coverage. It was becoming difficult but after watching it and hearing them announce that we'd raised close to £100,000 by then, I felt really proud of all of us.

We found that we'd inadvertently become spokeswomen for the older woman and we did quite a lot of local TV and radio which focused on the changing perception of the older woman.

It was odd because we hadn't set out to change anything, we just did it because we could. At these, Beryl, our oldest calendar girl at sixty-five, shone. Beryl said some brilliant stuff about relationships and older sex. She said that she didn't want to know about her children's sex life and they certainly didn't want to know about hers. She has such a twinkle, as does Mr January. We had to repeat a couple of bits because we had the cameraman laughing so hard.

But it wasn't all glamorous-sounding telly. Six of us went to a Bikeathon at Macclesfield for LRF. I drove and we only got lost once. We'd designed a sporty version of our calendar girl outfits: yellow sweatshirts with black caps. I looked mental in a baseball hat. On the back of our sweatshirts were the words 'Calendar Girls Appeal'. 'To whom?' quipped Ros's husband Chris. We had a stall to sell calendars, took loads, but really on a bike there is nowhere to carry a calendar. We gave out medals at the end and did interviews on local radio, then had lunch in McDonald's. We were brought down to earth when Ros asked a cyclist, who was looking at a calendar, if he was tempted. He answered 'not with those pictures'. She refrained from sharing with him that she was one of them. We needed to be brought down to earth every so often, the miserable biker.

Even when we least expected it, the calendar sneaked into our daily lives. We had our first yoga night in the new hut which had recently been completed. I felt a little anxious that it wouldn't be as good as in the old village hall, but it was fine. Lots there, including Sandra, Ange, Lynda and Ros, and atmosphere was good. The new hall was great, very in tune for yoga. A perfect way to forget about the calendar for a while but on the way home Ange, in her car with Carol, Lynda and Terry in theirs and Ros in hers all heard the Richard Stilgoe song 'Hi we are the WI' about the calendar on *Friday Night is Music Night*. We had heard vague mentionings about him and Peter Skellern including a song about the calendar in their present tour but that was the first time any of us had heard it. Ros, who had been brilliant and thorough about tracking down every bit of publicity we could glean, decided to track down Stilgoe and Skellern. There wasn't a number or address that Ros couldn't find. She found Richard Stilgoe's tour manager and actually spoke to Richard himself on his mobile. They were extending their tour and planned to record the song. They asked if we could be at their show at Leeds City Variety which was a thrill and something we all looked forward to.

The reaction to the calendar had been so amazing that we got a bit carried away with new ideas for raising money. We seemed fine as long as we stuck closely to the calendar but, for example, when we thought we might make a CD, we nearly came unstuck. Ros had contacted Neil Sedaka's tour manager to see if we could meet up while he was over here (we thought we might help revive his career). He didn't seem to need us but it gave Lynda the idea of releasing a CD with 'Calendar Girl' on one side and 'Jerusalem' on the other (or however that goes on CDs). Ian's band would back us and Dave, the lead guitarist (and husband of Carol, our adviser), would sort things out. We met at Carol and Dave's house. Dave organized the music and song sheets with different colours for different harmonies, which is all totally irrelevant when you are tone deaf. However, luckily everyone else isn't. All stood in month order. If we had thought about lining up for photos, Ros and me would not have been October and November, with ten inches difference in height. Dave took it all very seriously and was very patient. I had to speak my lines 'Romeo and Juliet on Halloween', I sounded stupid. Then Dave decided to hold auditions for 'Jerusalem' which would be on the 'B' side. I got that panic feeling inside me. Obviously I was not included, there aren't any speaking parts in 'Jerusalem' fortunately. The thought of singing alone took me right back to school, when my mam used to let me skive off on the day we had to sing scales, because I hated it so much. However, lots of the girls went along with the 'auditions', probably just getting caught up in another weird and wonderful thing from the calendar. Dave chose who would sing 'Jerusalem' and Lynda wasn't included, I couldn't believe it, she has one of the best voices. She accepted it very well, quite proudly, sat on the piano stool, head held high. By this time I was verging on hysteria and daren't look at Ros, who also hadn't auditioned. Time for more wine, I felt. Fortunately we all saw the light and decided against the CD. We were better sticking to something we knew about: posing in the nude.

Perhaps that's why the Christmas card worked so much better – it seemed a much more natural spin-off than the CD. Moyra came up with the idea of a Christmas card using the December shot from the calendar. A local businessman offered to sponsor us by printing 50,000 Christmas cards free of charge. But we would have to reshoot the picture because there were only nine of us on the calendar's December picture (not that anyone had noticed really) and all of us wanted to be on the card. We arranged the night.

I should have exercised more: there was a definite deterioration since last year. Too late now as always. I spent all day drinking water and trying to be firmer. We all arrived at Terry and Lynda's, with dressing gowns, pearls, lipsticks and Santa hats. The curtains were all drawn. Perhaps we would be a little out of practice with stripping? Lynda had trimmed up her mantelpiece to resemble the December photo. We all slipped into our dressing-gowns and stood in positions for Terry to set up. This time it was Lynda who flung her dressing gown off first and we all followed suit. My position was quite covered, I just had to watch out for the odd nipple slipping out on to Ange's shoulder. Two of them sat on Lynda's table again – would need more Dettol tomorrow. We had the same old song sheets and it seemed very funny singing carols again without clothes. Terry took reels of film, he was sweating a bit by the last shot with making sure that all the bits that needed to be hidden were. It was very amusing. Another wonderful evening of nudity. I couldn't wait to see the results.

The next day when he collected them, out of seventy-five shots, Terry said only one was right for the Christmas card. We all saw them the next night. There were lots of good shots, but each one had different girls' bits showing, apart from one. Lynda thought one of her bits (an important one) was showing, but we convinced her it was a shadow. Well, tried to convince her. She still wasn't sure.

We hadn't planned to launch the Christmas card immediately but it kind of leaked out and we got calls from the local and national press. Terry had to quickly produce a mock-up – no trouble. It did seem bizarre, a Christmas card in June, but then, what was normal? We hadn't any printed yet. The same story as with the calendar – we hoped it would be as successful. Soon after we unintentionally 'launched' the Christmas card the media attention picked up again. My dining room table was covered in press cuttings and letters, I needed to organize them into files. I would do it though, when I got a minute. Lizzi would help me. One day the calendar featured in the *Guardian*, *Independent*, *Yorkshire Post* and *Telegraph & Argus*. Headlines like 'Who bares Wins', 'And for that Festive feeling, here is the nudes', 'Bare we go again'. Everyone would know about the Christmas card, but unfortunately, like the calendar at first, we didn't actually have any printed ready to sell. Now we had letters asking for Christmas cards. We were off again.

Six of us had another visit to BBC *Look North* to do an interview with Claire Frisby about the Christmas card. We all met up at the studios, after several attempts to discover the correct road, but that was normal for us. The set was all Christmassy, with a tree with tinsel and baubles. They arranged us around the tree, which unfortunately was a foot smaller than me, so I looked like Gulliver. It wasn't our best interview, we looked a bit staged and quite stupid. It could have been set up a lot better, we needed Terry there. (We had photographers spend hours, days even, taking our photographs, but none were as good as Terry's.) But it was great publicity for the Christmas card. We chatted to Claire afterwards, told her some jokes, she loved the tomato sauce one. Ros asked about her documentary programmes and whether she would consider doing a documentary about us. We outlined all that was coming up: *Woman's Journal* Fashion Show at the Savoy, Woman of the Year Lunch, and who knew what else. We had contacted Stoney Creek in Canada, where WI originated, and thought of arranging a meeting with them. They were thrilled by the idea of the calendar but said they wouldn't be doing one themselves, they were too old. Claire seemed very interested in all of it so we would see.

Throughout all of this excitement, the reason for doing the calendar in the first place was never far from our thoughts, especially, of course, Angela's. On John's birthday, 1 June, Ange, Ros and I walked to the Sheep Pens and talked about him. We laughed about some of the birthday presents he had bought Ange, like the time he told her to look in the car for her present. She was really excited thinking he had hidden a ring or a watch, looked for hours, until he eventually had to tell her it was headrests, which matched the seats so were completely camouflaged. He liked to buy useful gifts. Ange, Rachel and the kids planned to go to Parceval Hall, where Ange had taken John for a picnic last year when he was so ill. It was sad, looking at the Pinnacle, 'Grandad's Finger' as Emma calls it. Angela and I both knew that John would love what we had achieved.

Ian's band played that night at the new Hall for a fiftieth birthday party. It was a hot day and I did a bit of gardening, very satisfying. Ange felt unable to come to the party, it was too hard with everyone in couples and no John. Unfortunately some people didn't understand how she felt and perhaps thought she should be over it. A year had nearly passed, but that didn't make it any easier. Her life had been so different with John, lots of plans, holidays and enjoying their lives. Out of everyone I knew, they genuinely enjoyed each other's company the most.

On the days when calendar business was light, I felt neglected. God knew I needed to get my feet back on the ground and start working again, if only to get Ian off my back, but it was so very hard with something new and exciting nearly every day. We celebrated our wedding anniversary, twenty-seven years man and boy, on 5 June. Ian wanted a romantic dinner for two, but in the end we just went to the Dev and met up with a few folk. It was quite a good night, still fractious though. I hoped we could survive the calendar. I had been at work more; however, most calls were not to order medical educational software but the Alternative WI Calendar. What could I do, I had to let it all happen, like it had been destined. Ian called it 'that fucking calendar' a lot now. Life was constantly changing, this was an amazing moment in mine and I didn't want to miss any of it.

Channel 4 had contacted us about a programme they were doing with Richard Whiteley about activities in the Dales. They wanted the calendar girls to be part of it and, just for a change, they wanted to film at Lynda and Terry's. We all met up there one evening and sat around the fire. Richard Whiteley walked in and sat in the middle, talked about the calendar and the Christmas card, asked if he could be the token man on the card. We said of course. He was quite hefty, just like he looks on TV, very personable and easy to talk to, wittier than I'd expected. We talked about Terry Wogan and how much he had mentioned the calendar on the radio. Richard was recording *Countdown* at Yorkshire TV and Terry Wogan would be appearing. Richard asked if we would like to go. *Did we!* We had a brilliant idea on our morning walk to the Sheep Pens: we would hire a minibus to take us to Yorkshire TV. Richard, true to his word rang Lynda to arrange tickets for all. Terry too, Terry Logan meets Terry Wogan. She knew of a farmer at Appletreewick who drove a minibus. She rang, but had to call back because he was at a funeral and his wife was milking. He called back and was thrilled to be taking the calendar girls on a trip. Miss July worked her charms again. The plan was to go on as a complete surprise between takes, with a signed calendar for Terry Wogan.

The minibus picked us up outside the Dev, all in our black, Lizzi and Mr January too. Beryl's Terry had been a star, helped us so much and enjoyed everything Beryl had been involved with. Ange hadn't realized just how much Beryl and Terry thought of John. Our farmer/driver was ace and we arranged for him to come into the studio with us. Richard met us in the green room, in a rather startling jacket, and told us when to come on. There were lots of wine and nibbles so we tucked in and watched the show on the TV. Lizzi, who had written in numerous times to go on the show, was an expert Countdowner, and here she was now. A young lady came for us in the second interval, we all lined up in month order, having met Paulie Walters (Terry Wogan's sidekick) in the queue backstage. He is very handsome and just as amusing as on air with Terry. Richard did a lot of preamble with Terry and Carol Vorderman, then introduced us, we all walked on one by one and gave him a kiss, Beryl first. Terry was surprised and just a little thrilled I felt! Lots of photographs, and the two Terrys together after Carol introduced our photographer. The audience were so appreciative, then we watched the next takes. I couldn't get any, Lizzi was brilliant at it, especially the conundrum. It seemed to take a lot of filming for such a straightforward programme, still we knew nothing about TV. People wait three years to be in the audience, we just waited a day! We had drinks in the bar afterwards, well champagne actually. All the contestants were there, plus Tel and Paulie, Richard and Carol. They signed our *Countdown* pads for us, which we had stolen. We did have more, but a guy on the set told us we had to leave them for the next show. I got autographs, even though I feel it is a crass thing to want, I was just carried along by it all. Having completely cleared the green room of food and drink, we were starving, so called at McDonald's on the way home. We looked a bit odd in there in our black with sunflowers.

*

By this point, (June) we had sold 23,000 calendars and needed more. We'd gone from the original printing of 3,000, to 5,000, then printing in lots of 10,000, which we thought was brave. After the first 3,000, we'd decided to have the calendars sealed in clear plastic, so Terry redesigned the back cover to include thumbnail photos of each month so buyers could see what they were getting. This time we decided to print another 20,000. We'd had a big discussion with some of us wanting to play safe and print 10,000. We were terrified of being stuck with loads. Ros convinced us all to go for 20,000. In any case Jennings already wanted 6,000 more immediately for back orders. Shit or bust again.

Some of our best events, where we sold the most calendars, were, appropriately, the various agricultural shows around the area where WI always had a strong presence. For these Ros's husband Chris had designed and supplied a marquee with a big sunflower on it. We had a trial run putting it up round at Lynn's, or at least the husbands did. Ten men to put up a tent – seemed about right. We called it our Erection Party and it was great fun – all the calendar girls and their husbands and the tent.

Our first agricultural show was the Game Show at Broughton Hall. Unfortunately we woke up to heavy rain on the morning. However, we were in the tent and out of the elements. It was fantastic, the husbands had done a great job setting it up for us and there was a good atmosphere with us all mucking in. We'd all packed picnics and there was so much food we could have sold it for charity. It was very cosy in the tent, especially with a primus stove. All decked out in yellow, sunflowers on the counter. It was a brilliant day. Mr January did a marvellous job pulling the punters in to buy a calendar. I hadn't really known Beryl's

Terry, Mr January, before the calendar, had even found him a bit scary. After all, he is a retired headmaster. But he is a lovely man with a great sense of humour, who turned out to be a natural at PR, wearing his 'calendar girl' baseball cap to every event. Beryl and he are a great couple, enjoying life to the full, involved in so many activities, they are an inspiration. And at the Show, what characters there were from all over. Some men loitered about shyly, then plucked up courage and bought a copy for their wives. The Leeds Pipe Band played in front of us, we danced (not for long), then sold them all a calendar. We took over £800.

We also had three days at the Great Yorkshire show in Harrogate, the largest agricultural show in Yorkshire. Horses, prize bulls, cows, pigs, sheep, rabbits, hens, you name it, they are all on show there. This was my first time there. Lizzi'd been with school, but never came out of the Radio One tent. We took hundreds of calendars to the Yorkshire Show ground and set up the stand for Tuesday, the first of the three days. There were boxes piled high, I couldn't think we would sell that many but it was a long way back to Cracoe if we ran out. There were over 3,000 calendars there, we hoped the security was good. There were WI members all over, working so hard, setting up the kitchens and restaurant as well as stands. Our huge photographs hung all around the stand, it looked good, but all one end was full of boxes of calendars.

The first day was glorious sunshine. We were so busy, there were at least eight on the stand at all times and we never stopped, bagging up the calendars, signing copies for extra money and being photographed in our frocks like celebrities. It was a strange feeling when someone asked to have their picture taken with us. It was fantastic, all so supportive. We sold 1,200 calendars the first day, that was £6,000. Not bad for a day's fun and laughter. There were lots of sad stories too, people who identified with Ange's loss. The WI women were great, working away in the kitchen and were so lovely to us in spite of the fact that all we did was swan about in black and sell calendars while they worked like dogs.

The second day was as hectic. We sold 800, that was £4,000, Angela ran backwards and forwards to the bank tent all day. There were some wonderful people, again, whose lives had been touched by cancer, too. With such a positive atmosphere, it was uplifting to be there. We did shift systems for coffee and lunches and it worked so well – what a team. I managed a little look around the show and it was impressive. We had tea with the dignitaries in the President of the show's tent.

For the last day, ten girls were on duty and Ian and Philip (Sandra's husband) came along later. Another marvellous day. Lynda and Ange went off to look at the horses. When they returned Lynda was covered in horse spit and oats all over the front of her dress. A few weeks before they had been to a demonstration by a local 'horse whisperer' so Lynda thought she was an expert and was demonstrating her skills to Ange, blowing up the horse's nose, when it sneezed and covered her in snot.

We met Claire Frisby, Pamela Rhodes, a sculpting vicar and Prince Charles amongst the hundreds. A steward told us Prince Charles was around and that we could meet him. The men took over the stand, with Mr January in charge. We split up and raced all over looking for him, because now he was running late and wouldn't be coming to the WI Pavilion. People kept stopping us for photos and to offer their congratulations. It was quite bizarre, this was the first time I realized that we were recognized. We saw the Prince in a massive crowd and didn't think we could get to him. However, some of the girls had got through, so we thought that's fine, we weren't bitter. We just stood in the crowd. Then a policeman recognized us and asked everyone to let the 'calendar girls through'. The crowd parted like the Red Sea and we ran through. We shook hands with the Prince and he talked to Ange. He remembered John and the Hawes Museum. One of the girls pushed Miss July (Lynda) forward, saying Prince Charles had just told them that she was his favourite and they were asking him why. He said it was because she painted like him. When asked if he would like her to paint him or be painted, his comment was that she would be far too expensive now. Lynda was glowing but soon stopped when an old lady from behind said, 'He will like you, love. You are the same colouring as Camilla.'

We sold over 1,000 calendars again, the total for the three days was over £15,000. In the WI Pavilion, those ladies had cooked all day again and all we did was sell calendars and have a brilliant time. They were so supportive of us and admired what the calendar has achieved for WI and 'women in full bloom'. We told them of a journalist's from the *Yorkshire Post*'s comment: that if WI had gone to Saatchi & Saatchi and offered them a million pounds to change the image of the WI, they could not have achieved what the calendar had.

*

After any of these 'away' events it was always good to get back to some sort of routine. The walk to the Sheep Pens had become our best catch up time. Ros, Ange and I made it most mornings. It was great to be out again. First walk this week, poor George. We had lots to talk about over the last three days, what an experience. I realized the calendar had helped so many people in different ways that we hadn't anticipated. This letter appeared in the *Craven Herald*, and it summed up the whole spirit of the calendar.

A dear friend elsewhere in the country had facial surgery for cancer. Knowing her as well as I do, instead of a bunch of flowers I sent her a Rylstone WI calendar. The consequences of my action have been: She has forgotten that she does not speak clearly and is talking freely. She has come to terms with her altered facial appearance and has started to laugh again. Instead of staying indoors until her hair grows long enough to hide the scars she is going out to meet her friends.

May I say thank you to the ladies of Rylstone for enhancing the quality of my friend's life.

Laughter is a strong medicine. It is more powerful than despair.

Ros knew the lady who'd written this and she told her how much her letter meant to all of us. What a wonderful comment on the power of the calendar. Laughter is a powerful medicine. It was especially meaningful for Ros, whose mother died around this time. Her mum, Eileen, was lovely, just like my mam, interested in life, never seemed old. Ros would miss her such a lot, she was a big part of her life. She used to read a book then wait for Ros to read it so they could discuss what they thought together. Just before Ros's mum died, Ros's brother-in-law, Peter, who was a real entertainer, always singing and in the panto every year, went to visit her in hospital. When Ros and her sister went along later, her mum was really poorly. While they were tucking her in, trying to make her comfy, they noticed at the end of her little thin legs, her feet were covered in Peter's stripy pantomime dame socks. He'd put them on her because her feet were cold. She would have laughed. It was a shame she didn't know more of the calendar, she died before Ros could tell her she had been invited to 'Woman of the Year'.

By strange coincidence, the room which was to be named for John at the Hawes Museum, which he had worked so hard for, was opened on the first anniversary of his death. Where had a year gone? That night, we all, husbands too, set off for the Hawes Museum. Micky, Lizzi and Adrian came with us. Such an emotional evening, especially for Ange, Matthew and Rachel. The building looked magnificent. It was on the site of the original railway station and John had wanted to bring a train back there as part of the museum. He'd organized the funding and travelled the length and breadth of the country to find just what he wanted. He nearly drove Ange crackers because he'd taken such a long time to decide. The train had been renovated while he was ill and he had managed one visit to check on progress during those months. It had all been realized according to John's vision and he would have been so proud of it. The extension was housed in an old railway car and it looked wonderful, just like the station had never closed. One of the girls who worked for him had made a sunflower tapestry for Ange. I don't know how she managed to speak, but she did. She cried as she opened the room, in front of the plaque with his name on. There was a wonderful light shining in the 'John Richard Baker' room. He would be there watching us, guiding us. Who would have ever imagined that we would be there a year after John's death, having experienced all this with his calendar? Sometimes life seemed very unreal.

Our lives didn't look as if they were about to return to 'reality' any time soon. If being Calendar Girls wasn't becoming quite a full-time job, organizing them certainly was. I hadn't realized the enormity of informing eleven people of every phone call, event, photocall and interview. But for my part and despite the strains it felt like the job I'd been born to do. I was loving it.

There was lots to look forward to over the coming months. As if to add to the sense of unreality, Claire Frisby, the presenter from *Look North* and her producer seemed to want to go ahead with a documentary about us. Ros had suggested it to them when we went to do an interview for the Christmas card. Well done Ros! It seemed that it would involve a crew following the calendar girls around and filming our various activities over the next few months. Everyone was very excited and keen to be involved.

We had several abortive attempts to meet with Claire to discuss this, on one occasion I suggested Lynda's house for a meeting. When I rang to warn Lynda she quickly put the finnie haddock she had planned to cook for tea back in the freezer – she didn't want the house smelling of fish while we were talking about middle-aged nude women! In fact that date didn't work out and when we finally managed a date, Claire Frisby and the producer Mike McCarthy met up with Angela for a quiet background meeting before the riotousness of all eleven of us together for a brainstorming. The noise level when we all get together can be horrendous.

Their idea was for a half-hour documentary filmed in Lynda's house, which they thought was just perfect for filming, and around Rylstone but also following us to the *Woman's Journal* Fashion Show at the Savoy, and the various other events, like Woman of the Year that we had planned for the autumn. I think they were amazed with us and all that was happening because of the calendar. They thought it would take about ten days to film and the plan was for it to come out near Christmas. It was all incredibly exciting. We were all thrilled with the idea and very animated throughout the meeting with lots of ideas.

There was just one sticking point, however. We had been, up till this point, adamant about not taking our clothes off again, refusing things like Richard and Judy, where they had wanted us to pose nude for them in the studio. Right from the very start we were very conscious about how easy it would have been to go too far and we didn't want to cheapen things. The film team, however, wanted us to recreate the setting up of the Christmas card shoot. They promised an all-girl team and they wanted to hang the whole programme around the Christmas card. I knew a few of the girls would be unhappy about it. At first we just said no but they insisted that it was essential. When they pressed me on it I decided to pass it on to Terry. If we did do it, he'd have to organize it all anyway, so I thought he could talk to all the girls about whether they wanted to do it again. He asked each of us in turn, very diplomatically, explaining the reasoning and in the end everyone agreed to do it. Result! I think they all very much wanted the documentary to go ahead. Personally, I didn't really mind and I think I'd have been disappointed to lose the documentary over this. A date was set and everyone was up for it.

What a night it was. All the calendar girls arrived at Lynda's to the now usual drawn curtains under cover of darkness, all eleven together, unlike the December shot where Lynda and Rita were missing. Sean Stowell, the assistant producer who'd taken over from Mike McCarthy, was already there setting up. We had met him before on a couple of occasions at *Look North*. He would be out of the room for the shot. We sat around in our dressing gowns drinking wine (very Noël Coward) and waiting for the camera girls to arrive. They arrived late having broken down on the A1. Eventually we set up around the inglenook, all trimmed up for Christmas – the fireplace that is, not us. First they filmed us in the back room as if we were getting ready for the Christmas card photo – shoes, lipstick, and a bra thrown on to the camera. We were all very lively. The two girls were great. Had us clinking our glasses, lots of abundance. Only seven hats unfortunately, but we shared, Terry organized us to look like none were missing. He set up the scene while they filmed him and Lynda putting scones out to look like mince pies, tea in the sherry glasses. I had to say, with my dressing-gown off my shoulders, 'My name is Tricia Stewart and I am Miss October on the calendar'. So did Moyra, Miss May. It was so late, about 11 p.m. and we were still only beginning the fireplace shot. Lots of shrieking and laughing, then we sang carols. Felt a bit strange being naked again at Terry and Lynda's, but we soon settled into it. The shot ended with us all shouting 'and a Happy Nude Year', then Ange threw a dressing-gown over the camera. I was interviewed afterwards by Sean, got home at 1.30 a.m., but Lynda and Terry were after me, they got to bed at 3 a.m.

We would all be knackered for the next day's filming. Vitamins, that's what I needed. Reminded me of the time I'd sent Lizzi vitamin pills to Uni in Liverpool, loose in an envelope. She'd been interrogated by the staff who thought they were drugs. I had led such a sheltered life, it never occurred to me about drugs.

One of the centrepieces of the documentary was the *Woman's*

Journal Fashion Show to be held in October at the Savoy. Back in July, the magazine's PR company had contacted me to see if we would appear as models at the show. Well, of course we were thrilled. Modelling with proper models – it sounded wonderful. All expenses paid (or so they promised). A free trip to the Savoy – sounded all right.

They were going to do a big piece about us in the October magazine to coincide with the Show. They sent a freelancer called Colin Dunne up to talk to us all in early August. In fact he had once worked for the *Craven Herald* in Skipton. Meanwhile the expenses for our 'free' trip were adding up. It turned out that the budget couldn't cover everything and we were gradually being asked to pay for more and more, including our travel down to the Savoy and our hotel. This caused a bit of trouble because, although we knew we could sell some calendars there, it didn't feel right to be taking money out of the tin for train fares. I felt that it was such a fantastic thing to be involved in that I didn't want to push too hard in case they told us not to bother. In any case I needed to book the train tickets on time otherwise we would miss the cheap ones. I wrote to GNER to see if we could have any concessions on the travel to London. I sent him a calendar, thinking perhaps 'Calendar Girls breakfast with GNER' might be a bit of good PR. Their PR man wasn't very amenable. I finally booked all the train tickets, absolutely no stress at all in that, thirteen different times and returns . . .

So our all-expenses-paid trip to London was vanishing and now we were paying train fare, hotel and nearly half of the 'free' tickets. Moyra was working on sponsorship from Marks & Spencer since it was their clothes we would be modelling and in the end they contributed a share towards the trip. It became a bit of a sore spot amongst some of the girls but I just remembered the saying 'You can't put a price on a good time' (probably explains why I'm always in debt).

Lynda was contacted by Jimmy Young's producer and they

arranged for her to do a live interview from the Savoy on the Tuesday, while rehearsing. We'd then go to the studio to meet Jimmy on the Friday. What fun!

We couldn't wait for October's *Journal* to come out with our four-page spread. Ros got it first and she rang round. I popped out to get it at lunchtime but it wasn't in any Skipton newsagents, finally got it in Gargrave. It was good, but he took so many photos, I am never sure why they choose the ones they do. The article was brilliant, and we all looked very good, healthy and wholesome!

Saks in Harrogate had agreed to do our hair free before the show because their team were to be at the Savoy as well. I talked to Bryn, the manager, who said they would organize press coverage of our hairdos. Ros was in Harrogate and called in to make some appointments. She told them she was Miss November and they said 'who?' She managed to book us in, seven of us together, all free, with the press in tow.

We heard from *Woman's Journal* that we were to have a *Times* journalist, Maureen Paton travelling with us to the Fashion Show. I hoped she liked noise. She would stay with Angela. Also heard that we would be fed at the Savoy with the models and dressers, good news, it would save us some dosh. We were also to be filmed by the BBC 2 crew, on the train and at the Savoy.

In the countdown to the Savoy, I tried to concentrate on Pilates which I was studying with a view to becoming a teacher, but found it was too easy to become distracted. Terry took some photos of Micks which I'd asked him to do because I felt Micky might make it as a male model. He had decided to leave Uni, no surprise there, he never really got into it. I wish he had been honest with us from the start and said he wasn't happy. He never actually lies, but is economical with the truth. At first he seemed settled, working, with lots of friends. Not everyone is suited to Uni, I know, although I thought Sports Science was the perfect course for him. Lizzi had loved Uni and Liverpool but it wasn't the same for Micky. If only he had left before partying for a year and running up so much debt. Still, he could be a model and get some dosh. He wanted to travel (don't we all), but first he needed to pay off some debts. With his looks and charm I thought he could earn some money as a male model and as I was going to be amongst them, why not take a portfolio? Such a rush to get them developed and enlarged. No trouble in the midst of a few calendar arrangements.

The morning before the Savoy was so fraught I felt I was going mad. It was pouring with rain and we were meant to be at a show at Pately Bridge selling calendars from the WI stall and, of course, being filmed by the BBC. We had an M&S photo shoot that night, a *Times* journalist to collect from the station, oh and my job. Ian had set off early to go to a London hospital, not at all pleased that I was about to take four days off. I popped into the office to make a few work calls and to check that the calendars had arrived at the Savoy. Ros's husband Chris, at his own expense, had arranged to ship loads down there to sell. We thought we might sell a lot because the calendar hadn't been available in the South at all.

The weather was still dreadful – driving rain. Ian kept sharing the motorway traffic and weather with me via mobile. On my way to the office I passed an accident on the Cracoe road. They'd just got some folk out and I thought I recognized the car as belonging to a friend of Micky's. I couldn't contact him for ages but he finally rang and was OK, thank you God.

What an awful day for an agricultural show. I collected Maureen Paton from the station, then we rushed back to Angela's, boots on and off to the Nidderdale Show at Pateley Bridge, near Harrogate in the pouring rain. Still torrential rain at Pateley, but I felt calmer and could appreciate how green it makes the grass. Maureen was a really nice lady. I filled her in on the background to the calendar as we drove. The showground was packed, but we got near the WI tent to park. Our stall was in the WI tent next to the WI publications stall which was selling their own calendar. I don't think we'd affected their sales, people seemed to be buying ours as an extra, not to put their next dental appointment on, but to treasure.

The BBC guys were already there, setting up. Calendars sold so fast, £700 in two hours, £1,700 by 4.30 p.m. I had not expected to sell so many at this show but people were queuing up. The *Times* photographer came and photographed us by a wet paint fence then on a wet bale of hay, we were soaked. He was amusing, trying to get some hills in the background in the pouring rain. The best bit was the woman from Alaska with a sheep. The *Times* guy got her, after Ros had asked the wrong woman to pose, who wasn't with the sheep and was very surprised to be asked. The real owner got her sheep to look at the calendar for a photograph then at us. Later we queued for the loo and the sheep was tied up outside crying for her. You can't beat a country show. All sorts of folk there, farmers, locals and lots of visitors. The sun came out too and it did in me as well.

Packed up at five-ish to rush home and get ready for the *Yorkshire Post*/M&S shoot tonight. Maureen took us to the café for a quick tea, then she read some letters while we got sorted. We rushed up to the Devonshire at Bolton Abbey to meet the lady from the *Yorkshire Post*. The Saks hair team were there to perk up our hairstyles. A glass of lovely red wine and I could feel the tension melting. The M&S clothes were great – white shirts, pashminas, black trousers, all casual but very smart, very M&S. I was given leather trousers but couldn't force them past my thighs so Beryl wore them and looked brilliant. She was a star with her Saks hair and leathers, she was like a young girl.

Home for cocoa and bed, knackered again. A perfect end to another manic day. Ian was in London so at least there'd be no arguments that night. To sleep, with the alarm set for 5 a.m.

In no time the alarm was ringing and I was up, showered and hair washed, ready for the cameras! I rang Angela to make sure she was awake (as if!), and Ros came and collected us to drive us to the station. The BBC crew were there waiting for us at the station, as well as Ange's dad, Frank, Emma and husbands, all waving us off, a send-off worthy of the *QE2*. We were all excited but controlled and so far, fairly quiet. We got on the train and found seats together and the film crew, who'd been out at the front of the train getting shots from across the rails, dashed on at the last minute to film us finding our seats. Tried to organize breakfast but not enough room for all of us, so only eight went to the restaurant and the rest ate bacon sandwiches in their seats. Throughout the journey the BBC crew was interviewing us about how excited we were and what had happened to us through the calendar. Everyone is so easy with it now, no worries with the camera. Maureen Paton was taking notes all the time. We made her sit with us, it was better for the rest of the carriage if we stayed together, it helped to keep the noise in one area.

Ros's interview nearly made Sean cry, talking about John, and how people's lives were touched by sadness. Then Lynda spoke about the reasons we did the calendar, how we weren't brave to strip off, people suffering from cancer were brave, their families and friends who supported them were the brave ones. It was very emotional for Ange.

We laughed, cried, talked, ate, slept and the journey whizzed by. When we arrived at King's Cross, there was Ian at the end of the platform with sunflowers for everyone. He came to the Savoy, which was great, I wanted him to feel part of this whole 'fucking' calendar experience, too. We stayed in a hotel not far from the Savoy and once we'd checked in and got ourselves sorted we walked to the Savoy on foot, only fifteen minutes' walk, all in convoy, it looked so good. Rod, the assistant producer, met us at the entrance and showed us the room which was to become home for the next three days – a little anteroom for eating and in the back room masses of clothes. Coffee and tea and all our meals would be in there. We all got a coffee and Karen Berman, from the PR company, came with Mikel Rosen, the show's director, to say hello and informed us that rehearsal was in ten minutes – scary. We watched the proper models perform – they were all so gorgeous. Terry and Ian watched our first attempt. They thought we were good. Of course we'd had catwalk experience before modelling for the Vogue Fashion Emporium but to be on stage like proper models was an experience. Mikel was impressed, we could tell. His dog Maurice was part of the show with a tall black model in a zebra skin coat and the dog on a matching lead.

Then it was time for the dress rehearsal. We stood anxiously by the rails of glamorous gear but we were in for a bit of a shock. These weren't our clothes but we were all to be in black with the obligatory white blouse. Well not all the clothes were awful but some were worse than others, mine especially. I was in a brocade frock (hideous, not at all what I would wear) with a jacket finished off by the white shirt. However upwards and onwards, if it weren't for these clothes, we wouldn't have been there. Ros had to wear black pleated front trousers, black polo neck sweater, white blouse, sweater round her neck and black gloves. She was leading us out. Angela wore a black petticoat, a black shawl (pashmina) as a skirt, and a white blouse. With a little black bag across her chest, she was pinned into the skirt. Lynda, who looked regal in her full-length velvet coat, said with a backward glance at me, that I looked like Mrs Merton. The awful truth was she was right.

Lynda did her interview with Jimmy Young from the toilets at the Savoy but she didn't tell him where she was. I had my legs up the wall, relaxing, but the lady asked me to take my shoes off, because they had just decorated. I had to come down quickly anyway, to tell people to put their clothes on quietly, because Lynda was live on Radio 2.

We did the first dress rehearsal, not looking quite how we'd expected, although some of us looked OK, even good. I felt geeky and so did Ros but she led us out brilliantly. She has guts. Just walking down on our own, then all together and turning back round to the audience. The routine was OK, we all grasped it fairly well, but Mikel told Ros to lose the gloves so she put them in her bag. My jacket kept falling off, but then it was never meant to be worn over a blouse. We went in to hair and make-up. They were busy with the models, then we were next. They were lovely to us, and we looked brilliant, once Ros got her eyebrows reduced. We had our nails done too. Chinzia, who did me, was brill, a very amusing Italian. We met some of the real models who were gorgeous and very nice, especially Axelle, who reminded me of Hélène, because she is French and calm. She bought a calendar for £50. The boys looked good, we thoroughly enjoyed watching them changing into their Kevins (Calvin Kleins). Just had to position the chairs correctly.

We had a yummy supper at six, with a bit of wine. Then we changed and the audience started to arrive. We kept going through the routine amongst ourselves. Chinzia touched up my make-up, a bit clown-like, but necessary for the lights. She said she would make me the best, the most bootiful lady of all and I was all for that.

Then it was show time. We watched the proper models doing their stuff, they were so professional and all looked wonderful. Maurice was a star in his cashmere dog coat. I felt a little nervous waiting on the steps so I took a Triple A. But I had nothing to worry about. We loved it and the crowd cheered. I could hear my sister Marg cheering from the audience. It was so good, we didn't want to come off. We waved and they clapped again. Then Mikel told us we were in the finale. Lorraine Kelly introduced it and was so good with our bit, describing the calendar, telling everyone it was on sale in the foyer. The finale itself was wonderful, Ange and Ros carried sunflowers. We were all crying when we came off. Everyone seemed to like us and it was very thrilling.

We quickly got changed and rushed to help sell calendars in the foyer. There were loads of women, all trying to find where to claim their free goody bags. Some were getting two. Marg was waiting there. She couldn't believe my frock, but said we did well. Champagne all round. Maureen Paton was in the foyer to see us with the *Times* features editor.

Terry had discovered a pub up the road in the afternoon, so we all set off there. It was very full and downstairs there was a private party. They said we could stay, but some girls went back to the hotel. We ordered red wine and discovered there was a tab, it was an 'end of contract' do for civil engineers and it was their tab. The young girl behind the bar had heard of the calendar and was thrilled to meet us, we promised to take her one next day. We had a great time.

We went back to the Savoy to find a taxi back to our Travel Inn. Apparently the girls who'd gone back early had spent an hour trying to organize our rooms which seemed not to have been booked properly. I was glad to have missed that. I got my bag out of the cupboard and my room key – 214 – or so I misguidedly thought. Tried my key in 214, but it wouldn't fit. It got quite hysterical because by now Ros couldn't find her room either. I didn't want to wake Ange, who I was supposed to be sharing with, but I knew she'd worry about where I was. Ros finally found her room and I decided I would have to sleep in her room. We met Beryl again in the corridor, still looking for her room. What a farce. We got into bed still laughing hysterically. Then we went through our goody bags, it was like Christmas morning. We ate the chocs and sprayed the perfume before we eventually got to sleep.

I discovered the next morning that my key had actually said

room 224, so I ran along in my nightie to find Ange, who thought I was just coming in from clubbing! We were pleased to find each other and we had a cup of tea before going down to breakfast all together, then off to the Savoy gardens for a photo call, as you do.

As we walked there a guy who had obviously slept on the park bench asked us about our sunflowers. When I explained he said he'd heard of the calendar and that he'd like one. He was delighted when I gave him a copy. Apparently he slept by the Savoy most nights. He didn't ask me for any money. Calendars to meths drinkers – what next? What a contrast to the opulence at the Savoy. Life is strange.

Our next shows were brilliant and we sold loads of calendars. We were all having such a great time, except maybe Ros, who was feeling crap in the clothes she'd been given to wear. She'd asked for something different to brighten up her outfit and they had brought her the latest fashion – ponyskin mules. They were flat and chunky and she couldn't walk properly in them, in fact she looked like she had cloven feet. I wanted to tell her that no way was she to wear them on the catwalk but the words couldn't come out for laughter. She laughed too at first but then was nearly in tears. In the end she bought a pair of Anelo & Davide shoes off a stand and he offered to give us all a pair for Woman of the Year. Not bad.

The male models were nice lads, so canny to us, some working while at university. Micky would have fitted in a treat, just his line of work, chilled, chatting and looking good. Mikel Rosen had seen his photos and thought he might have a chance – a glimmer of hope.

Our last show was amazing. Mikel wanted Ros to push the real models out of the way at the end and for us all to throw sunflowers into the audience. There was a taxi on standby for the girls who needed to go to King's Cross for the train that night – some of them needed to work the next morning and they would miss the finale. I didn't want them to go but even with only the six of us the finale was wonderful. We all threw our sunflowers to the audience, but I kept one and threw it on the catwalk at the end, for John. It slithered right down the full length of the catwalk, then stopped at the very end. The crowd gave us such a cheer. It was breathtaking.

We packed up our gear, in a bit of a frenzy now, and at the last minute they told us we could keep the clothes – typical with that frock. We gathered up the pony mules for Ros and all Chris's gear – free tights, goody bags, we could hardly move for stuff.

We sold a load more calendars, then packed up boxes. Bernie, the guy at the door stored the remainder for us for when we came back in a couple of weeks for Woman of the Year.

We rose early the next morning and left all our luggage at King's Cross while we went over to the BBC to meet Jimmy Young. He seemed a bit overwhelmed with us all, and looked older than I'd expected. He has such a strong voice on radio, and is really on the ball with current affairs. We had a very cheap breakfast in the BBC canteen, but we didn't see anyone famous.

Lynda, Ange and I didn't want to go shopping with the other girls, so we went into the church next door to BBC, it was called All Saints. There was a guy cleaning the steps, scraping chewing gum off – it was being tidied up for the following week. We sat in front of the altar and it looked like there was a light shining on the cross, right in the centre. When we left we realized it was from a flashing light on a roadworks van outside, weird that it shone on the cross. We just sat quietly, it was very calming. We left and had a coffee, then back to King's Cross to go home. It was a bit of a challenge to get on the train with all the freebies we had gathered, then to find a place for them. I was knackered by then, but couldn't sleep on the train for chatter.

*

The week after our Savoy trip was an anticlimax – I wanted to be back there. Ros and I were soon bored in between engagements. The good news was that we seemed to have gone down a treat at the Fasion Show. The bad news was that M&S wanted my dress back, apparently it was very valuable as a piece of fashion! No worries, I could easily return it and not feel too gutted. We needn't have killed ourselves carrying it all to the station. Apparently we should not have kept them after all. I didn't mind a jot but Lynda would be devastated – her gorgeous velvet coat. And what about Ros's ponyskin mules? Maybe they wouldn't miss those.

The *Journal* show was over but Woman of the Year was still to come. It was all still so exciting. I couldn't believe there was so much interest in us still. What times we were having. But it was a bittersweet experience for Angela, the thrill of modelling at the Savoy was one thing, but she came home to no John, no husband at the station to tell the stories to. Nothing can make up for that loss. We wondered where the calendar would take us next? Well, it was about to take an exciting and sometimes fraught turn.

Suzanne Mackie, from ABTV, who had written ages ago when the calendar was out of stock, had finally got her copy. I received a letter from her with a donation and the news that she was interested in our story for a TV drama. ABTV are a company in London who make films and documentaries for BBC and ITV. I thought this news through, it was exciting, sure but potentially difficult, invasive. I decided to pass it over to Angela before involving anyone else. It had to be handled carefully and anything like this really had to be Angela and her family's decision first and foremost.

At first she was very unsure about whether she wanted to go ahead with something like this, after all it would be a film about John dying. I was determined that she feel no pressure, no obligation at all to go through with anything that did not feel appropriate. She would discuss it with her children Matthew and Rachel.

With anything to do with the calendar, we had gone on intuition. If someone sounded OK, we'd trusted them. Suzanne Mackie rang again and I thought she sounded lovely, very genuine. They'd moved ahead already appointing a writer, so I arranged a meeting with Suzanne, the writer, who was called Juliette Towhadi and Angela, Lynda and Terry.

On the appointed day we collected them from the station and drove them up the dale. It was a wonderful sunny day, John was showing his dales off well. First stop was Lynda and Terry's house. They talked about their other ideas which had turned into feature films, done through their film company called Harbour Pictures. Amazing. Our intuition seemed to have been correct. They were lovely girls, very sensitive to Angela's ambivalence about the project. She was still very unsure though they tried to reassure her that the film would not be invasive and that it wouldn't portray us person for person. However, of course John would surely be portrayed, ill and dying, so it was a big decision for her. By the time they left, I felt there was still a long way to go.

I met up with Suzanne in London when I was there for a preliminary Pilates course and told her all our fears over the film – how John would be portrayed, that it not be sensationalized and stick to the reason we'd done the calendar. She seemed to completely understand, there was no pressure from her. It was a good meeting and I really liked her. I left feeling very confident about the film and about Harbour Pictures but of course it was not my decision. The plan was that she'd come and see Angela again in a couple of weeks and if she had decided to go ahead, Angela would ask the other girls if they wanted to be involved. For now though we kept the worries and discussions about the film to ourselves, little knowing that we were storing up trouble for later.

*

Meantime, although the calendar was never very far from my thoughts, Ian wanted a break from it. We spent a weekend down in Kent with my sister Marg. We had a lovely day at the beach in the sunshine, swam too. Ian and Ralph went fishing. We biked along to Whitstable and had coffee at the Hotel Continental, it was wonderful. I have always loved Whitstable and felt I could move there. It was rather nice to be recognized as a calendar girl on the promenade.

Lizzi had decided not to continue travelling and had found herself a 'proper' job. She was flying off to Chicago for training with her new job at Arthur Andersen. I was so pleased for her but I missed writing my letters to her. If I hadn't had that I would never have started the diary that I jokingly referred to as my book, little knowing. She was moving to Birmingham to live. This would be her final move from home and I'd miss her but there would be lots to occupy me. And, who knew, maybe Ian and I might get on better on our own.

We still received loads of letters every day with orders for calendars. Many of these we'd pass on to Jennings but we still did lots ourselves. Whenever we got a free moment, we'd meet at one of our houses to send out the calendars. Lizzi would have been proud of the system we'd worked out – we could shift piles in no time.

I had a wonderful yoga day with the girls at Margaret's. We sat out in her gazebo, which is beautiful, decorated with the same flair as everything she does. We even did some yoga, not just talked. I caught them up with calendar news and marital wrangles. They have been there blow by blow. My original teacher, Barbara, was there – she was seventy that month. God knew I needed some relaxation, the stresses of the calendar were building.

That night Ian, Ange and I went to Terry and Lynda's for a pheasant dinner cooked by Terry. We needed a few drinks to unwind from calendar exhaustion. It had taken over our lives. Ange, Lynda, Terry and I had given it such a commitment. The four of us had become a management team. Running the calendar had been like running a business, and I eventually realized that twelve people can't be in control of a project, someone has to be in charge. At the start everyone had been happy to have the lot come through me. As I had instigated and driven the whole project, the responsibility just settled on me. Both my office and home phone numbers went out with the first press releases, so I had handled it, but as the calendar went on I felt my position was being challenged by some. We had begun to have power struggles. I was beginning to think that Lizzi had been right when she told me at the start that I wouldn't feel the same about some of the girls ever again. We were eleven very different women who came together because of a tragedy, not realizing what a furore we would create and that it would go on this long. We had spent a lot of time together and discovered that, surprise, surprise, we liked some people better than others.

While it just seemed natural and easy for Ange, me, Terry and Lynda to more or less run things, perhaps it's not surprising that some girls began to resent this. We talked it over to see if we were handling it wrongly, how we could do it differently, but apart from talking to every single girl after every single contact, getting their opinion, then collating that information, we couldn't see a solution to the differences. I did feel we were doing a good job, keeping the spirit of the calendar and not turning the whole thing into a pantomime, which it could so easily have become. We still did things as a group of course, but some of the early enthusiasm had dissipated and some of the girls seemed to think that this was work. For me, though, it was still all great fun.

We were going up to the Kilnsey show where there was to be a ceremonial presentation of a cheque to LRF of the funds we had raised so far. The BBC, as ever, would be there to film and by now we had become accustomed to them following us around. Terry would just knock up a huge cheque, it was no trouble for him to paint one. The total would be nearly £200,000 when at the begining we would have been thrilled to raise £3,000.

The plan for the show was that we'd appear in the Grand Parade with Desert Orchid, the real star of the show – we never got top billing. I'm frightened of horses and kept thinking Dessie was Shergar – had to keep reminding myself who the dead one was. We had a great spot for a tent, no one would get past us without buying a calendar. On the day we were up there for 8.30 a.m. with coffee and bacon sarnies for breakfast. It was a bit dull but not actually raining. Everyone got there early, all bar Leni who had to work, so ten plus husbands, it was very cosy in the tent. We started selling immediately and there were such crowds, all day, that we nearly sold out. The cheque was presented in the ring, before the Grand Parade, to Harry Grayshon from BBC's *Look North*. Next was the Grand Parade with Desert Orchid, who was a bit wild, but then I am not at one with ordinary horses never mind famous ones. We drove around the ring in horse drawn carriages, waving at everyone, all applauding us. Then it was back to selling calendars. The Bishop of Bradford bought one and was photographed with us. We made £4,050.

In complete contrast, four of us went to an agrolurul show at Northallerton, which featured heavy horses and traction engines. Different folk, some extremely large, must have been hell in that heat. I drove a traction engine around the showground, really all by myself. We took £305, and it wasn't easy, not like all the other shows, where we were inundated with sales. Really we were spoilt; originally it would have been fantastic to make hundreds, but we expected more now.

The same day as Northallerton three of the girls went to Bradley show to judge the entries. They made £535 and were treated like royalty, lunch and drinks and a bottle of wine with a sunflower each. They had a brilliant day. You never could tell.

So though there was some disagreement and complaints about communication – the usual tensions of organizing a big group I suppose – we were all very excited about going to the Woman of the Year Lunch in October. Not to mention proud. I'd watched this annual event avidly and wondered what you had to do to get to it. Now I knew! We were nominated by Honorary Officers of the Woman of the Year Committee and invited as guests to the Lunch and Assembly. It's quite an accolade, it brings together 500 of Britain's leading women from a wide variety of backgrounds to celebrate each other's achievements and to raise money for charity.

I might not have even thought about it in connection with the calendar had it not been for a story Beryl told us at one of the events about an actress who'd written to her daughter, Louise, trying to get hold of us in connection with Woman of the Year, after seeing her name in the *Evening Standard*. Apparently Louise had written a letter to the *Evening Standard* after they had published an article insinuating we were making money for ourselves. This had incensed her and she had written a reply putting the matter straight. Beryl couldn't remember the actress's name, only that she had big teeth, so we went through Esther Rantzen, Janet Street Porter, Bugs Bunny, then just before she went home, she remembered it was Maureen Lipman. Fancy her not being able to find us when we've had a suspect letter from a Dutch seaman on his ship, on yellow lined paper, addressed to 'WI calendar, England'. Shades of Captain Pugwash.

I thought how wonderful it was to be nominated and I wrote back to her immediately and a few weeks later was thrilled when I came home to a message on my machine from Maureen Lipman's secretary. She wondered how many women there were and where was Miss December. The invitations were on their way but I wouldn't believe it until I saw them. Angela and Beryl received theirs first but no one else did. Perhaps they were alphabetical. Of course we all got them in the end. What a thrill. Even better, I got the impression that we were going to be on Maureen Lipman's table, with Linda Gray who was Sue Ellen in Dallas.

On the morning before the lunch we left Skipton station at 9.13 a.m. for King's Cross. All present except Leni who had to work. We stayed in the same hotel as we had done for the *Woman's Journal* Fashion show two weeks before, in fact even in the same rooms as last time. We did a bit of sightseeing, saw the London Eye and all had dinner in an Italian restaurant. We got to bed early, but I had quite a disturbed night, could have been excitement, so I was a bit tired next morning. Needed extra concealer.

We were up and off early, all in black with our sunflowers. We walked to the Savoy and were recognized by the doorman and the guy who sold our calendars last time. We met up with Beryl and Terry who had stayed with Beryl's daughter, Louise. Then we went up to the Assembly which was full of amazing women. Joan Armatrading sat next to us, fancy, and first there was a fascinating debate on GM foods. We were introduced to Maureen Lipman and I thanked her for nominating us. After the debate, we all were directed to the reception, followed by the BBC crew (who, of course, were still tailing us). I was wired up and never sure whether I was switched on so I was mindful of my language.

Everyone was announced into the reception where they were met by a line of dignitaries such as Lady Lothian, Floella Benjamin, Lady Helen Windsor, Virginia Wade to name a few. They called out our names and we filed through but then the BBC wanted it again, because they had missed it. So everyone, all these talented, famous, achieving women, like Esther Rantzen, waited in the queue while we were announced and walked through again, amazing. Recognized so much because of our black with sunflowers. Maureen Lipman spoke with us and said how she admired what we had done, then did an interview for the BBC crew. Filmed with all sorts of folk in the reception.

We met Helen Carey who was to be the National Chairman of WI the following year. She had supported the calendar throughout. Champagne, cocktails, sherry and wine all on offer but I didn't drink them all, I held back. Ros who is ace at recognizing stars saw Molly Weir, Linda Gray, Esther Rantzen, Jenny Bond, Shirley Conran, Linda Lee Potter, Linda La Plante, Fiona Phillips, Germaine Greer, Lorraine Kelly. Linda Gray spoke to Ange about John, saying he would be there with us. She'd heard about the calendar at 'home'.

We were all on separate tables but I was with Maureen Lipman. On our table were a physician, the youngest leader of the BBC Welsh Orchestra, the director of the Lottery Film and Arts Council, a Labour MP, the Associate Editor of *The Times*, the Vice President of the Fire Brigade Union, a farmer and a woman who had rowed the Atlantic single-handed. When I looked at the menu it said seabass. As I hate fish I tried to ask the waiter for an alternative. The youngest leader of the Welsh Orchestra joined in with me but the waiter didn't understand English so it all became a bit embarrassing. This as the woman who'd rowed the Atlantic was talking about the challenge, the waves, the swell . . . We thought then that if she could do that, then we could eat the bloody fish and we did!

After the lunch Ange was signing calendars at the top table for Lady Helen who was interested because her husband had had lymphoma too. Ange asked her to sign a card and she was about to sign, when someone next to her said that royalty didn't do autographs. There were some fascinating speeches on human rights, political prisoners and the torture of prisoners. Floella Benjamin told us that when we got home and were asked who had been the Woman of the Year, we had to say 'me', because every woman present was a Woman of the Year and had earned that right. Made me go goosepimpled. We all bought our Woman of the Year badges, an Elisabeth Frink sculpture of a bronze eagle. The Frink award is given every year for outstanding achievement in overcoming disability. Lots more filming and photographs, even by *Hello*. We all lined up in what had been the changing room at the fashion show. Two weeks before we'd been scrabbling around there for free tights! Then guess what was under our seats, goody bags, with all sorts in including three really big books. So exciting looking at the freebies. Lugged it all to the train again, it was all too exciting. Red wine on the train and forty winks. What an experience.

I was still on a bit of a high the next day – it was difficult to come down and get back to reality when the BBC were still filming what felt like our every move. Today they did all the Rylstone and Cracoe scenes. We had become good friends with Sean, the producer who'd taken over from Mike McCarthy and the cameraman, called Keith. Roy, the postman was filmed first, delivering all the calendar mail and talking to dogs. He had delivered hundreds of letters, knew who was which month and never complained. He's also kept each of us informed about who's been receiving what – the joys of community life.

Next on to the Dress Emporium and Ros. There had been no customers all morning, but as soon as the cameraman set up, the shop filled up. Ros spoke about how her son James had seen her on TV in Australia the night of the launch, then moved to another rack of clothes for another shot. It all took ages to do, all for seconds on screen. They had got permission from our president to film the WI meeting that night. It was Angela's posy bowl. (Each month a different member does the flower arrangement for the President's table.) She was panicking, looking for flowers. This night's monthly competition was four decorated buns. (They'd had a similar theme the year before but had misspelt it in the Parish magazine, so it read 'decorated bum'. So Lizzi and I made one out of marzipan, decorated it with flowers and entered it.) So I didn't enter this time. Ange and I were late for the meeting. The whole day had been hectic. Sean, the producer, was late leaving Ange's interview, so had had a very chaotic time setting up in the Village Hall. Our President had already ticked him off for being late but he took it well. We opened every meeting with 'Jerusalem' and this time we sang it three times for the camera, each time in a different key. WI business first, and Sean and Keith were sent into the kitchen. They filmed the cookery demonstration, then the supper and raffle (another monthly fixture), I won a candle. It was a different sort of meeting with a camera crew there but very amusing. We met the men in the pub afterwards for a post mortem. Sean had been taken by laughing fits all night. Keith the camera-man had found it hard to contain his hysterics too. What a night!

All along we'd been getting great support from the WI, locally and nationally. Lots of individual members had written and it felt very important to us to get this response from our own WI women. We were asked to speak at the Autumn Council WI meeting of our North Yorkshire West Federation at Aireville school in Skipton. I had never been to one of these meetings before. We hadn't expected a large meeting but there were over 400 women there. Six of us were each doing a three-minute slot. It was scary because they looked intimidating, sitting with their arms crossed as we walked on to the stage. But they were an appreciative audience. Christine was petrified. We thought she looked cool leaning on the lectern but she was trying to stop herself shaking. It was brilliant and we sold out of calendars. In fact Christine rang her husband John to bring more down to us and we sold them too. Such expressions of admiration and support, if we had doubted we were reassured after that day.

We were getting practised at these sorts of speaking engage-ments and had worked out a format which worked with however many of us could attend specific events. We were all getting requests to appear or speak, so would bring them to the now fairly regular calendar meetings we'd instituted and see who could go. I kept updating schedules and handing them out. We had to remember that this wasn't a job and that no one was expected to attend anything unless they wanted to, or take lots of time off work. There was no pressure. We had started this as a voluntary project and that hadn't changed.

I felt it was important to do the small local events as well as the big flashy stuff. We didn't want to forget the people who had first supported us. We did a local presentation to raise funds for the Village Hall, Hetton Chapel and the WI Project to help the Women of Romania. We sent out lots of invitations and called it An Evening with the Alternative WI Calendar Girls. We raised £700 for the three causes. Instead of being in the background as usual, Terry also spoke that night about his role as photographer. People are fascinated with his story, how it was for him as Miss July's husband, photographing her friends in the nude. He told them how Patrick Lichfield had written complimenting the photography, especially as his models hadn't been the usual young, perfect ones but real middle-aged women.

Much as the calendar felt like a career, it wasn't of course and it would end one day. I had decided to do a Pilates training course which entailed twelve monthly two-day modules in London. It would complement my yoga classes. I was a bit nervous about it. I stayed the first night in a hotel which was scary on my own, then with Amanda, the woman I'd met up at the medical conference in Scotland. I got up early to get to Kensington on time. The studio was very London. The first moments of a course were always difficult until you gel. Wondering who else would be there, whether I would like them, or they would like me and worrying whether everyone else would be really good at Pilates.

I needn't have worried, it was brill. I thoroughly enjoyed the weekend, so interesting, I loved it. Pilates is definitely the way forward for exercise. Nine girls, well women, one guy. A few dancers, one actress (darling), fitness teachers, a physio and me. It would be all I expected and more. Only eleven more modules to go. And I didn't mention the calendar.

If I needed any more reminder that the calendar wouldn't last for ever, our experience in Wigan was it. We had been asked to meet up with Ian Botham on his last fund-raising walk for LRF. He'd raised so much money for them over the years but had decided that he needed a break, so he was sort of handing over the baton to fellow fund-raisers. The nearest point to us was Wigan, not somewhere I had spent a lot of time, just knew about the pier really. Christine, Lynn, Moyra, Rita, Angela and I set off. I drove and only got lost twice this time. We stayed at a good hotel and had a great night at the dinner laid on for the walkers. We signed calendars. It was a great crowd, with a good spirit. Matthew and Georgina came with their little baby Helena (two months), she was so good, she is a cutie. Matthew loved meeting Ian, I suppose he is one of his heros.

The next day after breakfast in the hotel, we tried to find the stadium in Wigan and got lost again. We eventually got there to see the walkers set off. They set off at such a fast pace, I was relieved we weren't walking with them like I'd wanted to at first. Instead, off we went to Asda collecting for LRF with buckets. We set up a table with calendars and Christmas cards, unloaded the cars in the pouring rain, brought out six boxes of calendars and Christmas cards, must have been about four hundred.

We sold a grand total of four calendars all day long, six of us standing in the rain. No one had heard of us. They gave generously to LRF in the buckets but obviously didn't want calendars. A very humbling experience, we were so used to being recognized and everyone loving the calendar. Just think if it had all been like that. It's like Lizzi had said: I'd been lucky not to have people shouting at me in the High Street to put my clothes back on! We did our shopping and bought Christmas presents. It was very tiring, no buzz, a bit soul-destroying really. Torrential rain as we loaded up. We had a last cup of tea and set off. Wigan had had a calendar bypass.

7

We wondered whether maybe Wigan was a sign that things had peaked. Certainly the publicity was winding down and though we still did regular talks it looked as if our time in the media spotlight might be coming to an end. There was still a big demand for calendars, which would probably be increased when the BBC documentary was shown in December. And of course there was the possibility of the film; Angela was still talking with Harbour Pictures. But day-to-day life was returning to normal. I was spending a lot more time in the office, although the atmosphere between Ian and me wasn't exactly blissful.

Up until now any disagreements between the calendar girls had been minor and probably to be expected in a venture such as this had become. But the subject of the film really seemed to set the cat among the pigeons. After much thought and deliberation, Angela had decided that the film could be a good thing. It would mean more money for LRF and another wonderful dedication to John. She had built up a trust and friendship with Suzanne and Nick Barton from Harbour Pictures, as well as with the writer Juliette. We needed to know what everyone else thought now, so arranged a calendar meeting for late November at Angela's house to discuss the proposed film. Angela took the meeting and outlined the events leading up to this moment. Rita and Sandra

'Radiographers wed' was the headline in the *Sunderland Echo*, 7 June 1971.

Me and Lizzi.

Micky's photo, taken by Terry.

Angela and John.

This page:

Not all of these shots made it into
the calendar.

Miss Aquarius. I thought this was far
too discreet.

The
Alternative
WI
Calendar
for 2000

When the ladies of
Rylstone & District WI
drop everything
for their traditional crafts,
"Jam and Jerusalem"
will never be the same again!

Miss February (Angela) out-take.

The original Ros (Miss November), crocheting a blanket (with her jeans rolled up above her knees).

Chris (Miss September) poses with teapot. We nearly called this one 'more tea, vicar' but didn't want to offend the church.

Miss July (Lynda) looking regal at her easel.

Our 'president', Beryl (Miss January).

Posing with Harold while fundraising
for Kirkwood Hospice, Huddersfield.

Ange handing over £50,000 to complete the outpatient unit at
Leeds General Infirmary.

I told the kids we'd be on a billboard.

Ange and Beryl strutting their stuff on the catwalk at the Savoy.

On the mobile, dressed for the finale at the Royal Variety Show.

And in the circle bar afterwards.

Calendar signings at the bookfair at UCLA.

Our names in the window of the
Madison Bookstore. Fancy!

Me and Ian back together.

were quite definite they did not want a film. They were understandably worried about the content, that the writer might make things up that hadn't happened, and about how they would be portrayed. Ange explained that she would have rights on the script, that it wouldn't be us as us, but characters based on us, and what we had achieved with the calendar. We would all need to sign a release contract, but if anyone didn't wish to sign, they wouldn't be portrayed in any way. It would be difficult to feature eleven characters anyway. Beryl made the point that as long as the story of John was portrayed sensitively, she wasn't worried about anything else. She said she'd be quite pleased to be portrayed as a nymphomaniac! The general consensus from everyone was that really it was Angela's decision as so much of the story concerned her and John. The next step was to see copies of the releases and go from there. I felt it would be amazing to have a film about the positive reaction to a tragedy, but there was a long way to go yet. What I hoped for was a film about the reasons we did the calendar, to capture the spirit of it. But it would have to be an individual choice for each of us. That meeting broke up with everyone agreeing to think about it. The crux would come when we were sent our releases to sign.

It was later, at another calendar meeting at Terry and Lynda's house to talk about reprints, that the subject of the film came up again. This night we seemed to firmly divide into two camps over it: six plus Terry for it (me, Ange, Ros, Beryl, Christine and Lynda), five (Moyra, Sandra, Lynn, Rita, Leni) against; perhaps against was too strong a word, but not for it. I felt that a touch of bitterness had crept in to the group. It was as if the film became a rallying point round which to build up all the little niggles that had dogged the organization of the calendar till now.

Still there was much fun to be had from the calendar. We all went off, en masse, to the Leeds City Varieties to meet Richard Stilgoe and Peter Skellern. Lynda had organized our Appletreewick farmer minibus again. We arrived at the theatre to be met by Sean and Keith from the BBC, still filming for the documentary. They had spent so much time filming, however would they whittle it down to thirty minutes? We had a drink in the bar and then set up a place to sell calendars and cards during the interval and after the show. Our seats were right at the front. We realized that Richard Stilgoe and Peter Skellern were sitting amongst the audience along our row because that was how the show started. The show was brilliant, they are so very clever. Our song was at the end, it was hilarious, then they repeated it for the BBC to get a different angle. We stood up for the applause when they introduced us. During the interval we sold loads of calendars, then we met Ollie and Wil again, the students from Leeds University, who had us on their first Student Radio broadcast in April. They managed to get in as BBC with Sean and interviewed Stilgoe and Skellern. Canny boys. It was great to see them. Drinks in the bar afterwards with the stars and Richard Whiteley, who was in the audience. We signed more calendars, then home in the minibus. Our driver/farmer enjoyed it too.

We seemed to be receiving as many letters as ever. And then, a bit of a blow. At the beginning of November Jennings, who had been so fantastic, shipping out the bulk of the calendars – nearly 50,000 – had to stop the mail order because they would begin to be too busy with their Christmas trade. They had originally expected to sell a few hundred calendars but in the end had had to take on three extra staff, at no charge to us, and never let us down. The girls were so pleasant and they must have had days when they never wanted to hear the Alternative WI Calendar mentioned again. We were indebted to them. Without them we would have been in a mental asylum. We would have to do them ourselves now, after all, it would only be for two months. We'd decided to stop selling in December if we hadn't sold out by then. Some of the calendar girls suggested we outsource the lot now but that would have taken money out of the fund. Terry had looked into it and discovered that it was costly and we felt sure we could do it ourselves. Besides, if we gave it to someone else we would miss reading all the letters. This was where Lizzi's training would show! In the summer, Ange had continually worried what she would do all winter, when the Tourist Information Centre closed, well she knew now.

By this time we were waiting for our latest reprint of 10,000. From our original printing of 3,000 calendars, we'd now got something like 70,000 and we thought this last batch would take us through to December. Two thousand calendars went straight to Jennings to cover their back orders and, from then, it was down to us for mail order. We would cope.

In the end we came to dread the letters ever so slightly but we actually had some good times doing fulfilment. We couldn't complain, after all, we'd decided to do it ourselves instead of paying someone. It was very fulfilling, maybe that's why they call it fulfilment? Angela had a team of regulars: Beryl and Mr January, me, Ros and anyone else from the village who dropped in to help. On these occasions it took Ange a while to sit down and actually do calendars, so occupied was she with serving coffee and toast. She'd be able to run a café after this experience!

After packing a load of calendars one of us would drive them down to one of the local post offices. I usually went to Grassington Post Office where they were lovely. Chris, the postmaster, and his wife, who was pregnant, would sit many evenings sticking stamps on our envelopes. I would just dump the lot in the shop and they would sort them out and work out the cost, then we'd pay later. I'd park right outside the post office and often kindly passersby would help me unload. Eventually we worked out a great system where we would know the weights of different numbers of calendars in envelopes, so we'd write down how much, work out the cost and they would stick all the stamps on afterwards – saved us hours of time.

After a broadcast or event, we'd get a pile of letters and Ange's team would rally round again, along with the villagers (sounds like a Dracula movie). Ros and Mary would do them in quiet moments in Vogue. Christine and John took piles of them home to do them there. Others helped when they could. It was a marathon, but reading the letters was wonderful. It was actually what the whole thing was about. Letters like this:

Dear Unknown Friends,

My name is Diana Akerman, I'm from Argentina, and I'm coming to visit your country in February, I've lots of things in common with you, in first play, I'm 52 years old and leukemia take away my husband in May 98. But when I read the news today I thought that I did nothing to help the suffering people.

My husband was 52 when he left us. He was medicine doctor, his name was Ricardo, and we have words of love for him all days.

Ramos Mejia is a pretty city in Buenos Airies, I hope to have notices of you if you come to Argentina in any occasion. I'm going to London, with Malena (17) and Laura (16) next month and I'll try to know you.

I beg your pardon for my English, but we haven't opportunities to practise it. I hope to see you next month. Or to have notices of you to give my respects and special to Ms Baker. Perhaps your husband and mine are in the sky speaking at us. See you soon.

I wrote to her and sent a calendar, but I never heard anything else from her.

When Maureen Paton's article about us appeared in *The Times* in November, focusing on the WI angle, we were completely inundated with requests for calendars. In the article I was quoted a lot about WI, and I worried I would be excommunicated for my comments. It came across as a criticism, but that wasn't at all how I had meant it. It could have been read as if we were disappointed with WI Head Office's support for us, but we didn't expect promotion from them, just their blessing, which they'd more than given us. We knew well that as a charity they could not be seen to promote another charity. In fact, since doing the calendar I'd come to realize just how much the WI meant to me and to the rest of the calendar girls. What a part of our lives it was, how many friendships I had gained through WI, all different types and ages, women I probably wouldn't have met otherwise. Hundreds of the letters we had received were from WI members, full of admiration for what we had achieved for WI. The overriding message was 'more power to your elbow'.

Speaking of elbows, Ange needed two lots of cortisone injections to try and cure her calendar elbow, which I'm sure was caused by lifting boxes in and out of the car, garage, house and into the post offices. Roy arrived each morning and would tell Ange how many letters today, it must have increased his workload so much, but he was always cheerful. Each day piles arrived, all wanting multiples of calendars: could we send one to Aunty Jane in Cornwall and one to Uncle so and so in Gloucester. We never really knew when the demand would die down.

I went down to London for my second Pilates module, which I was really enjoying. If only I had had more time to study but each time it seemed as if the demand for the calendar was waning, something would appear somewhere to stoke demand. We were nearly out of calendars, which was how Terry wanted it, a sellout in December. We deliberated on ordering more, but no one would want a 2000 calendar in January 2000, would they?

Christine asked us if we would present the awards at Craven College, where she works. It was quite an honour and Chris spoke on her own. When the calendar was first launched, I don't think her colleagues could believe she was on the calendar, naked pouring tea. Certainly her family were taken by surprise. She didn't tell her mother, who lives in Canada, anything about the calendar, just sent a copy along with her sister when she went to visit. Imagine her mother's surprise as she flicked through the calendar to see her daughter standing naked pouring the tea. She has become a bit of a celebrity at work, much admired and totally supported with time off for calendar 'engagements'. Her speech was really good, she was so confident now, although she said she was petrified. She, like me daren't give the vote of thanks at a WI meeting, we still don't offer! Now she can talk to an audience of over 400 in the nude (or so it said in a misprint in some publicity material for something or other).

Just before Christmas the BBC documentary went out. Ange, Christine, Beryl, Ros and me watched at Lynda and Terry's. I wasn't sure whether the other girls got together to watch, neither camp had mentioned it to each other, but we were better watching documentaries apart now, in case expectations weren't reached. Sean had done a wonderful job, I didn't think it could be criticized. He'd included some good stuff, very poignantly put together, it made us cry. We watched it twice, scenes from the fashion show, arriving at the Savoy, Woman of the Year, WI meeting, on the 'Pride of the Dales' bus, walking up to the Sheep Pens complete with yoga poses. Even the dogs, George and Sky featured, so we have George for posterity. However Polly, Ros's dog, wasn't on, I hope she wasn't too upset. We rang Sean to congratulate him, he was celebrating at home. We hoped it would be networked even though we were nearly out of calendars and could do without a massive demand now.

Around this time, a guy called Warren Höge, who said he was from the *New York Times* rang the pub looking for us. He had followed our progress, had all the press cuttings and wanted to come up and see us with a photographer. The *New York Times* – hell! I thought we'd made it when we appeared on the Women's page of the *Guardian*. He was based in London and tried to arrange an interview up here but something always seemed to intervene. Once the Belfast peace talks broke down again, so he had to go over there to report on progress, or lack of it, and put the Alternative WI Calendar on hold for now. We left it that he would contact us after the Christmas holidays. He sounded very nice.

Christmas was OK, it could never be the same without little children believing in Santa. I felt quite lonely. Ian and I were not as one over the festive season but we had some good nights out. Amanda came for a Yorkshire Christmas. By the time she went home she could have written a thesis for Relate, not just from us, there were lots of tensions around with other couples too. It seemed ironic, when Ange and John had been so happy together and he had to die, yet there were so many other couples not appreciating each other. We had lots of walks with George, did Pilates and watched black and white films on the telly. Ian had been busy with last minute organization for the village hall do on New Year's Eve. Lizzi and Adrian were coming for it. I had promised we wouldn't argue and bring on Adrian's nervous cough! I wouldn't have to sob at midnight if she was here, I always missed my mam so much on New Year's Eve, I would ring her from whererever I was, put the phone down and cry. Micky would be out with his mates, but we would probably see him New Year's Day, if he surfaced. He stayed neutral with Ian and I, but it affected him a lot.

The do was a huge success, everyone danced, the food was great. Half a year of calendar girls – March, June, July, August, October and November – were there. Angela had gone to friends in Devon – running away she called it. Ian had cooked the starter for 200, a fish dish in an Italian sauce, masses of it. Everyone said it was delicious and he got lots of compliments. I loved Lizzi being there to celebrate the millennium. Amanda decided to stay on for it, bought a frock in Harrogate and gained even more counselling skills.

New Year's Day we had our usual village walk, this year around Grimworth Reservoir, but it was very foggy. We all ate sausage and mash in the pub afterwards. Ian didn't walk but he met us there. Amanda said a strange thing sitting in the pub afterwards, looking around at the calendar girls and their husbands – that all the husbands were petrified of me and where I was taking their wives. I felt surprised, I had no idea of that, it made me feel sad. There was nothing negative in the calendar, it was all positive and uplifting, nothing to fear.

Finally, Warren Höge from the *New York Times* was coming. His visit coincided with our monthly WI meeting and I got permission for him to come. There was no equivalent in America so he needed to experience it first-hand. I had arranged to collect him and his photographer, Jonathan, from the station in Skipton. Would I recognize them, or would they recognize me? As it happened they stood out from the Leeds commuters, not least for Warren's matching pink shirt and socks! We drove up to Terry and Lynda's house, pointing out all the calendar landmarks on the way, the Village Hall, Rylstone duck pond and the Devonshire Arms pub. Only Angela was missing. She was on her way back from Devon, hopefully in time to see them. A very noisy interview, all shouting over each other just like with Cosmo Landesman, but he seemed to cope well. Jonathan took a Beatles album-cover-type photo on the green, beside the ancient stocks. They were nice guys. Warren is married to a Brazilian lady so had celebrated the millennium on Copa Cabana beach, how good is that? Couldn't compare with Cracoe Village Hall.

I arranged for Ange and Terry to meet Warren while we were at WI, before they came to the meeting. Everyone needs to speak with Ange to understand the heart of the calendar, something they can't get from any other of us. After the raucous interview in the afternoon, he could have got the impression that we were just having a good time and forgotten the sadness behind the calendar. It was a bit fraught at WI for me with suppers and setting up the tables. I didn't introduce them properly to dignitaries, mainly because I was serving, pouring tea and washing up. We went back to the pub, where it was buzzing, full of characters, farmers with no teeth, all playing darts and dominoes. Couldn't have been better for men from the *New York Times*. What a character talking to Lynda, no teeth, permanent fag. Alan Bennett could write plays for the rest of his life from Cracoe alone. We had asked Roy to come and be interviewed about the thousands of letters he had delivered and he'd asked should he wear his uniform? Well, absolutely. A bit of an English farce, in the nicest possible way. They must have felt they had landed on another planet but I think they enjoyed it.

Every day there were still letters for calendars and we were returning cheques now with a standard letter saying sold out. If it was a really touching letter we tended to send one of our own copies, but we needed to stop because one day there would be none left. Terry suggested we keep ten copies each of the original and a few of the second version (When we'd put the months on the back). I had kept signed copies for Lizzi and Micky. The nights we have sat around Lynda's kitchen table signing hundreds of calendars, passing them from month to month.

The priority now, apart from getting some orders in at work, was to finalize the arrangements for the handing over of the cheque to the Leukaemia Research Fund with the total money raised. We were aiming for as early as possible in 2000. I just needed to organize dates with all the girls, then the pub and Douglas Osborne, the Chief Executive of LRF. Andrew Trehearne from LRF was organizing cardboard cutouts of figures for the amount which was, at a good approximation, £331,200, not bad eh? LRF were thrilled with what we had achieved. Graham Kennedy at Jennings offered to arrange the pub, as he had done for the launch. He would also organize the press releases as for the launch. He had been the mainstay of this calendar, without Jennings' input we wouldn't have achieved this success.

The date was set for Friday 14 January. We needed all the monies in by then, which could be difficult. Perhaps we could put an approximate amount on the cheque. LRF were fine with that. We invited anyone who had helped and supported us, families, friends, lots of whom we hadn't invited to the launch. I told Lizzi and Micky to book time off work. I couldn't imagine it would be as big a deal as the launch but there seemed to be a buzz in the air. I heard from Radio Sheffield, *The Times*, *Mail* and *Express*, all interested in the presentation of the cheque. Perhaps we were underestimating it? (We'd done that before with the calendar.)

What a day it turned out to be. Lots of press and TV and all the folk who had helped us so much. The pub soon filled up. Not quite as packed as the launch, but well attended by all the media. It was a lovely day, very emotional. We handed over £331,200 approximately, everything hadn't come in yet, but it was near enough that amount. Who would have thought. Douglas gave us all a framed photograph of our month and made a wonderful speech, thanking us all. Douglas Osborne said that he and LRF had been thrilled with the calendar's success, not only for the money raised but for the raising of awareness of these blood related cancers and the research being carried out to fight the disease. He had always been very caring of Angela and sensitive to her feelings. Ange's dad, Frank, was very amusing, after we announced the amount, he shouted out to Ange that he had another £5.

And it looked like there would be more to come. Ange had a message from a girl at Floyd PR wanting us to do an advert for a household product, a secret product. Ange and I arranged to meet Floyd – who we soon discovered was really Freud PR – at L'Oréal in Sloane Square for a breakfast meeting. They sent train tickets and a car met us at King's Cross and whizzed us there. It was a good meeting – they wanted a Peta-type photo shoot (the fur campaign models in the nude), which sounded wonderful. At first they only wanted five of us for the shoot but Ange explained that wasn't possible, they either offered it to all or none, that was the way the calendar worked. They offered what seemed to me a large amount for LRF, but Angela negotiated them up. At the end of the meeting they asked if we were going shopping to Harrods, like we were country bumpkins down from the sticks, but we said no we were off to the office of the *New York Times*! On our way, we found a white feather on the steps of the tube. It (the feather) struck a chord because over the Christmas holidays Ange and I had watched a programme about angels with Amanda. It included real life experiences of seeing angels when loved ones were dying or after death. I had always thought that everyone has a guardian angel, and a palmist (not the same one who said I would write a book in my fifties!) told me that Ian's mam, Eleanor, was Lizzi's guardian angel. I could believe that, she would want to look after Lizzi, who was born a few months after Eleanor had died. Some of the people on the programme had felt the presence of an angel after the death of a loved one, as if they had become an angel and were now looking out for that person. The significance of the white feather is that it is a sign from an angel, when there is no way a white fluffy feather could be there – like at the tube station! We joked about 'parking angels', but sometimes, spookily, there would be a space.

We met Warren and he told us that Freud PR is the hottest property in town, he chuckled when we explained that we had been unimpressed due to the fact that Ange had called them Floyd for two weeks.

A few days later it was the public opening of the Hawes Museum – John's project. Angela was asked to represent John and it was a very sad day for her, it would have been so different with John there. She met John Prescott, who said he had a calendar in his office. The ceremony was in John's room. He would be so proud of her. I was sure we were sticking to his plan – he had been directing us – I was trying to think things through slowly, like he tried to teach me – I felt I was learning.

But what would John have made of the next bit of news we received: Warren rang to tell us that his article about us had appeared that day on the front page! The front page of the *New York Times* – whoever would have thought it?

The Jam Hits the Fan

8

We had 60,000 orders for calendars in the weekend after the *New York Times* article appeared. People had somehow found Daelnet Internet Services website, who were nothing to do with us but were an Internet company with offices in Bordley, a village a mile from Cracoe. People must have found Dael as in Dales and the location and assumed it was us. Before this their biggest response had been to the 'Knitters of Dent' website (Dent being a Dales village famous in years gone by for its knitters), which made Ange and me chuckle. We had once bought, via John, a load of 'Knitters of Dent' birthday cards, and for years everyone we knew got one! They were getting 200 hits a minute on their email – 60,000 emails mostly from the US wanting a calendar. And not a single one to be had because we'd sold out in December. That didn't seem to stop the flood, however. The guys who ran the company were brilliant, they did a reply for us saying the calendars were sold out. They charged us nothing and invited us to read the letters, some amazing ones. One in particular from a lady who had been a nurse and now had breast cancer. She'd been feeling really low and bad about herself but hearing about the calendar had raised her spirits.

We had press interest from around the world; offers from Hollywood film directors and stars' agents to do a movie – nearly everyone I spoke to seemed to have directed *Sixth Sense*, or worked for the director who did! Angela was thrown into a panic by a call from a Hollywood producer asking about the film rights. She told him we were 'taken'. Not to mention renewed interest in the UK press covering the story of what a hit we were in America. NBC sent photographers and a senior correspondent; and a producer from the ABC show *20/20* (which we quickly learned, was a big deal over there) rang for a chat and said, 'Why don't I hop on a plane and come see you?' – and she did.

Just when we'd all thought that was it, now it was off again. Angela thought that the calendar had a mind of its own and that John was guiding it somehow. She said, and she was so right, that if the US reaction had happened earlier, we couldn't have coped with it, but the way it was working out was just the way she imagined that John would have planned it. The difference this time was that by now we knew some of the difficulties that this renewed brush with 'fame' could lead to. We looked forward to the next stage of the calendar with excitement and not a little trepidation.

I think all the girls might have echoed Ange's thoughts about the calendar having a mind of its own but that seemed to mean different things to different women. There had been tensions before over various issues and of course there was still the unresolved issue of the film, but it was really only once the *New York Times* created the huge upswell of interest again that unresolvable problems set in. Maybe it was because the stakes had been raised or maybe it was just inevitable anyway but some of the calendar girls began to feel they'd had enough of the calendar, that we had made our point and that it was time to get back to normal.

I couldn't have felt more differently and I had little patience with that attitude, which probably didn't really help matters. For me, and for all of us, life could never be the same again. The calendar had changed things. It had been the most amazing experience, we had really left a mark and achieved so much, raised such a lot of money. I was thrilled to think that it might carry on and not only because I enjoyed the new world and experiences that the calendar presented but because I knew we could still raise lots and lots of money for leukaemia research. Besides, there was never any pressure on any of the girls to do anything they didn't want to do, it was voluntary fund-raising after all. Not everyone was as impatient with the 'enough is enough' attitude as I was and Angela in particular wrestled with the decision about the film and the ramifications of her decision to go ahead with it.

The cracks were in evidence at the shoot for *People* magazine, an American weekly with an enormous readership of nine million people. We gave the interview in the Devonshire at Bolton Abbey and all of us were there. From the beginning it was a bit fraught because the time had been changed which some of us didn't know. We ate lunch, while having lots of photographs taken and then went back to Lynda and Terry's for more photos. I wasn't struck on the journalist who seemed to have no charisma, he interviewed us typing on a laptop. But the photographer was a nice guy and we made friends straight away, which he used to get Terry to strip off, as if Lynda was painting him in the nude. A brilliant idea for a different shot, or so it seemed at the time. Terry was sat on a chair as if posing for Lynda to paint him, he was naked, but just showed above the waist. However, as soon as they'd done it Terry wished that they hadn't, but it is so easy to be carried along with these guys. No doubt it would be tastefully done, they shouldn't worry. I was getting a bad feeling about the whole thing, thinking well, the magazine was made of thin paper, what do you expect? But I don't suppose I should judge the merit on that. All in all it was a bit of a fraught, screamy, competitive day.

None of that showed in the final piece which turned out OK, after all, even Terry's nude shot, although Terry did get some disparaging comments from a few disgruntled husbands. Not long after it came out we were playing WI darts at Skipton Rugby club. The ladies from Lothersdale came over to see us straight away to ask about the calendar's progress. One of them was Gladys Emmott, a farmer's wife, who was famous locally for converting one of their barns into a very posh hat-rental agency. They are brill women and they had a copy of *People* magazine, which one of the ladies' daughters had sent from America. She said that they had been practising darts in the pub, not scoring well until she showed Gladys the photo of Terry, then she scored double top, took another look and scored another double. Lynda said she would tell Terry because he was a bit embarrassed by it. It was a good night and we left arranging darts in the nude for next year. We were rubbish at darts but at least we'd have the edge on the nude front!

Our next adventure was the Surf shoot, or Scurf as Beryl had christened it. As if to prove that we could carry on as a good calendar team despite our differences, we had a super day when we travelled down to London for it. Well, at least ten of us did. Rita had decided that she didn't want to take her clothes off again, which was fine. The rest of us were ready and willing and I'd been putting lots of cream on my body, waxing and detoxing (or at least giving up chocolate for a day or so).

We took the afternoon train down to London for the scheduled Surf shoot arranged by Freud (at this stage the product was still supposed to be a secret). I got a phone call on the train from Hollywood about a film – again – which I also tried to keep quiet! There was enough trouble with film talk. I always liked the train, sarnies, coffee and chat and it was a good journey. We were collected at King's Cross in two cars and booked into a lovely hotel. We unpacked and went downstairs to meet up for a meal with the Freud team. We looked at contracts over dinner and straightened out a few minor details. We went to bed quite early, we needed our beauty sleep.

The cars collected us again the next morning and took us to the studio warehouse for the shoot. Once again there was an all-female crew. One of the make-up team named Rae had a feather in her hair so we talked about angels. It took all morning to be made up and organize the set. Loads of girls working, I would love a job like this. They made us look so good, well marvellous really. The set was all white and wonderfully lit up. Then Ange took her dressing-gown off and sat naked on the set – she looked wonderful. We all followed, dropping dressing-gowns as we walked into the lights and took up positions. Those who wanted to be at the front were told to sit there. Fortunately there was no contest, five wanted the back, five the front. Phew! I went to the front, you guessed. Five at the front, sitting with legs covering all bits. Five behind, kneeling up. The back row held giant sun-flowers and in the front we had packets of Surf. They directed us, taking polaroids, which looked great to me. The photographer was very clever. After a while it became really uncomfy sitting on my foot for so long, over an hour. I'd never been pressed up against so much bare flesh for so long before, especially female. I was enveloped in the girl behind me. It was warm but it was a good atmosphere. They played Abba music and we sang along. I think this was one of my best days.

We adjourned for lunch, which was good, with a glass of wine. The next photo was naked again, with an orange banner held along the line of us hiding our bits. It was tricky for Ros and me, when my bottom was covered hers wasn't – needed to manoeuvre a lot. We dressed for a hats and pearls shot. They posed us sat astride a bench, looking like we were wearing just pearls and hats, but we had bras on. It looked good. The last shot was on the idea of *Friends*, sat on a big orange sofa. They supplied black outfits for us, big orange cushions and of course packets of Surf. That was it then. We finished and waited for the cars to collect us. We all felt really tired. It is hard work being a model. The cars were late, the traffic atrocious, so we missed our train.

The five in the first car just caught it, but not us. We were exhausted by then but there was nothing we could do but wait. We got home very late and very weary.

It had been a brilliant day but it was clear that by now, after over a year of the calendar, we needed a break from each other. Things would quieten down soon. They had to, we had no more calendars. And I needed to be in the office more before Ian and I ended up divorced! Things between us seemed to have deteriorated to rock bottom. We argued all the time and the rows mostly started about how much time I was spending on that 'fucking' calendar and not spending on the business. I understood but I just couldn't stop now. I'm afraid I offloaded a lot on Lizzi and she understood how I felt and empathized with me, but must have got sick of me complaining but not changing anything. I felt like I needed a complete switch-off and, ages before, I'd booked a meditation weekend with shiatsu Hélène which I thought couldn't have been more perfectly timed. Wrong. I would have been better sleeping all day. The morning started badly with foul weather right up to Malham Tarn. Ian had to drive me and he was really cross about that. He kept saying couldn't I do something normal like staying at home for once and why did I always have to be doing something different. It was a very tense trip and I wished I hadn't arranged to go. I wasn't ready for this type of meditation, it scared me at first. Then we had to be very quiet, hardly speaking, which is difficult for me. The guy who led it, AmSa was like a native American Indian with Jesus eyes. I chilled into it a bit, but it wasn't the right thing for me at the time. Later, in the evening out by the lake, I spoke to Ian on my mobile who had had a horrendous trip back and was still really annoyed. He picked me up the next morning and though he'd calmed down a bit, we were still not really speaking.

Maybe it would have been better for Ian and for some others who were having problems with the calendar if we knew when it was going to end but it seemed that every day brought some new thing from some corner of the world. One day it was the front page of *Le Monde*, ooh la la; a Mr Gonzales from Brazilian TV in London faxed me via *Le Monde*. How international is that. He wanted to arrange to film us. Warren Höge, from the *New York Times*, said we should do that for the women in Brazil, they are perceived to have 'had it' at our age. Unfortunately, despite a few more calls, mostly to Lynda who developed quite a fondness for Mr Gonzales, he didn't have the money to get up to Cracoe to interview us, so we weren't able to further the cause of the middle-aged woman in Brazil – guess you can't do everything; a New Zealand radio station wanted an interview; the choreographer of the Bluebell girls in Paris wanted a calendar; Japanese Newspapers were interested. Dallas Windsor, not very Japanese, I know, rang to arrange to send a journalist. A journalist called Toshi came up to see us in Cracoe and he was lovely, but difficult to understand, specially with my accent too. We were chatting to him, when Lynda disappeared, to return with an old-fashioned photo album. It was her scrapbook for her Japanese penpal, with all his letters and cards and a photo of him. Toshi said he must have been well educated because he wrote in English. She had only stopped writing to him at nineteen, when she got engaged to Terry. We developed slowly in those days. She asked Toshi to look for him, see if he remembered her or knew of her now as Miss July. He promised to send us a copy of the paper, we could look at the pictures.

Tense times, busy times and often it was still an awful lot of fun. Filming for the *20/20* news show for example was a real laugh.

Ene (she did hop on a plane), from ABC TV in New York had spoken first to Terry, then me and she was so interested in it all. I called her Henna for a while, but got to grips with it eventually. A couple of researchers also rang to get background for Ene. Shortly after, she and her entourage arrived and booked themselves into a local hotel. I picked her and her assistant Carolyn up and drove them over to Lynda's where all the calendar girls had convened. She met everyone and said what she wanted for the programme – she knew what she wanted OK. She had the week planned, who she wanted where. I liked her and Carolyn. They would be here a week, including a camera crew arriving at the weekend. We would be filming bits and pieces practically every day.

We spent all of the next day filming with Ene, walking in the fields beside Lynda's house, over and over again. Up and over the same hill, good exercise for us, at least. She wanted the sheep in the shot and tried to get them to come to us, as if. The crew were great, they were chuckling at the sheep. Whilst in the field, I got a call from *You and Yours* on Radio 4. They wanted an interview that lunchtime. I have always listened to that programme. I told them I was in a field, filming for *20/20*, and agreed to do a recorded interview when I got back to Lynda's. Which I did and it went well, they asked good questions. Fancy being on *You and Yours*.

Ene had moved to the Devonshire at Bolton Abbey, she didn't like the facilities at her first hotel. Americans expect more than us! They needed someone to drive them around, so I suggested Micky as he was between jobs. We insured our Mazda for him and he was in, at £10 an hour. He was thrilled and they loved him, who doesn't? Perhaps he could drift into media, modelling hadn't come off but at least we had some good photos of him!

Next Bob Brown, the correspondent from the *20/20* show, arrived. I thought Ene would interview us but apparently not. That took the team to nine. Or ten with Micky. The BBC only ever had a team of two, there's the difference. Ene wanted to film us doing a few calendar girl events. Firstly we were at a farmhouse in Hebden to launch a Hat Agency. Ene filmed us doing it. Lovely place, wonderful hats. Ene and the crew then got lost in the Dales, Micky wasn't driving that day. They found us eventually, filmed us on bails of hay. Ros and Beryl looked brilliant, and there was lots of traditional cow muck for Ene to see and walk through.

We then had one more full day dedicated to ABC. Lynda, Moyra, Beryl, Ange and I sat around Lynda's table, drinking coffee, being filmed catching up on calendar stuff. Later that evening all the calendar girls met up at Lynda's for filming. So much happened each day, I had loads to share, so I took advantage of the times we were all there together. It was getting more difficult to get together like this due to everyone's commitments. Moyra had been contacted by another US TV company wanting to do a documentary piece on us. Ene, naturally, said not to do it, it would take the edge of hers. I could see that, she came first, and was a real professional. A few objected, but she explained her position well and smoothed the troubled waters.

The crew had set up in Lynda's lounge. If Terry had been charging location fees, they could have made a fortune, the number of times their house had been used. Ene arranged us all on the sofa in front of the Inglenook. Bob sat in front of us with a list of questions. The conversation flowed, Beryl was brilliant, nothing fazes her, she's so natural. Everyone had a say, but you never knew what would stay in. This would be seen by so many people, I should have made up better! Ange was interviewed on her own and had them all in tears. She was worried that she had opened up too much about John's illness but I didn't think they would exploit her. An exhausting day in many ways.

Had a chat and walk to the Sheep Pens with Ange the next morning. She was worn out with all the filming. Today she was taking them to Leeds General Infirmary, to interview Dr Childs, who had looked after John, and to see the ward. That would be hard for her. Micks drove them all day and Ros and I just worked. When I rang the hotel after work, Ange was having her nails done and Micky was in the pool, this was just the job for him.

Next up for Ene was the WI meeting experience. The crew was all set up before we arrived with bottles of wine and cheese for supper. The other members have been great, putting up with the media, although lots have said they have enjoyed it all. I would say 98 per cent totally support us, although we don't ram it down their throats, only update people who ask. The rest have been a bit sour, but there would always be a negativity in some people. Ene chatted to our president and secretary, she had already contacted them for permission. She was so professional, a fantastic lady, I would have loved Lizzi to have met her. Ros and Lynda were on suppers and they served us beautifully.

At the end of the meeting we had to say goodbye to them all, which was very sad, we had become close, but I felt sure we would keep in touch. Micky whipped them away and would take them to the airport the next day. Ene thought he was very intelligent and would achieve a lot. My mam always said 'that bairn will surprise you' and he constantly does.

A few weeks later, in February, the *20/20* show went out and Ene said it had come together well. We eventually saw a tape and it was fantastic. The American reaction to the calendar was overwhelming really and continued to be. Beryl developed a funny routine about how her stereotypical attitude to Americans had been completely revolutionized since the calendar.

*

While she was over, Ene told us we could sell the calendar in the US. She said we needed a publisher over there but first we needed an agent and she knew a guy in Canada, a friend of hers. What an idea, there were no objections, from anyone, which made a pleasant change. Terry contacted Ene's agent/friend and organized the whole thing. What an amazing amount of work involved, faxing Canada, looking at contracts, Matthew helped with that. It all had to be done in such a short time.

Our agent found us a publisher. Workman Publishers in New York would do the US calendar. Terry sent all the technical stuff, I had to put together a package of background, press cuttings, résumés of ourselves, letters, a sample of nearly a whole year of calendar stuff. Ian suggested we halve the royalties between Leukaemia Research Fund and the equivalent society in America which seemed only fair when it was to be sold there. Ange would organize that. The day she rang Leukaemia and Lymphoma of America in New York, there had been a thunderstorm and people couldn't get in to work. She spoke to the lady on the switchboard, explaining why she was calling. The lady listened then said, 'Well my dear it is marvellous what you have done, you will make a million and it may be just that million that will find the cure.' That is exactly what Ange hopes for. It was also what kept her going if ever she had doubts that she should continue with the calendar.

I sent more background stuff to Workman by Fedex. I was au fait with the system now, on first-name terms with the Fedex man. Terry spent so much time on this, organizing the plates to go over, checking proofs, they wanted a more colonial look than ours, perhaps a Victorian look. He'd become so involved with the calendar, he had probably forgotten how to paint. I talked to Ellen Morgenstern, the publicity director at Workman who was lovely and so thrilled to be involved with the calendar. It was so exciting to think there would be an American calendar. Workman wanted to publish the calendar in early May. They aimed to launch for America's Mother's Day on 16 May. It was going to be a nineteen-month calendar starting in June through to December 2001. Workman took a chance launching a calendar halfway through a year. I could feel it all starting again, bubbling away, I loved all the organizing, but not much time again for proper work, Ian was sick of the 'fucking' calendar again.

We seemed to be back to the starting blocks again, except this time there was the troubling problem of the film playing in the background. Before the calendar, I could never understand why groups like the Beatles or the Spice Girls split up. They were making money, all they had to do was churn out songs. I understood now, too many differing opinions develop after starting off with the same intention, it becomes impossible to all work together as a team any more. We were relieved to have gone some way down the road with Harbour Pictures when the American furore erupted, otherwise we would have been completely bamboozled by all the film interest now. It became tricky enough as it was . . .

By this stage Angela, Matthew and Rachel had formed a good relationship with Harbour Pictures. I knew that Beryl, Christine, Ros, Lynda and Terry felt the same trust as me. Suzanne and Nick (from Harbour Pictures) were at the Sundance film festival in the USA and rang to say they had met Buena Vista who were interested in the film. Buena Vista is the UK arm of Disney. We needed to be signing contracts. Harbour Pictures offered to pay for us to have an independent lawyer of our choosing for the film contract. Matthew said he would organize that, investigate in his law firm. We would have a showbiz lawyer!

As if to add fuel to the fire the *Daily Express* picked up on the Hollywood thing. On the front page was a picture of Julia Roberts, with the headline 'Will Julia Roberts strip for the WI?' The article suggested we were to do a Hollywood movie with American actresses, completely untrue, though we had had calls from everyone and their dog's agent, Meg Ryan, Meryl Streep's a few times – can she do a Geordie or Yorkshire accent? Even more *Sixth Sense*, I must go see this movie of a thousand directors.

And then some interesting news: Moyra heard via a builder she knew who was doing work on Victoria Wood's house that she wanted to make a film now. Moyra was very excited about it.

It was obviously following up from the front page of the *Express* with Julia Roberts 'stripping for WI'. I talked to Ange and Lynda, we couldn't understand why she hadn't contacted us before and why via her builder. How come she hadn't looked at the calendar to find all the names on there, mine, Logan Studios, and the printer. She had had a copy since June 1999. Ros had sent her it and received a card, saying she thought the calendar was brilliant. She gave Ros Julie Walters' agent's address, but no donation, which was fine, stars must get lots of charity requests.

How would we have felt if this was our only offer or if it had come earlier? Probably very differently, we would have been thrilled to have Victoria Wood's interest. I know five of the girls were very much for her, but as we have all said, ultimately the final decision was Angela's. No wonder there are world wars, when we couldn't agree over a film; how would we deal with more serious problems? We wanted to keep this civilized. Any adverse publicity would damage the relaunch of the US calendar and the press were always looking for a downside or 'split' as they call it.

Ange thought it only fair that Victoria Wood knew the situation with Harbour Pictures. She was unable to get Victoria's home number so I rang her agent. I explained that as the film was so close to Angela and her husband's death, I felt Victoria needed to speak with Angela first. Victoria phoned me first and I gave her Ange's number. She rang her later and Ange clarified the situation. Ange was worried that it was unfair to give false hope when she had built a strong relationship with Harbour Pictures. However a meeting was set up for the following Friday night at Moyra's after yoga. I knew it would not be easy.

I spoke to Suzanne and Nick at Harbour Pictures, who also wanted to come and talk to everyone. I arranged that for a few days before the Victoria Wood meeting (they would need to bring Madeleine Albright). We'd thought we were at a stage where those who didn't want a film could just opt out and the rest of us could go ahead as Angela saw fit. It was hard for Angela because any dissent was hurtful to her. She tried so hard to be positive and fair with everyone, but sometimes people have to agree to disagree.

So the meeting with Harbour Pictures took place at Terry and Lynda's house. On arrival, the atmosphere seemed very tense, or perhaps it was just me. Matthew spoke well, in a very moving way, outlining his initial thoughts on a film, how he hadn't wanted any further attention on his father's death, that he had thought it should end with the calendar. However he had met the people concerned and built up a relationship, realizing what this could raise for LRF, which of course was the whole point. He trusted them, but would look carefully at the contract and take advice, liaising with our 'film' lawyers, who had been recommended by knowledgeable lawyers in his firm. It was heartrending listening to him talk about John. Some tough questions followed. Lots of points were raised, some perfectly valid like would they make up things like affairs to spice the story up and who would have rights on the script, but it still felt aggressive. Ange felt, very strongly, that by agreeing to the film with Harbour she'd got about as much control over the end product as we were likely to get. The thing was that any filmmaker could have made a film about this story without us. At least with Harbour Pictures anyone who signed a release was entitled to read a script. This seemed more than fair to me. And, as long as we were involved, LRF stood to make substantial sums of money from the film. Suzanne and Nick handled it well, but by the end of it I felt cold and my legs were shaking. I said nothing, but felt ashamed that I hadn't intervened at the unpleasant moments. Still, that would probably only have made matters worse. The two camps seemed even more divided and entrenched now that there was another offer. Ange was so upset after it. I wondered whether Victoria Wood would get the same sort of grilling come Friday.

The next morning, during our walk to the Sheep Pens, I talked about the film problems with Ros and Angela. It appeared the main complaint was that I hadn't told everyone sooner. But I hadn't wanted us to make any decisions until Angela, Matthew and Rachel had confirmed or dismissed the idea. I had felt it was not our decision in the early stages. We chewed it over again and again but I didn't really see what I could have done differently. I dreaded the Victoria Wood meeting.

We had yoga before the meeting, so we were a bit late. We rushed in to find all the others surrounding Victoria and her agent, Phil McIntyre, who was sat at the top of the table. Matthew and Rachel were already there. Introductions were made. It was a totally different atmosphere to Wednesday night's meeting with no nasty questions. Victoria Wood clearly felt a very strong connection with the story and pitched determinedly, talking about how she would write it herself. But it worried me, this wasn't a *Dinner Ladies* story, there was so much depth in this calendar. It was very difficult as this was the first meeting with her. Although she had been close to the story geographically, she didn't know any of us. It felt to me though that there was not a lot of reference to the heart and soul of the story, in fact Ange was hardly involved. It was decided they should go to Ange's house with Matthew and Rachel – Georgina was there with Helena – to have a family discussion. We all agreed, or so I thought, that it would be down to Angela, finally.

Once Angela and Victoria Wood had left I'm afraid I just couldn't not speak up. I said I thought they had given her an easy ride with no nasty questions. How did they think Victoria Wood would portray them anyway? I brought up the complaints of Wednesday. There had been lots of comment on where they thought I'd gone wrong in handling the publicity, criticism levelled about 'lack of communication'. I felt it was easy to say 'I didn't know anything', or 'no one told me' when I knew that I'd passed information on by phone, and printed out schedules, taken letters to meetings, as we all did when requests came through to us. Well, I got a lot off my chest. Terry was criticized for agreeing with me about Wednesday. There was a heated discussion, ending in me being told I was on the biggest ego trip ever. A few people left after that, well stormed out, but I felt it was time for these things to be said. The remaining few smoothed things over, agreeing that the decision on the film was Ange's. Good job Victoria had left otherwise she would have got a much better script. Lynda, Terry and me called at Ange's to share the experience, so glad Ange had not had to sit through it. I must say, I felt better for speaking my mind.

But Ange was worried. They had clarified their position on the Harbour Pictures film with Victoria, explained the situation and their feelings, the relationship they had built up with Harbour Pictures and Victoria and Mr McIntyre left, saying if that was the decision they would bow out gracefully.

But that wasn't exactly what happened. Roy the postman delivered a recorded letter from Phil McIntyre to all – as Roy said, 'you've all got one.' I don't think he's signed a secrets contract. It outlined their interest and enthusiasm for the film and offered us a lot of money for it, more than Harbour Pictures had put up front. I had breakfast with Ange, and she said that despite the letter she and Matthew and Rachel were still certain they wanted to keep faith with Harbour Pictures. That was my feeling, too.

And that wasn't the end, along came another offer from Phil McIntyre, once again to all of us, except Terry, who they obviously did not consider to be a major player. They had increased their offer of money up front, it seemed they desperately wanted to do the film. Far from bowing out gracefully Phil McIntyre unwittingly caused even more problems between us.

The opening line of his letter implied that Matthew had spoken for all the girls when he'd conveyed Ange's decision to Victoria Wood, which of course Matthew would not have done. Matthew represented the views of and spoke for his family, not all the girls. Victoria Wood had, however, made it clear from the start that she was only prepared to go ahead with Angela's approval, so I guess for them it added up to the same thing.

Well, it seemed we needed some outside neutral help to resolve this. We arranged for all of us to go to London to meet the media lawyer that Matthew had found for us, a man called Reno Antoniades, who had quite a formidable reputation. A media lawyer now, well doesn't everyone have one? Before we met him we had a meeting to discuss our questions for him. Once again we all convened in Angela's kitchen, the scene of many meetings and discussions, it could be the title of a book. A cut and thrust sort of a meeting. The aim was to sort the issues out regarding the film. The main issue had changed from some girls not wanting to be involved with any film, to now wanting to be involved in Victoria Wood's film rather than Harbour's. They argued that the money was better and that Victoria Wood would have a particular affinity for the story. They meant that she was English, having swallowed hook, line and sinker the line about the Harbour Pictures film being a 'Hollywood' one. We were divided.

Lynda, Terry, Angela, Lynn, Moyra, Rita, Sandra and I travelled to London for the *Parkinson Show* and we had arranged the meeting with the lawyer to coincide. Ros and Christine both had to work so would miss the fireworks. They'd join us later for *Parkinson*. Eight of us together on the early train, as so many times before. We were booked into our usual Travel Inn. Like a school party, the eight of us took the tube to St Christopher's Place to meet our media lawyer. The offices were very tasteful and Reno was a handsome young man, just back from hols in Cuba. He handles stars like the Spice Girls, so would be totally au fait with girls groups. We should be a piece of cake, or not. It was a good, informative meeting. He handled all the issues well and gave good advice to all who were open to it. He is a clever man. I felt he had an immediate empathy with Angela and that we could trust him. Ange sat next to him, then me, Lynda and Terry at the other side, we said very little. He outlined both offers, the monetary remuneration, implications of distribution, control over scripts and the signing of releases. It was all very comprehensive. It wasn't just the money up front to consider; the better the film the more it could make in the long run. We wanted, of course, to make lots of money for Leukaemia Research, but a sensitivity to Ange's role in all this was paramount. That seemed to be the crux of it. His advice was sensible and neutral, so much so that each camp interpreted it in their favour.

We nominated a spokesperson from each group; Ange from our side and Moyra from the other. What a shame we had degenerated into this. We set out to sell 1,000 calendars, dedicated to John, raise £3,000 for LRF, with no idea it would take off like this. Perhaps we had done well to survive so far. To be fair we had been challenged by a major event, of our own making. We needed now to consider the image of the calendar, and maintain our dignity. People admired us for our guts in doing the calendar, the friendship for Angela, the way we had handled 'fame'. We couldn't blow it now. The only way forward was a democratic vote. All seemed happy with the meeting. We weren't to talk to either contender for the film for a week, then we had to write to Ange or Moyra to say who we chose. We left the offices and went for a drink in the square nearby. We didn't mention the meeting in the open between the two camps, but obviously spoke separately.

We moved on amicably to the *Parkinson Show*. Back to our hotel, to change for 'Parkie'. John, Mr September, was with us because there had been a spare ticket. He was excited to be going to the show, like all of us he loved watching it. We met in the foyer and ordered two taxis to take us to the BBC. There was a buzz about the whole place. On the show that night were Harry Connick Jr, Kate Winslett and Jimmy Tarbuck. First it was drinks and nibbles in the green room, then we took our seats, reserved in a good spot. It was such a thrill to be there, the guests were brilliant, especially Kate Winslett. After the show, we went back to the green room for wine and yummy food. I chatted to Michael and his wife Mary, Jimmy and lots of interesting folk. Wondered if one day we would be on the show.

The next day we'd planned to go to LRF head office. We tried to call and see them when we were in 'town' (as Maureen Lipman calls it). Ros and Christine went back early for work, some went shopping while Lynda, Terry, Ange and I went to LRF. Andrew Trehearne from LRF had contacted Workman's agent in the UK to meet us and Douglas Osborne was in the office too. Whereas the American deal had initially seemed like a wonderful bonus, now that we were openly in dispute over the film, the minutiae of this deal, too, was becoming an issue. Unlike with the original calendar, where all the money had gone directly to the charity, there would not be the mega amounts of money from this calendar. It was now a business deal, with agents, publishers, printers, PR, marketing etc, all to be paid for this time, not free as we'd done it. But as Douglas said he would rather have 1 per cent of something than 100 per cent of nothing. Our agent in Canada had got us above the normal calendar royalties, so it would amount to a fair bit. However, this was later to become an issue when we, and in particular Terry, were criticized for not getting a better deal. Oh well.

Perhaps we should have insisted that the other girls come with us to this meeting, but in the event it seemed a bit of a relief. There was such bad feeling over the film and we had completely different approaches now. In any event we had a really good discussion with the guy from Workman on how we could promote the calendar in the UK. We had him mind boggled, there was so much happening. He was sure there was still a market here. We were still getting letters all the time. It would be great to have a calendar to sell again with all that was going on. In April there would be the billboard, still a secret product, we couldn't divulge it. I'd told the kids we would be on billboards, mind I hadn't envisaged forty-foot ones. The BBC2 documentary was due to go nationwide in April, around the same time as the LRF conference in Manchester (where a billboard would be). He went away with a lot of info. Lots to use for promotion.

What an exhausting day. Ange and I decided to stay overnight and we had supper with Ene, who was still in town. She reassured us that we were doing the right thing over the film and it was good to hear it from a professional like her. Of course we sometimes had doubts, going a lot on intuition as we did.

The next morning we had breakfast in a café, like Southerners, then to King's Cross. Upgraded to First Class, Ange's charm! Slept and talked about all the problems. It was so hurtful for her, she coped well with it, but it was saddening. It was like a betrayal, I know that sounds dramatic, but we started out all for the same purpose or so I thought. Now that seemed to have altered. Some of the girls said they did the calendar for LRF, not in memory of John. Perhaps I should have realized at the outset that we didn't all have the same view of the calendar and then I might have handled things differently – better, even. Lizzi often tells me I shouldn't assume people always think the same way I do. Having been so close to John, for me this calendar centred around him and Ange. And I couldn't forget that whatever we did, whoever we met, wherever we went with this calendar, Ange came home to no John.

Once the split was acknowledged it was as if the floodgates had opened – lots of other contentious stuff came up, and it was open-season on me. I was asked how I came to the approximate amount for the handing over of the cheque, the £331,200, which we had agreed upon. It was suggested that I had overestimated by £7,000, figures scribbled down on a bit of paper, for me to justify. Ange was worried, but there was no issue. It was discussed with Jennings and LRF, we added up all monies to come in and agreed on the approximate amount on that basis. There was no missing money. In fact, when all the monies came in it would probably be more than that amount. This was the first time a money issue had arisen. We were all handling money every day, a lot of money, then it was passed to Ange, so it had to be on trust. I had never had the slightest mistrust of any person involved.

One of my efforts to 'improve communication' went wrong. Prior to another of our calendar meetings to discuss the film, I sent a newsletter around, with an update, trying to explain how Ange felt with all the arguments over the film. It had completely the opposite effect I'd intended, causing more bad feelings. I was worried that we forgot why we'd done the calendar, we would lose the success. Angela is the heart of the calendar, her input and depth. It is difficult to explain, but she has a strength and truth that have made the calendar.

Things like this were frustrating and hurtful but I tried to keep calm about it all – not that easy for me. Beryl (Mrs Kissinger) suggested that we needed a chairperson to run our meetings, a neutral party – they would be queuing up for that job! Which masochist would want to take that on? What a comment on us. There was now a telephone chain, to improve communication. Seemed complicated. It would be like Chinese whispers. This was of course a direct dig at me and I looked forward to sharing the problem of communication. It took the pressure off me, it had been hellish at times.

The calendar went on regardless. There was lots to come with America, and I wanted it to continue but not be spoilt. Our biggest fear at this stage was that news of the split would get into the papers. We thought that would be the end. We would have to agree to disagree over the film – the democratic vote was 7 to 5. Terry, Lynda, Beryl, Christine, Ros, Angela and I were for Harbour Pictures. Naturally, Terry had a vote, to some of the girls' surprise, but he was the photographer, instrumental in the production, development and distribution of the calendar. Angela wrote and told Reno the decision and he passed on the information to both parties. Harbour were delighted and thanked Ange for 'keeping faith' with them. They would shortly issue a press release announcing the film. I didn't feel this was the end of it, though.

In April 2000, a year after the launch, we were in many of the national papers and on a billboard with Surf, we were off to the LRF annual conference in Manchester, where there was a billboard, and the BBC documentary was about to be shown nationally. Saatchi & Saatchi couldn't have planned it better than that.

In the midst of all this, on a whim, Carol and I went to Bradford to see a clairvoyant. It's the sort of thing you do when looking for 'something' in your life. We were a bit apprehensive. If it had been the house next door, we wouldn't have gone in but we'd come all this way. Carol was first, I sat in the other room and looked at Buddhas, spiritual books and videos, so felt OK. Carol came out mouthing 'amazing' to me. It was tarot cards, which have always scared me. This is what she told me: I was unhappy, I lived with a depressed person, difficult and moody. I needed to sort it out, move on, sort out finances. She saw a house-move, sell up and share out the money. I would be betrayed by a dark-haired woman, whom I thought was a friend. She turned a card over with the swordsman on, he was waiting for me, he would blow my socks off! Also the Ace of cups, the highest card for business, my new career would be very successful, I will make lots of money. She saw a much wanted baby, we would find out in June/July. Also someone having a heart attack. Never mentioned the calendar, not any reference to it. I always wonder if they can see what they can, why do they live like they do? I know you have to be careful, but it was a bit spooky. Carol's was very interesting and correct. I think she had Ian sussed at that moment. I wondered if we would stay together, made me think.

We travelled down to London again for the Surf launch. Away for another two days.

Ian took us to the station, stopping on the way at the newsagents to buy copies of the *News of the World* which would have pictures of the billboard. You always worry a bit with a paper like that, but the photos were good and the report was fine. We looked good, the hair and make-up were excellent. That shoot had been one of my best days and I think it showed. I met the other girls at Skipton station.

All smiling together as we set off. I suggested to all the girls that we didn't talk about the film to the press. They would surely ask. I didn't really know what to do. But felt everyone should know that Harbour Pictures would put out a press release the next day about the film. We had not talked about the film together since the final decision had been made (though naturally it was often the subject of conversation between ourselves, hell we were forever more casting ourselves and John – Ange had her heart set on Michael Palin) but it loomed unspoken between us any time we were together. Cars picked us up at King's Cross, we were getting used to this sort of treatment. The launch was at the same hotel as for the shoot. All afternoon we did interviews with the *Express*, *Mail*, Press Council and lots of photographs. Then we went off to Soho Green with the *Daily Telegraph* photographer. We ate in the hotel which was very posh. Ange was not well, she thought she had caught 'slap-face' from Harry. The meal was lovely, Lynda and I took Ange a plate of cheese and biscuits, sat on her bed and ate it with her. We needed her on top form for tomorrow, make-up would have to cover up the slap-face!

We had ordered loads of the morning papers but it was only in the *Express*, how disappointing. John Clancy planned to open a fish 'n' chip shop to use up all he'd bought today and over the months, which have had no mention of us. I had brought all my Pilates books and file, and tried to study after breakfast, while Ange did the *Sunday Times* 'a life in the day' interview. How brilliant is that. It was the first article I read on a Sunday morning. Steve Wright wanted me, Sandra, Ange and Lynda later that morning. I always listened to his show. We were collected by car. It was a very amusing interview, Lynda was ace, very commanding, we managed to mention Surf, in spite of no advertising. Waiting outside for the car we bumped into Parkie, who recognized Ange and hugged her.

Ange, me, Lynda, Sandra and Ros went for a shop. There was a camera/radio shop next door to the hotel and we asked in there for a cheap radio to listen to ourselves on Steve Wright but it was £40. When we told them who we were he got one out of the window and we listened all together in the shop. We showed them the piece in the *Express* and signed the photo for them. We had such fun and then we all bought a handbag torch for walking around Cracoe with no street lights. I was just losing the anxiety of the film conflict and chilling in Habitat when the *Express* journalist from yesterday rang to say he'd received a call from a source telling him all about the split, how Victoria Wood's offer was more altruistic, how much more money she had offered, and that five of the girls would not sign for a Hollywood movie. This was just what the press had wanted, a negative slant. I tried to play it down and at least he had had the decency to ring me. He had got the impression that we disliked Americans, I emphasized how much support we had received from America, about the US calendar and the money going to Leukaemia and Lymphoma Society of America. This could affect the launch of the US calendar, I felt sick that someone had gone to the press with this. Lynda took over, made me slow down and think. She was right, the way to go was quiet, try and haul back a bit of dignity. I spoke to LRF and Harbour Pictures to warn them of the bad press coming. They were disappointed but their main concern, as always, was for Ange's feelings. We'd just have to keep our fingers crossed.

As if that wasn't bad enough there was an awful article in the *Telegraph* about the split. The journalist named all five 'rebels', but an anonymous spokeswoman said, 'This is not a minor difficulty but a definite difference of opinion as to which offer should be accepted.' There were sentiments like worrying that Rylstone would be invaded by American tourists and Moyra was quoted as saying, 'The American project is more risky. If they're going to make a film then good luck to them, but I don't particularly want to get involved in it. Having said that the last thing we would want to see happen is for Angela to get hurt.' The *Express* one was OK, at least he put both sides. And he mentioned John.

And so it went on, but then you can't just court the press when you want them. The *Daily Mail* was next. A really nice photo of me, I don't know where that came from. I hadn't worn that suit for months, but I may drag it out again. There were lots of insinuations, about leaving the door open for a rival movie, that the split would mean we could no longer make money for leukaemia research. Not if we had anything to do with it.

This had set off another wave, Surf has had so much extra free publicity! We were contacted by news organizations in Germany, South Africa, New Zealand and Canada, to name a few, all wanting to know about the film. Harbour Pictures sent out a press release. Will a film have ever had more prepublicity? We were being advised by a team of people including Diana Holmes, the publicist for Workman Publishers in the UK, Andrew from LRF, Suzanne and our lawyer, all working together and advising us what to do, it was like the spirit of the war, we could all go on holiday together. Lots of newspaper reporters were on to us, looking for 'dirt'. One, Sebastian O'Kelly from the *Mail on Sunday*, arrived despite being told we wouldn't do an interview. He turned up at Terry and Lynda's, so Ange, Ros and Chris came to talk to him. He had spoken to Moyra on the phone. He wanted separate photographs of the two groups but we refused. That was the first time we had asserted ourselves, we hardly said anything, Terry talked mostly about horses. Ros and I didn't like him or his photographer. I think they felt it. He wanted to write about the split. He had just returned from Eritrea and said this interview was worse than being there! Angela and I were off to London to do a live show called *Loose Women*. Lynda told Sebastian to organize everyone to go to the station for a united photo and my God they did. Brilliant. All waved us off on the train with Sebastian. He has the worst case of dandruff I have seen, but I held back from giving any advice. Made small talk, then he went into First Class.

What a chewing night, we went to three hotels before we were in the correct one. Then finally in our correct room, we put the TV on to the *Eleven O'Clock Show*, which I have never seen before, and a guy was saying the WI are making a film, it will be called 'Baggy Puss', very amusing, made us chuckle after a harassing day.

Loose Women was brilliant and then we did a *Guardian* interview – everyone wanted to talk about the film. She seemed an OK girl so maybe she'd put our side of the film story. We then went on to Harbour Pictures at Chelsea Harbour. It was a lovely place and wonderful to see Suzanne, Juliette and Nick after this week. We had made the right decision and I was sure it would all progress as it was meant to. I read the *Express* on the train home and my picture was in as part of the quiz of the week referring to the Surf advert.

What a whirlwind. I'd decided I didn't have to take my Pilates exam which was scheduled for the following week. I would cancel it on Monday – what a release. All weekend would have been hell trying to cram it all and I didn't want to do a crap exam. Lizzi would think I was chickening out, I suppose that's true, but I would take it next time and be prepared. I had had a lot on!

Another article appeared in one of the papers referring to the Rylstone Five. It made me so cross but I was just going to have to learn to put up with this sort of thing. But one comment in particular was hard to let go by: that Ange had been in negotiations with Harbour Pictures for a long time before involving anyone else. That was the time when she was trying to decide whether she could bear a film about her husband's death. I didn't think it would harm the calendar, though. Crap for Ange again. Better if she hadn't read it.

The adverse publicity didn't seem to be having too bad an effect. At this point we still did some things together, though actually that was becoming more and more difficult. Any time we were together with the 'Rylstone Five', as the papers called them, we simply didn't mention any of the press articles, the film, or any other of the contentious issues between us. I don't really know why, it just seemed the best way to handle things. Some of the newspaper articles suggested, melodramatically, that the row had split the village. Well, not so I'd noticed. Life went on, we saw the five at WI, at the pub quizzes and we never mentioned the calendar. Sometimes it was as if it had never happened.

Meantime I was trying to revise but it just didn't stop. I had started a little Pilates group to practise on with Christine and John, Terry and Lynda, Ange and Ros. It worked well, good for my teaching practice. I had rescheduled my exam for later on in the year. Work was hardly ever on my mind now and Ian was completely fed up. I was always away and he was always in the pub. Nothing changes. Maybe my angel would look after me.

Lynda had had an invite from Preethi, the Indian girl we'd met at the bookfair, to go to her book launch at Dover Street, by the Ritz, on Thursday night. It was the same day as a shoot in London for the *Mail*'s *You* magazine. Lynda had sent her a calendar, which was in her office. She was having a stressful day organizing her launch and when she went in her office, the calendar fell off the shelf. So she phoned Lynda who was also miserable and the depression lifted for them both.

So once again we caught the early train to London. I couldn't believe we were still doing this. A car took us past a huge Surf billboard to the *You* shoot in a wonderful building in Battersea – a converted school. We had an exhausting day, outside in the rain, walking across the road on a zebra crossing, like the Beatles, not quite. All day inside, outside, walking up the road, sunglasses on, sunglasses off, with attitude, without it. It appeared over three pages under the headline 'Resevoir Dolls'.

Ros, Lynda and I decided at the last minute to stay over and go to Preethi's launch. We booked a double room at the Travel Inn thinking we could sneak three in, there is always an extra single bed in the room. It would be cheaper. We got out of the *Mail*'s clothes and back into ours, and bought ourselves some toothbrushes. Around the corner was the Ritz, so as we had time to spare, we popped in for a gin and tonic which cost £10 each. We ate three bowls of free nuts each and stayed ages watching people who thought £10 for a G&T is normal. We walked to the restaurant where the launch was to be held and Preethi was thrilled to see us. The first thing we saw was masses of sunflowers in vases in a beautiful water shrine. Sunflowers mean happiness and are Preethi's mum's favourite flower. We met her mum and dad and lots of her friends and drank champagne. Her book focuses on following your dreams, following the African dancer. Later after speeches an African dancer appeared and a band, it was brilliant. Lynda danced and did her African 'click', from her childhood days in Africa. A lady from South Africa came to meet us and held my face in her hands and told me we had done a wonderful thing and she didn't think we realized how wonderful.

After lots more champagne and food we were the last to leave. An Aussie couple put us in a black cab. I was so pleased we had stayed down for this. We decided in the taxi that Ros and I would book in, while Lynda hung around discreetly, so they wouldn't know there were three in the room. She went to the door first but it was locked and when the guy asked her which room, she swept past him. Ros and I went to the desk, probably looking drunk, but trying to be coherent. We stood filling in the forms and Lynda came floating past us. She was meant to be discreetly waiting around the corner. We ignored her, but back she came again. I mouthed for her to go away. The stupid thing is the guy on the desk probably didn't give a stuff how many were in a room. Verging on hysteria and dying for a wee, we finally booked in then collected Lynda who was now hiding! We opened the door to the room and guess what – only a double bed, no single. We were in fits now. No jamas and three in a bed. Ros got into bed in full make-up, with me, the biggest one in the middle, then Lynda, bathed and in Ros' T-shirt, at the other end. We slept really well, not touching each other!

*

The calendar was still taking us to places we'd never been before but the best was yet to come. Our American publishers, Workman, had decided that they needed some of us for an American tour when the calendar was published there in May. We knew that Angela would be chosen but the great news was that they had decided on four of us and I was one of them! Ellen Morgenstern wrote a lovely note outlining their reasons for who they'd chosen and hinting that there may be a second trip later in the year. This was beyond my wildest dreams. Angela, Beryl and I would go first to New York, then meet up with Lynda in Los Angeles for the *Tonight Show*. Lynda had had a feeling all along that she would be going, she had no idea how. Jolie, the producer of the *Tonight Show* rang her at the gallery and asked if she could fly out all expenses paid, to LA, next Thursday, to arrive in time to meet up with us three for the show on the

Friday night. Very calmly she said yes, but could she fly on Wednesday so that she could get over her jet lag before the show! She agreed, then asked her all about her royal connections. What a trip this would be.

Would it never end? This was my life now and I could hardly remember the other one!

The morning before we set off for America Angela, Beryl and I walked to Rylstone to the churchyard and put flowers for John, then went to church at Hetton. It was a meaningful service, full of thought and kindness. Ange's parents Joyce and Frank were really canny, wished us a lovely time, Joyce said she would pray for us to keep safe. I was so looking forward to the trip. I could hardly wait. I had never been to America before and to be arriving at JFK in New York, then on to Los Angeles, Santa Cruz and San Francisco was so exciting. What a relief to leave all the problems at home behind, both with Ian and the 'rebels'.

In the days before we set off, as we planned for the trip, I had to keep pinching myself to prove that it was real and that we were going. What a thing, a tour of America, we had no idea our little venture would come to this. Ellen had sent a schedule over. All sorts of people wanted to see us. She said the schedule was expanding every day. Over dinner at Terry and Lynda's one evening, with Beryl and Ange, we talked 'America': what to take, what to travel in, size of cases, etc. We decided on lots of black and to wear our sunflowers and pearls at all times – the official calendar uniform. We needed to take copies of some of the wonderful letters we had received for Workman: like from the Queen and Queen Mum, thanking us for their calendars and sending their sympathy to Angela, some of the many heartrending ones, poems and the international ones addressed simply to 'Calendar Girls, Yorkshire'.

Planning for our trip was so thrilling that I wondered if the reality could begin to meet our expectations. I'd had a shiatsu session to boost my energies for the trip. Hélène said she worked on my basic energies, trying to remove negative energies – I was afraid there was only one way to do that and I would have to have the courage to do something soon.

I had spent the weekend before leaving with Lizzi in Birmingham and it had been lovely to see her. She seemed far away, geographically, at the moment. We bought clothes for America, lunched and talked about all sorts – Ian, the palmist, the calendar (of course). She felt Ian and I would be better apart and that I would be happier on my own. Sometimes I felt that too but it seemed such a drastic step. I knew it was me and me only who could sort my situation out, instead of just moaning at her all the time. It wasn't fair to offload on her and it was destroying her relationship with Ian. I fantasized about being offered a job in the States, a sabbatical for six months – the solution to all my problems. But that would be running away.

The night before we left I packed, trying to take little which wasn't easy with all these black suits. Ian was driving us to the airport and said we needed to leave at 6.30 the next morning. He wasn't thrilled about my going but didn't try and stop me, though he did remind me frequently that I'd be away for his birthday on 25 April. I was fighting the guilt. I set my alarm but didn't really think I'd get much sleep.

I was up at five, bathed, hair washed, make-up (no George to walk, he was on his holidays at Terry and Lynda's), then I walked round to Ange's, to find her trying to force another jacket in her case, so I encouraged her. Drove up to Terry's to collect him, he was coming with us to do a recce for Lynda's flight on Wednesday. We would meet her there after we'd done a few days in New

York. We filmed her waving us off in her nightie (no flashing this time) and left shouting 'see you in LA on Thursday'. Beryl was next to be collected. Out she came with her green case on wheels and hat in carrier – kiss for Mr January and off we went to Manchester. It was a lovely misty morning and Ian started shooting the video we had promised to record – or rather I had for a Sky TV programme.

Ange tried to get us upgraded but no luck today, even though they knew about the calendar. However, our seats were OK and the lunch was good, then tablets, sleep, afternoon tea and time to get off in New York. A guy with 'Stewart – Ladies of Rylstone' on a card ushered us into a tasty car and whisked us off to the Roosevelt Hotel. Very nice, posh hotel – all in separate rooms – they do not know that we sleep three in a bed at the Travel Inn in Putney. The rooms were lovely, but Beryl was on the ninth floor, a long way from us, so we changed her to ours. We unpacked a bit, then rang Ene from the *20/20* show and she came for tea in Teddy's, the hotel café. It was great to see her again and catch up on all the calendar news. She had sensed the differences between us, a very astute lady, she missed nothing. Her advice has always been let it go, continue to handle it with dignity.

Then Ellen Morgenstern arrived with the latest schedule – just as I expected she was lovely, what a sussed lady. She had organized this tour fantastically, there were pages and pages of things for us to do. We were to have dinner that night with Carolan and Peter Workman, our American publishers. We got ourselves a taxi – well the doorman did – and he dropped us off at Union Square – we didn't know the name of the hotel or anyone's phone number. Ange spotted the restaurant and it looked lovely. With Carolan and Peter to meet us were Ruth Sullivan, our editor, Jim from the Leukaemia and Lymphoma Society of America and another lady from the local chapter.

After a lovely dinner, we walked back with Carolan and Peter through the streets of New York, past Barnes and Noble book-store and Carolan suggested we go in and look for our calendar. I looked up and saw a sign advertising a Michael Palin book signing on Wednesday night. This seemed like destiny; we'd talked about how he was Angela's favourite to play John in the film. We'd try and go. We walked to Carolan and Peter's flat, then got a taxi back – what big girls. We were a bit tired now. We had all got along so well, especially Beryl, who talked to Jim all night, then when we got back to the hotel, desperate for the loo, Beryl said what a nice man Robert was or was it Rick – we laughed so much we nearly wet ourselves, trying to find the loos at the Roosevelt.

We were up early the next morning for the *Today* show live. Make-up and breakfast. Our first interview was with Katie Curran for the *Today* show. Her husband had died of cancer two years before and she had an empathy with Ange. It went really well, all three of us talked together as a team letting each other speak and chipping in when needed. Not all our interviews had been like that and it was a good one to start with.

We spoke to various people to set up more interviews through-out the day, our schedule was crazy but we just went along with it all. We were dropped from CNN who were covering a live broadcast by the President – we'd been ousted by Bill. We walked to the Barnes and Noble branch where we were doing a signing later that week. Amazingly the window was full of our calendars, with enlarged photos from the calendar as posters – it looked wonderful. I took photos and video – I was getting the hang of this video camera now. We were knackered by now and returned to the hotel for a rest and Ellen went back to the office.

Beryl and Ange went for a walk while I tried to sleep, but I had phone calls and faxes – so no change there. They went to St Patrick's cathedral, where there was a service and singing, and lit a candle for John. They saw a few shops and found a good

Deli. Beryl wasn't feeling well at the Deli, she'd had no sleep last night. We decided to let Beryl go to bed with a sleeping pill and Ange and I would do WCBS-TV. A lady called Dana, very petite and glam, interviewed us. Ange had her lines off pat: 'We are so pleased to be here in the USA to promote the American version of the calendar, which is a nineteen-month calendar, from June 2000 to December 2001, the royalties being shared between LRF and Lymphoma and Leukaemia Society of America.' And then we had to get in that the calendar was available in bookstores now.

Back to the hotel to change for the Leukaemia and Lymphoma Society of America's 'Man and Woman of the Year' awards. Beryl was ready when we got back having slept for a few hours and was feeling a lot better. A stretch limo arrived for us – the first of many – and took us on a wonderful ride through Central Park to the Tavern on the Green. What a place, all lights on trees and privet animals. We met Jim again and Mary, the Executive Director of the New York chapter, who was lovely. We circulated and met two young girls who fund-raise and were running the New York marathon soon. Beryl was at a table with a couple from Texas who had been on a tour of China and not enjoyed the food – chicken, chicken and rice – they took her through the whole trip, Beryl would have no need to visit China now. A guy sat at our table and chomped through the speeches – he looked like he was wearing his teeth in for Mr Ed. He seemed determined to stay with us and was enamoured with the calendar. I asked him to video our presentation, not sure whether he was drunk or daft. The evening was brilliant and we signed calendars, selling them for $20 each. Mr Ed asked us to sign a calendar to him, 'Selfish Bob' and I thought he must be aware of his failings, then realized he meant 'Sailfish' – he had a boat.

We drank some lovely wine, not too much because we were definitely on the sleeping pills! Left earlyish, although I wanted to stay for the reception for a 1,000 guests of Al Pacino after a film preview. Better to have an early night though – or so Beryl and Ange told me. They wouldn't have got me and Ros away!

We were up early again the next morning for the Rosie O'Donnell show. The crew (mine) arrived at 7 and did a little cameo filming in the bedroom, wearing my robe. Beryl had come to dry her hair, then Ange arrived (she was still trying to get to grips with the fact that she had no dressing-gown – robe here – in her room and Beryl and I had massive fluffy white ones). We were taken by car, once again, to NBC studios where breakfast, make-up and hairdressing were all laid on for us. So exhausting! We went into a studio to rehearse the intro which was all written for us in massive letters – they must have thought our sight was failing! We then sat in the audience and listened to the manic warm-up man. Under our seats were goody bags with books and other heavy things which made our hearts sink thinking of getting them home. Then it was our cue.

The producer had warned us not to say 'nipple' on air and when Rosie showed the calendar my nipple was covered up by a pink post it. I said it was always like that. Beryl said we'd been told not to say 'nipple', so Rosie made us say it all together. After all, the previous week she had been discussing the 'Vagina Monologues'! She was great fun and we didn't want to come off – for a change.

I had to leave at the first break to go to the Bronx for a radio interview. Kim, from Workman, took me and Ellen stayed with Ange and Beryl until the end of the show – they saw Michelle Pfeiffer – then they did a TV interview later at the hotel. Kim took me on the Brooklyn Bridge and I looked over at the Hudson River. Then on to the radio studios in the government building there. Lots of security and checks. A downtown New Yorker called Joan interviewed me – she was brill, got it all in again. We hadn't really changed anything for the American market, perhaps explaining WI a bit more, which Beryl usually did, as she knew the most. It was so easy to speak about the calendar, I knew every bit of it and we all felt passionately about what we were doing. Then out of there to another studio to do WNYC-FM/NY to be interviewed on the Leonard Lepate show – like our BBC Radio 4 – how highbrow.

We were met at the door by a girl called Sarah who took us up to the studios. I sat down and put my bags on the next chair. I heard someone else come in and went to move my bag for them to sit down and looked up and saw Michael Palin looking down at me with laughing eyes. I couldn't believe it, he looked so handsome and cool. I said hello and he knew about the calendar. I told him we were coming to his book signing tomorrow at Barnes and Noble and why we were in the US. I also told him about the film and Ange wanting him to play John. I am not sure whether he thought I was serious, because he made a joke about taking his clothes off. He'd already done that for *GBH*, so no secrets there! I told him where else our 'tour' went, and he said he couldn't get on the Jay Leno show. His interview was after mine, but he listened to mine and they turned it up for him, and Sarah told me he was really excited about meeting the calendar girls. Leonard was good, asked really interesting questions and I was on a long time. Met Michael Palin again at the door and he told me it was a good interview and I said we'd see him tomorrow. Kim said I had been really cool and seemed unexcited at meeting him. Good. I couldn't wait to tell Ange and Beryl.

Back to the hotel and high tea with the Media. We had about ten minutes to get ready in frocks, hats and pearls – Ellen's idea. Beryl looked like she had walked off *Murder on the Orient Express*. We walked in to a room filled with media folk – Ellen said there were people there who never came to anything. Beryl sat with two old men (there's a change), not knowing who they were and thinking just another two old men, but apparently they were VIPs in magazine land. We circulated as Ellen had told us to and were photographed so much. Ene came, Ruth Sullivan, Mary and Jim (or Rick as Beryl knows him) from L and L. There were cucumber sandwiches and nibbles, silver service and tea – just what we always ate at WI meetings! The hotel manager came to meet us – the Roosevelt Hotel, who give a lot to the Leukaemia and Lymphoma Society, had donated our rooms so we thanked him. Ellen finished her introduction by thanking the Ladies of Rylstone for 'caring, sharing and most of all baring', and we gave our presentation. We talked, so easily, although not for Ange. Her bit was to explain the significance of the sunflower and it was always so sad for her. But she handled it so well, moving but never too sentimental. She has some guts, John would be so proud of her. It was a magical afternoon and worked so well.

Ellen finally went home after another hard day's work – it was hectic for us, but Ellen was constantly organizing, rescheduling and checking the itinerary and I knew from what I had done it took a lot of energy. Back to our rooms for a little wash and brush up and to change out of the frocks, then out of the hotel to find a taxi to see Michael Palin. We were on our own now and there were loads of people waiting. We couldn't get a taxi to stop and then a guy with a stretch limo offered to take us with another passenger for $30. The other passenger paid $15 and he said it was a good deal, so we hunched over into another stretch limo.

Barnes and Noble bookstore was full to bursting, but the girl said 'hello ladies, your seats are at the front' and took us right to the front row. Then Michael Palin came on to give his talk, which was very amusing and lots of questions afterwards – mainly about *Monty Python* – I should have asked him about Sunderland Empire and the parrot sketch some thirty years ago. He finished with 'now to the filthy lucre, if you don't want a book, fuck off'. No one was offended and I had been holding back! After his talk we were invited up first to have him sign books for us and we signed a calendar for him – magic. We had a coffee upstairs then taxi home and to bed because it was a 4 a.m. start in the morning.

A 3.30 a.m. alarm call. It was still dark when Beryl and Ange arrived at my room, no make-up on. Looked and felt very 'naked'. Kim met us with a car to go to Murray Hill studios for seventeen satellite interviews. We knocked at the studio door and were let in to get ready for the satellite media tour. Photographers and technicians set up the room. We'd brought sunflowers from the Roosevelt to place the heads on the table in front of us, to show on the screen. The producer arrived, looked about twenty, same as the make-up girl, who said she could see John on my shoulder before she even knew why I was there. We looked better after make-up. I sat with Ange first, then up on the screen comes Chicago – Roy and Kim – we talked to them for a bit, then on to Phoenix with Kyle and whoever. Then Beryl swopped in for a few – Atlanta, Washington, Little Rock. We tried to get all the info in each time and I think we did OK. You had to concentrate on looking at the right camera. The lights went on above the one we needed to look at and without appearing to, we had to turn to that one. If we didn't do it the guy waved his arms around frantically, but it was hard to see him in the darkness. Eventually we got the hang of it. The controller kept reminding us and saying we were doing OK. By 8.30 a.m. we were finished.

After more coffee and breakfast, we were off to Rockefeller Plaza to record the *Later Today* show with Florence Henderson who was Mrs Brady in the 'Brady Bunch'. We were taken to the green room which was bustling with folk – it was 'mother and daughters' day all over the US. Moms took their girls to work with them for the day. They did our make-up again, we should look good by now but we needed lots of concealer for the dark shadows. Beryl was holding up so well, she looked the best of us. Florence was interviewing Julie Andrews before us, and we expected her to break into 'The Hills are Alive'. She looked good on the monitor, talking about osteoporosis. Then Florence got changed because they are all meant to look like different shows.

On the set and in she came, face looking younger than sixty-six, although Beryl is a contender for better, naturally. She was lovely to us, very compassionate, got all the relevant stuff in and the audience reacted well. This was for transmission the week after we left so it would keep the momentum going. I wished I could have stayed to do six months' promotion.

We headed back to the hotel with Ellen to eat a picnic lunch in our rooms. Beryl and I had a sherry to perk us up, we felt a bit weary now having been up eight hours! Next was the calendar signing at Barnes and Noble – we were worried no one would turn up and I would have to drag them off the street. However there were people already queuing throughout the store – I couldn't believe it. They had a table set up for us and we started directly, signing, talking, laughing. CNN was filming all the while with a great lady reporter – Jeannie – who talked to lots of the people about their reasons for buying calendars. We signed over 300, it was a brilliant experience. We were just signing some to leave in the store when a young man called Bruce ran in to buy a calendar for his mum. He was sweating buckets, he had run six blocks and was dripping. Angela was worried about his calendar getting drips on and was dabbing at it and then Beryl got up and wiped him down with a serviette – CNN filmed it all – he hoped none of his friends would see it. He was from Sussex and his mum was still there. People of all ages were buying it, many for Mother's Day presents. Mother's Day is a massive celebration in the US. Ange and Beryl broke into 'Jerusalem' – it sounded brilliant – I did not even attempt to mime! We could have stayed all day and looked round the store. US bookstores are so different to those at home, a place to go and really look at books, to stay and read and have a coffee. Barnes and Noble stores are tasteful buildings, very period, wood, sedate calming places. I liked them.

We, however couldn't stay because next stop was JFK airport to fly on to Los Angeles and meet up with Lynda. As we left the store people waved us off, a lady with a sunflower T-shirt and filmed again by CNN – I waved my sunflower through the car window. Back at the hotel there was a fax from Suzanne at Harbour Pics – Buena Vista would like us to meet for lunch if possible on Friday. We have a window! Ellen thought it was a good idea to meet them or rather for them to meet with us, she felt sure they would be impressed and it would benefit the film for them to know what we were about.

We were struggling so much with our suitcases, having been given books, sweatshirts and mugs by different shows, it was so hard to force it all in. I had to sit on my case, which was not a good idea. On the flight Angela did not feel so well, she was not keen on all the flights. By the time we were through the airport and the limo arrived she looked dreadful. She managed the ride to the hotel, but felt worse, probably travel sickness.

We arrived at the Beverly Hilton in a limo bigger again than Angela's lounge and Lynda swept out of the door to meet us. Like royalty. The hotel was fantastic but Angela could only just reach the couch in reception. Ellen booked us all in – separate rooms again – mine and Beryl's were poolside – can you believe it! Mine was right by the pool, Beryl overlooked it. Angela went straight up to bed, so Lynda helped her with her gear. We all unpacked and met back at the restaurant for a light supper. I opened a bottle of wine in my poolside room before dinner – very nice. Then to bed with plans for a swim in the morning. Lynda who had already had a day here and sampled the luxuries, said the pool was lovely.

I woke to a wonderful sunny morning having slept well, but then I knew I would. Lynda rang at 7 for a swim. Gorgeous, then coffee by the pool. We did an interview for San Francisco live radio at 7.45 a.m. Good news – Angela felt a lot better and in this hotel she had a robe! We breakfasted together in the restaurant. Then Lynda did the *Roadside Café* (Santa Cruz) live radio interview from my room. We got our clothes ready for the

Tonight show with Jay Leno. First we were going to Disney at downtown Burbank for lunch with Jerry and Jason (the head guys at Buena Vista). Two limos arrived for us, and drove us through Beverly Hills, lots of work for housekeepers and gardeners here, but not much chat going on over the garden walls.

Arrived at Disney – we knew we were there by the stone dwarves up on top of the building – no Snow White though. We were met by a guy called Jerry, whom we thought was the doorman at that stage. He took us up in the lift to the executive dining room and we were very animated about dwarves and Snow White on the way up. Mickey Mouse was everywhere. Then the 'doorman' came in with us and introduced us to Jason. We now realized these were top Disney executives, but nothing wrong with being natural, was there? We all sat down for lunch. Mickey Mouse was on all crockery, his head shape cut out of the backs of the chairs. I filmed Lynda and Ange holding salt and pepper. We calmed down and the conversation was easy between us, although Jerry very cool – chilled. We ordered – only Ellen and Jerry ordered starters, we all ordered a main course of mixed field salad. Starters arrived plus a salad for Beryl, who although surprised, dutifully waded her way through it. She only managed half, then the waiter took it away and brought her the main course – a bigger bowl of the same salad – we said nothing just looked at each other. It was delicious and Beryl valiantly struggled through a lot of it. Meanwhile Jason was putting ketchup on his fries, having difficulty with sauce running out and had to use two hands – I daren't look at Lynda and Ange passed on sauce completely. By now Ellen was intrigued by the tomato sauce joke but it was one that needed to be visual, with the actions – we could only refer to it and chuckle, like Terry Wogan and Paulie do all the time with the Country and Western joke about Preston. There was a director called Richard (we must start paying attention to who is who) – he had directed *Sixth Sense*, another one! When I asked him if he had rung us he seemed bemused so he must have been the real one. He thought the photographs were wonderful and complimented Terry. Thought Judi Dench should play Lynda. We told a few stories and Jason made a few notes, especially about the golden flying penis. Lunch was nearly over and we all went to the loo together, as girls do. Ange called out of her loo that we had to watch out if Beryl started hopping and rubbing her whiskers because she had eaten so much lettuce. Beryl came hopping out of her loo to hysterical laughter.

We had a tour of the complex, Mickey Avenue, Goofy Drive, I filmed a bit. There were sunflowers in the entrance to the shop – wherever we were, John was there. I bought a few bits in the Disney shop, a ponyskin bag for Ros and a Mickey candle for Christine. Then it was time to be collected by the *Tonight Show* car – now that was big, bigger than Ange's lounge and kitchen together, it would never negotiate the lanes of Cracoe. I filmed the dwarves as we departed but still no sign of Snow White.

It was just a short way to NBC studios, well it was in a limo that long. When we arrived in the car park Jay Leno's car was pointed out to us – apparently he has lots of them. We had proper dressing rooms with our names on the door. Met Jolie, the producer I'd spoken to at home to arrange this. On the phone she'd kept saying, 'oh that's so furney', without ever once laughing. She was quite serious but nicer than on the phone – a different drawl in her accent. It was Jay's fiftieth birthday so Ange had brought him a book about the Dales and we all signed a card. Fruit, food and drinks as usual, but we were stuffed from lunch. We relaxed a little, told Ellen the tomato sauce joke, but a bit tricky because the main word meant nothing to her. Did a press interview. We rehearsed a bit between ourselves, then went out to see Jay and have some cake with him – in fact he called us up first to have chocolate cake and ice-cream – massive bits. Then it was back to the dressing rooms for hair and make-up as usual. More rehearsal, but we knew what to say. It would be more light-hearted than the other shows, but still it would sell calendars.

We were the first guests on. Lynda sat next to Jay on the sofa, then me, and Ange and Beryl behind. He concentrated a lot on Lynda and she was brilliant – all about Terry and taking the photos. He asked how long we had been strippers, introducing me as formerly known as 'boom boom'. He was very amusing, obviously clued up and spoke to each of us. Ellen was pleased with it. We watched the rest with a glass of wine. As a gift, there were enormous baskets of goodies, very nice, but how on earth would we get them home? At the end we went back on set to say goodbye to Jay. The audience cheered us again, they were staying to test out Jay's presidential address for the White House that weekend – he had a vicious wit.

Slept well, again, and woke up to a gorgeous morning, again. I swam with Ange and Lynda, then breakfast outdoors by the pool. We were off to the LA Festival of Books today where I was hoping to bump into Michael Palin again. The sales guy from Workman picked us up and Ellen drove a car to the bookfair at University of California. We arrived to a sea of marquees which looked great. There were lots of people about and a good atmosphere. We found Duttons' site, where Workman had arranged for us to sell our calendars. I could have looked around for ages, but we went straight in to signing calendars. Red hot, too hot for Beryl, but Ange loved it. Michael Palin was due to be here until 12.30, we were booked till 1.30 and I didn't want to miss him. Nor did Lynda who hadn't met him yet. It was such a sunny day that I'd worn my Wolford gobi (the same colour as the desert) tights instead of black but it was so bright that Ange said my tights were dazzling people when they came to buy calendars – but I couldn't take them off and have bare legs. We were very busy for the hour and recognized so much from the TV shows, it was such an experience. We had to finish on time, because we were flying from LA to San Jose that afternoon and needed to go back to the hotel and collect our cases etc. We hadn't seen Michael Palin but Ellen said we could walk back that way, so we all set off and found him, still signing away with a small queue still there. If only we could stay longer and chat, but at least Lynda met him and he recognized her from the Jay Leno show, then we had a photo or two taken. Beryl kissed him goodbye – any excuse – and off we went to the Beverly Hilton.

Another stretch picked us up and dropped us at the airport, where the driver got a parking ticket. When he left I realized my vanity case was in the car. Ellen got on the phone to the car company while I tried to stay calm although my tickets, glasses and contact lenses were all in there. Luckily the guy returned because he'd spotted my case and all was well. We checked in and I gave my *Tonight Show* basket to the check-in girl for her mom on Mother's Day. What a relief to be rid of it. My case was absolutely stuffed and I had to sit on it to shut it.

It was a very relaxed flight – the flight attendants in shorts. I persuaded Ange to have a gin and tonic, hell they were strong, but did us good, chilled into the flight. A bit of a mishap later, not my day really – my case came around on the carousel – open, with a heel of a shoe sticking out and the foot of a gobi tight – very glam. Everyone found it hysterical. Collected our car/carrier and forced the luggage in, tricky. I slept all of the way to Santa Cruz.

We arrived at the hotel with only minutes to unpack and get ready. I was sharing a room with Lynda and it already looked like we'd been burgled. We struggled with the coffee maker and managed a type of beverage, then met in the lobby. We had all scrubbed up very well. We drove to the bookshop; our first impressions of Santa Cruz were that it was very fifties and a bit hippy still. When we arrived at the bookstore it was packed and they cheered us when we entered. Kelsey, the manager, opened up the evening, saying lovely things about us. I started off, then Beryl, Lynda and finally Ange did our by now well-rehearsed routines. There were lots of laughs and sad moments, especially when Ange talked about the sunflowers. There were questions and answers next which went on for about half an hour, everyone was so interested. It seemed a very feminist town, lots of dungarees. We set up a table and signed calendars for nearly 250 people – it was amazing. Lynda was first so she had to write the dedication, it was good for her, challenged her spelling powers. One strange lady, with lots of blue eyeshadow, talked to Lynda for ages, all about the queen and all sorts of utter rubbish. While she spoke I noticed she was wearing a home made badge, but couldn't make out what it said – all I could see was 'fuck'. Lynda looked discreetly, Beryl tried, but couldn't make it out. Then I lent further over and realized it said 'I fuck to come, not to conceive'. After the initial shock, we thought perhaps that the chance would be a fine thing for her. Beryl had a little chuckle, but didn't think she'd be making one for herself. When we had signed all the calendars, Kelsey spoke again, said such wonderful things, it was heartwarming.

Ellen asked us if Kelsey and her girlfriend could come to dinner with us, we were OK with that – hell, we come from Cracoe, where anything goes. The restaurant was avant garde, very free, as were the waiters, especially Bernard, our waiter. He described the food like a work of art. The meal was the best of the trip – we all agreed. At first conversation seemed slow and Antonia (Kelsey's partner) was a little shy. She looked very butch, because her hair was short. She explained that she had had long hair, but was ill recently, so cut it short and was experiencing such a different reaction from people. After she said that we all relaxed and conversation flowed – for a change. Beryl spent most of the night chatting to the guys on the next table and sampling their food. Kelsey and Antonia told us about a meditation kind of place that they go to, with hot tubs and beds for massages. We all listened to the directions, but didn't feel we would go. Perhaps we weren't quite ready for that yet. Some wine, then liqueurs, then back to the car, lots of hugs and say our goodbyes to Kelsey and Antonia. When we got in the car we had to laugh at ourselves, because we thought Beryl hadn't known what was going on but of course she knows more than us. Bed, pills – it was heavenly falling asleep when you wanted.

Lynda and I were up early and out for a swim. We called for Ange, because she didn't answer her phone. She was out of it, she had taken a melatonin – only 1 mg – but she couldn't wake up. It was a good job she hadn't taken one of Beryl's 3 mg – she would have slept through San Francisco. Lynda and I walked on the beach where there were two men metal detecting – one recognized Lynda from the Jay Leno show. I paddled and Lynda videoed and panned round the beach, much faster than me because Ange wasn't there to tell her to go slower. We'll probably be sick when we watch that bit, like when Ange's mum and dad videoed the bulb fields in Holland from the coach – everyone who watched it felt ill. Moved on to the swimming pool, which was a lot colder than the Beverly Hilton pool. The hot pool was good. Beryl and Ellen appeared from their walk on the beach and we all went in for breakfast. The restaurant overlooked the sea and breakfast was wonderful, absolutely loads of food. Beryl and Ange shared the massive portions to help reduce Workman's bill – we will be 12 stone when we leave. Ellen was meeting her friend from school so we were like children released for the morning. We decided to do the boardwalk – that was one of my favourite songs and now I was on one – amazing to think how I came to be doing all this.

In the lovely sunshine, Lynda wearing my black hat, Beryl and Ange in baseball caps – we walked on the boardwalk to see the seals. I had been so looking forward to seeing them and straight away I saw two swimming out in the sea. An enormous bull was sleeping on the wood struts underneath the pier, a pelican sitting on the rail being fed bread. Then a whole flock(?) flew over us to catch the fishing boats coming in – perhaps it's a plethora of pelicans – I needed to ask someone who had just sat their 11-plus.

I decided I must have a swim, even though I was warned it

was freezing. But it couldn't be much colder than the North Sea at home. Beryl and Lynda sat on the prom, like sedate WI ladies. Ange staked out on the beach and I braved the waves. Lots of seaweed, tricky exposing the purple/white thighs though. Everyone was right – it was freezing, but I did it – not for long, but I managed about four strokes. Dried off a bit in the sun, then we all trailed up the beach, like refugees from Blackpool, only to be recognized as calendar ladies even without our black and sunflowers – though Lynda still had her black hat on. She had made a real impact on Jay Leno.

We sat and had an ice-cream and filmed the chat. I was ready for a glass of wine now.

On the way to the seals we had passed a shop with a T-shirt in the window, depicting a young body in a stars and stripes bikini. Beryl wanted it to wear at WI next Thursday but it cost $25 – too much. On the way back Beryl looked round for a present for Mr January – and Lynda asked the young guy in the T-shirt shop (who was from the Isle of White) if he could put a hole in the T-shirt and reduce it. He recognized Lynda from the Jay Leno show – even in her hat and gave Beryl a discount.

Angela must have looked at us, laughing, crying and experiencing this incredible time and wondered why John had to die and this calendar become the phenomenon it had. Was it all part of a bigger picture? It seemed meant to be, the whole thing had evolved as if it was destined to, with John's spirit behind it, well not really behind it, but in the heart and soul of it. How wonderful it would be to talk to him about it and all the other happenings in our lives. Ange had handled the total loss of her beloved life, not only without bitterness, reproach or self pity, but with dignity, strength, humour and truth. Whenever I thought about Ange and John, it led on in my mind to Ian and me. I was beginning to feel, more and more, that we were in an impossible situation. I was very unhappy and I thought he was, too. I thought a lot about what to do, should I heed the advice of the fortune teller? Had she told me what I wanted to hear?

We were setting off that afternoon for Palo Alto on the way to San Fran – yippee. Palo Alto was a lovely place, very middle class, tastefully kept. The bookstore had been an old cinema, now converted, with a café/restaurant. Ellen worried that the evening was not very organized and that the event had not been advertised enough. The manager was lovely, apologetic for the lack of people, but we were OK. Set the table up, with the help of Beryl's WI cooperative table skills. A few folk, but not like Barnes and Noble. We looked round the shop after signing a few calendars. Wonderful books, but I couldn't carry any more. Also got very large Michael Palin – couldn't ditch that.

Then it was on to San Francisco – no flowers in our hair, just in our lapels. I slept all the way, so it would be a lie to describe the journey. Ange woke me for the Golden Gate bridge. We arrived at the Maxwell Hotel which was very authorish, the type of place you could have imagined Agatha Christie staying at. Ange and Beryl had palatial rooms, with mega beds, could get five calendar girls in easily, also splendid views over the city. Unfortunately mine and Lynda's was not in that league, it was double with no view at all. Luckily we weren't bitter.

We tried to revive ourselves to go to our last dinner with Ellen. We had just realized, sadly, that this was our last night with her. We would miss her so much. We hadn't known she was leaving in the morning and we hadn't organized a present. I suggested the pearls that Angela had bought me, because I had the case and we could pin a sunflower on it. Lynda thought it was a brilliant idea. I explained the plan to Ange, on the phone, when suddenly Beryl's voice piped up saying what a good idea. Ange said how was Beryl speaking and I said 'isn't she in your room?' but she wasn't. Beryl was speaking from her bathroom where the phone had rung as well as in Ange's room. An unintentional conference call.

We did a few more interviews in San Francisco, some good ones with interesting and interested people. One asked Beryl if she was on the internet, Beryl said the only net she had was a hairnet! And we had to say goodbye to Ellen. It was so sad, we didn't want her to leave us. We gave her the present and all were 'full'. Beryl shed a tear and hugged Ellen. We had so enjoyed being with her. She said she would come to Yorkshire and see us.

We had a day off before leaving at 6 the next morning for JFK. We decided to pop into Macy's again – Lynda wanted undies for her boys. I just stayed on the ground floor and looked at the empowerment bracelets, for tranquillity, health, luck, strength, etc. All things which would be wonderful to achieve by buying a bracelet, if only – we bought some anyway! I bought health for Lizzi, because it was turquoise like American Indian stuff, wisdom and inner peace for Amanda, luck for me and health and wisdom for Micky – there wasn't one for a job.

We had lunch in a Bayview restaurant and told each other stories. Lynda's story was about her mum, on the set of *Bonanza*. A graveyard scene was being filmed. In the silence, when Lorne Green was trying to do his burial speech, they kept hearing a creak and stopping the filming. After three interruptions, they realized it was Lynda's mother going backwards and forwards in the rocking chair. Beryl spoke about her sex education or complete lack of it. It was a lovely finale.

We assumed we could just get a tram back, but the queues for the trams were massive, and we needed to get back to leave for the airport, so in a bit of a panic, we got a stretch limo from outside a hotel. The driver looked a bit suspect – Ange and Lynda thought we were off to the white slave trade, but we were fine and only $4 each. Back to the Maxwell, goodbye to San Francisco, collected cases and off to the airport. I really wanted to stay, or perhaps it was that I really didn't want to go home.

Next was our flight – lots of induced sleep and food. Drank

this time, not worried about looking so good now. Manchester – no cases for me and Beryl. All the videos were in my case. Surely they wouldn't be lost after all those hours of 'filming'. Fortunately they eventually turned up. Ian picked us up. The atmosphere between us was quite strained. It felt strange to be home. Ian had worked hard on the house in the two weeks, sorting the garage out and gravelling the garden, very Mediterranean, it looked great. Pity we couldn't have done it together months ago.

It was straight back to work, no jet lag as yet. Ian asked me if I had missed him, and truthfully, I answered no. I told him that if I had been offered a job, I would have stayed. This was my opportunity to finally say what I'd been thinking for some time. I told him I wanted to separate. It seemed inevitable to me but it took him completely by surprise. He was devastated, more than I had ever anticipated. We had had such a horrible time, I would have thought he would have expected it. I felt a great sense of relief when I said the words, but confused at the same time because Ian was so upset. I could see no other way forward for us. I talked to Lizzi from the office, she was relieved, told me not to be scared, I would be OK on my own, and eventually so would Ian. I hoped so.

As always when there is a crisis, at the same time there would be something that I felt I couldn't miss, tonight it was WI! We talked a bit about our trip but not a lot until Beryl gave the vote of thanks. She had her coat on, then at the end took it off, showing her American T-shirt and said America hadn't changed her. I didn't mention Ian and me yet. I felt numb, not frightened, but quite controlled.

We needed to visit Ian's dad, but didn't want to worry him with all this mess. Micky came with us, we told him we were thinking about splitting up, he didn't say much, but he had hated all the acrimony. Ian got really upset again, I was calm and was pleased I had taken all the video tapes for Dad and

Jenny to watch, it was easy to talk, they would feel like they had been with us after hours of USA. They were still enjoying all the calendar stuff, but we didn't say anything about us.

We went around to Ange's to tell her. Ian was really upset, an awful day. I didn't really know what to do or how to do it. She wasn't surprised, she had known all our problems but the news upset her although she thought a little time apart would be good for us. She felt sorry for Ian but understood how I felt. She said John would have known how to help us, he had worried about us even when he was ill.

Meantime newspaper articles appeared in the *Telegraph* and *The Times*, saying the American media tour was one Madonna would die for. I wondered what the papers would make of Miss October splitting up from her husband. Everyone would blame the calendar. Ellen rang to say the calendar was selling well after the tour. Barnes and Noble sold hundreds in the week after we signed there. There was still so much going on. Workman were thrilled with the success of the tour. They were less thrilled, however, with Diana's plan for us to appear on Jerry Springer's new-style show, not his disgusting one, he was trying for a new image, more Jay Leno or Parky – some chance. Ellen was worried about it and Peter and Carolan dead against it. Lots of discussion. They only knew his lowlife show and were horrified what would happen to us on there.

And then the BBC2 documentary was screened nationwide. I was at Pilates in Harrogate, so I missed it, but Ange cried all the way through, remembering the closeness of those early days. The way the girls spoke on the film, the reasons for doing the calendar, where had the compassion gone? How the situation had changed. We went to the pub afterwards and none of the other girls mentioned the documentary. Not a word, no one even asked Ange how she was coping, nothing any more.

Strange, Ian was not drinking alcohol or eating much. He was really trying, but I felt it was too late.

10

The screening of the BBC documentary kept the calendar fire burning but I had resolved to really concentrate on the other things going on in my life. Now that I had decided to try and make a life of my own without Ian I really did need to get a job. I had not earned much throughout the last year, not contributed a lot to the business. Ian had supported me financially really. I was convinced that Pilates could be my future, I loved it and that meant study, study and more study. I'd already postponed my exam once but I was determined to be ready for the rescheduled date at the end of June.

Ian and I were still living together, trying to get used to the idea of living apart, but after nearly thirty years of marriage it was hard to take the steps required to truly break up. He constantly asked me if I had changed my mind, if we could stay together but I was indifferent to it all, as if I had finally closed down to him. I wanted us to be calm, quiet about it, tell no one else, just see how we were after a few weeks. I didn't want a constant barrage of questions of how I felt, whether we could sort it out. I wanted peace. Ian found that hard to accept, he said he wanted to try again, that he would change and he could not envisage life without me. Now and then I felt upset, but my mind was set and I suppose my heart was hardened.

Even though the calendar had become folklore as that 'fucking' calendar because of Ian, he had totally supported it, spoken positively on interviews and never told how we really were, which would have shattered the image of the calendar. How we really were was sleeping in separate rooms (my decision). He had been really loyal though. He had often said out loud (but never to the media) that he had needed to buy a calendar to see me in the nude, people thought he was joking. I talked to Lizzi a lot, asked her what she would feel like if her Dad met someone else, I knew a few who would move in quickly. She said she felt she would get on better with him if we were apart and she would cope with whatever happened.

Life carried on still together but separate, almost as normal except with the knowledge that it would soon all change, which caused a certain amount of stress. Ange, Lynda and Terry came around one night for dinner in our newly pebbled garden. Ange had a burst pipe in her kitchen, which she only discovered because she went home early to escape an awful argument between Ian and me. There was water pouring through the kitchen ceiling, which, left much longer would have wrecked the kitchen – God is good you see. It's an ill wind.

Ian was very unhappy, I couldn't do or say anything to change that. Lizzi came home for a couple of days. She believed I was doing the right thing, that I would never be lonely, Ian and I would be happier apart. I agreed, but who would be Ian's friends, he had felt ostracized with the calendar, how would it be apart? He looked so much better for losing weight with the misery. Why didn't he do that before now, perhaps I should have threatened to leave sooner?

Lizzi and I cleared out her wardrobe, bed drawers, and cupboards and filled ten binbags for the Salvation Army – very satisfying. We found Lizzi's letter to the tooth fairy:

Dear Tooth Fairy,

    I thank you very much for taking my teeth. I would like to go to where you take the teeth. My daddy says you make the stars with them, do you? I would like to give you this elephant. Please write

    From Elizabeth Stewart. I like you.

Ian replied:

Thank you Elizabeth but tooth fairies are too small to carry these presents. Guard each tooth you lose with this elephant and we like you too.

    X

Where did those lovely times go? It must be both our faults, drifting apart, full of bitterness. What about grandchildren, we won't be together to enjoy them. What a waste. I felt very sad. I sorted out all my calendar cuttings and then cried at the movie *Meet Joe Black* – again.

    I was glad to have Lizzi here with me, Ian was very much on the edge. We walked to Rylstone to light John's candles. Lizzi still found his absence so hard to believe. Later we found all her Teddy cards from John, that he had sent while she was studying for her degree, they were very amusing, telling her to study and how many days she had left – it was so sad to read them again. There was also an Easter card that John sent to her in Oz on 7 April 1998. It just summed up how brave he was and how he was more interested in Lizzi than in his own problems. This was what he wrote:

Dear Lizzi,

    Just popped out for a couple of pints – not the black stuff but the red stuff from Airedale. I need a boost and by tonight I'll be jumping five barred gates. Apart from that I am coming on OK – slowly but surely and according to plan. At long last. Yes, it has been rather horrific but there is much of the last two months which I just don't remember. But everyone else remembers all the details and that is something I think about a lot because it has affected so many people – Ange in particular, but such a lot of other people as well. The support and prayers I have received have been overwhelming and I'm sorry if I got rather emotional when you phoned from the beach. However enough of my thoughts on the meaning of life – we'll discuss them later in the year when you are home and I am fully recovered.

You know all the news because I think (know) how much you talk (fax) your mum. She has been a great help to us – our Angel.

I had a call from Adrian on Sunday. He seems to be on top of the work on the last lap. I know you are in a dilemma about future plans but I said to Adrian that you had endured the worst of your separation (first 6 months) and you must do what you feel you should do whilst you are on the other side of the world. This opportunity will never come again in this form. Later you will be middle class and want to do things very differently. Adrian seemed to agree and you should encourage him to finish graduation and prepare for next year. It won't be the end of the world if he doesn't come out this time, you have plenty of time to do things together in the future.

So, here I am philosophizing on all things and doing nothing. Some Australian sunshine would be nice, but that will have to wait until next year. In the meantime you enjoy the Aussie experience and have a big thankyou hug from me.

Lots of luv,
　　John xx

What a spirit to write such a letter. I must give it to Ange to keep. What would John think of Ian and me, he tried so hard to sort us out, even when he was so ill. One of the problems was the comparison of John bravely battling his illness and Ian just seemed to be doing nothing to enhance his life.

Lizzi and I had a very blubbering time, finding all these letters, plus old photos of happier times. We had been a really happy family, had great times when the kids were young. In fact I couldn't ever remember being unhappy until these last couple of years. Ange was at Frank and Joyce's for tea, so we got out of our misery and picked her up later. Went on to light John's candle, asked his advice, then walked home with George. Then Lizzi set off for Birmingham. She was very upset for me. It made me sad, but it had to be like that for now.

It was a very unsettling time for me and though I was trying to concentrate on my future, actually the calendar kept me sane. Compared to my personal life, it seemed uncomplicated. Calendar, Pilates and reading Michael Palin (which I was enjoying even though it was making me very unsettled and yearning for a little apartment in Paris or Italy) kept me occupied.

We'd heard news from Suzanne and Nick who'd been down to the Cannes Film Festival that there was a buzz about the film – our film. Suzanne and Juliette were due up in Cracoe before the end of May with the first draft of the script. Angela and anyone else who'd signed a release would read it. I looked forward eagerly to seeing what they'd made of an experience that already felt to me like one out of the movies.

The calendar was back in Skipton in Maple Leaf's, the photographer's shopwindow. The American nineteen-month version was now available in England. Life as a calendar girl went on.

After much discussion Diana had finally reassured Workman that the UK Jerry Springer was OK for us to do but I think perhaps we wished we hadn't. Although it sold calendars! Diana decided on Lynda, Angela and me to do the show. So we went down to London for it and were collected by car and taken to the BBC studio where it was filmed – very Jay Leno-like set but

nothing like the energy and buzz of that show. It all seemed
pretty desolate. We were first on and Jerry Springer seemed very
nervous. He told Lynda he wasn't used to having normal people
on his show! It took three takes to do the introduction. Still we
had a great time with Diana.

We'd also arranged for the Leukaemia Research Fund people
to meet the film people, and Diana. Apart from the trouble
we were having amongst ourselves over the film, everybody else
involved in the calendar got along great together and propelled
things along with positive energy. We had forged some everlasting
friendships. Diana arrived first then Douglas Osborne and
Andrew Trehearne. We went off to a restaurant called something
like Orifice! Suzanne and Juliette were already there, all introduced to each other, then champagne. Talked about film and
Cannes. Our film was the talk of Cannes – could be there next
year – well I'd predicted Woman of the Year Lunch, billboards,
and America, so could be Cannes next! Wonderful arty restaurant,
saw Harold Pinter just sitting having lunch, as you do.

Harriet, a journalist friend of Diana's from the *Telegraph*,
joined us later. I saw her stop as she came in. The next day she
told Diana that she'd seen John smiling down on us. She didn't
say anything at the time, in case she upset Ange. She was a lovely
lady, wanted to do an article about the calendar and us at this
stage. Unfortunately as we'd already agreed to do an update with
Georgina Howell for *The Times* Harriet couldn't do it. Diana
was worried about the *Times* article because she thought they
would focus on the negative side – the split, rather than all the
positive things the calendar had achieved. It was all good fun and
everyone got on well.

The *Esther Rantzen* show, which we'd filmed over a year ago,
finally went out. I remembered it as a good show, with very
interesting people on, but wondered whether we would look
dated after a year – I needed Triple A then. I watched it with
Lynda, because she was at home – Ange was at work again, telling

visitors where to go in Grassington – literally, soon I predict. We were impressed, none of us looked nervous, Ros looked so bonny and we were very cool. Lynn looked like she had lost at least two stone since, but her photo wouldn't have epitomized WI without that two stone then. Esther included us a lot, especially sitting on the podium. It was a good show, and we had changed the stereotypical image of WI and middle-aged women too.

Incredible to think what we'd done since that programme had been filmed and how we'd just sort of integrated the calendar into our lives. Some things were still as they'd been before but really everything had changed. We still had our daily morning walks to the Sheep Pens whenever we could fit them in – our catch-up time. But poor old Polly, Ros's dog, had died, so even that wasn't exactly the same. WI, however, continued much as it had always done. We still went to the monthly meetings, entered the competitions and enjoyed the friendships. I dashed back from one London trip, can't remember whether it was calendar or Pilates, maybe both and was quickly returned to reality. Ian picked me up from Skipton and whizzed me up to Grassington for the Bulb Show. I couldn't wait to see the judges' comments for Ros's entry, which was a poem about the calendar. She got a silver star 19½. Miserable lot, could have made it 20. Here it is:

Thoughts on The Millennium (Calendar)

A way to raise money was the main aim
Eleven WI ladies all of them game
Perhaps a nude calendar – what a sensation
Brilliant idea – it would shock the nation
They posed behind crafts – tastefully nude
Photos done in sepia – certainly not crude
Beryl starts the year off with 'dress barely formal'
Chairing the meeting – you'd think it was normal
February's Angela playing 'Jerusalem' for all she is worth

And her 'countenance divine' certainly did 'shine forth'
Lynn behind a sieve looking ready for action
'No need for baking powder' a most popular caption
'Guarding her tender blooms' in the potting shed
Leni's a lovely picture it has to be said
Moyra arranging flowers as the Daring buds of May
A lot of people thought the vase got in the way
Miss June is Sandra with not a stitch to wear
An elegant pose – she does look good bare
'A nude painting' for Lynda as Miss July
Prince Charles's favourite – it's easy to guess why
In front of the Aga is Rita making jam
'Beautifully preserved' August does look glam
'One lump or two?' Christine has to ask
For September a large teapot – quite a dangerous task
Tricia works hard behind a cider press
October 'Fruity and full-bodied' in a state of undress
November arrives and the weather turns cold
Ros 'knits two together' – she's not very bold
For December all together exuding good cheer
Wishing 'a Merry Christmas and a Happy Nude Year'
Sunflowers featured on every page
And women of a certain age
Clever photos taken with lots of care
Only hats and pearls to wear
With a dedication to a special man
Everything went according to plan
Would anyone buy it – how could we guess
It went worldwide – it was a huge success.

                                Rosalyn Fawcett – Miss November

   Still she had done well. Low marks on the biscuits and they
looked great, so fiddly. If I had spent all day piping patterns
on biscuits, I would have been gutted to get 9 out of 20! Lynda
was awarded a silver for her painting of a pink giraffe, the judge

thought it could have been further to the right in the picture. What!

My Pilates practice group was getting into a good routine, though the cooling of friendships over the film trouble meant that this class was smaller than my original yoga group had been. Wistful as some of these losses made me, I certainly didn't hanker after the old life. New experiences kept coming our way.

Like the calendar signing we did down at Hatchard's bookstore in Piccadilly, next door to Fortnum & Mason's. That morning I was awake at 3.30 a.m. but I'd discovered a nifty trick for getting back to sleep. I'd put the mask from the plane on and maybe because of the connection with temazepam – it induced sleep, I'd go off like a light – champion. I was able to get back to sleep till 5.30.

It was an absolutely gorgeous morning, we should really have been up the Fell with a picnic but never mind. I travelled down to the station with Ros, Moyra was in Ange's car, and the rest were there waiting. Hatchard's is a wonderful store, over 200 years old and our calendar was in the window – amazing. They had never sold calendars in the store before. I borrowed an upstairs office to make a phone call and there on the wall was a relief sunflower picture. There was always a sunflower from John. I asked if we could take it downstairs for the signing. We signed 1000 calendars and it was all very animated with lots of chat and banter, telling jokes and making profound statements, like Ros's – 'same bed – different dreams', or, 'the son of a duck is no mean swimmer'. The average onlooker would never have guessed we had our differences. I talked with some brilliant people, like the lady from Tuscany, who'd overcome her fear and moved out there. She said fear stops us doing the things we really want to do – how right was that. An American lady, from Seattle, who bought eleven calendars and works for a cancer organization raising funds, asked when the new calendar started. Ros's reply of June 1st made us realize that the new version of the calendar began on John's birthday – what a perfect coincidence. Workman had chosen the date and Ange had not realized either – well done John.

We signed the Visitors' book – the Queen and Winston Churchill have signed it. When we'd finished at Hatchard's, where we signed over 1,000 calendars, we walked over to a hotel called Browns to meet the lady from the *Sunday Times*, Georgina Howell. She had already met us at Hatchard's, chatted while we signed, then helped us choose books to read. Ange spoke a long while with her about John, feathers and angels. Browns is on Dover Street just opposite the Indian restaurant where Preethi's launch was. The name of the restaurant means soul in Indian. That was a wonderful evening, another magical result of the calendar. Tea was organized at Browns – cakes, champagne, scones £26 a head. It would have only been £19 without the champagne. It was so posh, Christine took photographs of the loo! When Beryl and I worked out the cost, we were stunned. Beryl said we should have gone to a café and shared the change from the £260. What was left was packed up for on the train. Couldn't bear to leave it at that price.

These calendar signings were always fun and often very moving: meeting people who had been touched by cancer made us remember the serious side of the calendar. We did one signing at Waterstone's in Leeds. As we were leaving, Maggie, one of the nurses who had looked after John rushed in. She was so pleased she hadn't missed us, and bought calendars for us to sign. She cried when we talked about John and she said he had been a very special man. They were still so busy, the ward was full. They all appreciate so much what we are doing. Why was there so much of these diseases now?

My twenty-ninth wedding anniversary – 5 June – oh dear, oh Lor! I got a sad card from Ian saying what are we doing. I still felt numb, not really making any effort to leave, or plans for the future but going along separately. He made me laugh remembering twenty-nine years ago last night he had curlers in the side bits of his hair to keep it smooth. I had forgotten that, not that we were together – I was at my mam's, he was at his. I tried to study, but messed about a lot. I walked in Grass Woods with Lynda and Terry, Preethi (she was staying with Terry and Lynda), George and Sky. Preethi talked about how she published her own book, *Gypsy Masala*, then promoted it. There were uncanny similarities to the calendar and how we had handled everything ourselves.

The journalist from the *Sunday Times*, Georgina, was there that day and would come to Lynda's tonight with Angela, Beryl and me. All the others were summoned to Moyra's at allotted times. Georgina had been met and organized by Moyra and Rita. By the time she reached us, she had interviewed everyone and their dog. Finally we talked to her around the fire, more about the spirit of the calendar. I felt she had the heart of it and was very in tune with Ange, although we would see what she wrote. Diana remained unconvinced. By now, with the split over the film public, we worried that any interview would focus on that to the detriment of the calendar as a whole. Particularly as the other girls, the Rylstone Five, seemed less reluctant to discuss this aspect of things with the press than we thought appropriate. I hated that it had become their version versus our version, but what could you do? Preethi spoke so warmly about the calendar, surely she couldn't remain untouched. Her words were beautiful – she wished Georgina could have spent four days in our company like she herself had, because we had a generosity of spirit.

Georgina came with Ros, Ange and me the next morning up to the Sheep Pens after spending the night at Angela's. Sad without Polly. Ros shed a tear for her. It was a beautiful morning and Georgina loved the walk where so much of our planning had taken place. She said her time in the Dales had been wonderful, very busy but she had met some exceptional women. Complete breaths and corkscrews. Breakfasted at Ange's, where Georgina gave her a copy of her book – *Vogue* – which was very tasteful, she had written a lovely message inside.

To the office – calendar phone calls all day, no work, but when I am bankrupt, I can say I did a good calendar. The realization that we were actually doing some good made us keen to carry on with the calendar in any way that we could that didn't seem cheap or sensationalist. One evening Ian, Ange and I were at Lynda's for tea. We spent a lot of time with Lynda and Terry, they had been really good with our problems, we had got to an easier stage and laughed and joked about 'splitting up'. It still seemed unreal and we had made no move to do anything permanent as yet. After dinner and some wine, we discussed how we could do another calendar for 2002: 'Going to the movies'. We thought of lots of titles, Marilyn in *Some like it Hot* with the dress blowing up; Jane in *The Outlaw* in the hay with her cantilever bra on; Vivien in *Gone with the Wind*; Marlene in *The Blue Lamp* – but Lynda wanted all the best parts, in fact all the parts. Thought she might let us be Bette Davis or Greta Garbo. We had a good laugh about that but this time didn't follow through – probably for the best. But at least six of us still felt that if there were ways to continue raising money for research, then that was good enough reason to carry on. We'd become by this point one of the highest fund-raisers for leukemia research and Douglas Osborne and the LRF were always very involved in any of our plans for the future. The fact that we were having the time of our lives was almost by the by.

Though I could easily see a future for the calendar, my future with Ian was still far from clear. We spent a weekend at Whitby with my sister Marg, Ralph, Helen and Keith, her husband. The journey was very traumatic. Ian wanted me to listen to R. Kelly's song 'Why did I ever let you go', I didn't exactly say no, I just didn't want to get into an intense discussion, but he ripped it out of the tape player and threw it out of the car window. We turned back once, but then continued. It would be a difficult day seeing them for the first time since our 'troubles'. The beach was lovely, we walked right along, just talking, Marg was so concerned. George and Bailey (Helen's dog) had a wonderful time running after sticks on the beach. Whitby was very packed – a bit like Blackpool, but nicer. Ian bought me a silver bracelet with a stone of Whitby jet, which was lovely but I wished he hadn't. Emotional day, really. Marg and Ralph are very sad about it, they have watched us deteriorate, but we have all had such a wonderful time together over the years, all the kids close, growing up together in spite of the geographical distance.

One of our big problems was that Ian resented the fact that now I was always popping off somewhere or other either for the calendar or for Pilates, leaving him alone. In fact the Pilates training was becoming much more intensive and I was off to London quite a lot. What a contrast to when I'd begun the course and was afraid to be lonely in a hotel on my own. Now when I went down to London, there was always someone to stay with and someone to see. The calendar had brought me so many new friends. I often stayed with Amanda, or sometimes with Preethi, or Sabine, the girl we met through the *20/20* show. When they weren't off somewhere on their travels, I stayed in Kent with Marg. Now the studio was in Covent Garden it was easier from there. If I had free time I called in at LRF head office or tried to meet up with Suzanne Mackie for a coffee, it all evolved into a pattern.

My exam was looming, but I had worked hard, enjoyed relearning anatomy, found the Pilates, just as described 'the way forward for exercise'. I had enjoyed learning more about the whole subject. I planned to stay with Preethi the night before my exam, then after the exam Marg was taking me (as a treat) to stay overnight at the Fishermen's Huts on the beach at Whitstable, which would be great.

Ian took me to the station, wished me luck and off I went. I met Preethi at Wembley after quite a bit of study on the train.

It was very calming at her house, she, as Lynda described her, is like a 'gentle breeze wafting through our lives'. The morning of the exam I woke early, dozed again, looked at a last few definitions. Meditated with Preethi, if only I was disciplined enought to do that every day, I could be calm. She doused – it said I would pass! Read some poems. I got the tube to Covent Garden and met Marg for lunch, then went on to Neal's Yard for my exam. I felt nervous, it was thiry years since my last exam. None of my own group were there and I felt lonely. But I managed to write for the full three hours and felt, at the end of it, that I could have just passed or just failed. I took a late train back to Marg's, completely knackered. Tomorrow we were off to the Beach Huts at Whitstable for the night.

We spent a relaxed morning, paddling, I nearly swam but it was just a bit too chilly. We ate breakfast on the beach. The huts were ace, Lizzi would have loved it here. I felt so much better for being there with my sister. We talked about what I would do on my own, where I was going really. I needed to earn my own living: set up a Pilates business, perhaps write my book. I had talked about writing a book for ages, a bit like the calendar, in a joky way. I had continued my 'letters to Lizzi', as I called my diary, after she came home so had a diary of all we had done – and some. Whenever there was an amusing anecdote, someone would say 'put it in your book'. Two palmists had told me I would write a book in my fifties. Who knows maybe I could and earn some money to keep me going!

That morning Ian rang to tell me he was putting the house up for sale! He would not wait around any longer to see if I was going to change my mind. Was this the right thing to do? It felt OK. He sounded more positive than for ages. Something had to happen, but I hadn't really thought about what. Marg and I walked along the beach and talked about my future, I felt quite relieved I suppose. Ian seemed to have moved on out of the depths, which was good. I have always loved Whitstable and encouraged Marg to move there, perhaps I could have a little beach hut. We wandered along and looked at houses, then had a meal at the Hotel Continental. We walked back, I was tempted to swim again, but resisted. I had a good, relaxed night's sleep. Ian seemed very calm and determined now. He was moving on.

I had a Pilates training day in London the next day. I did better that day feeling more confident in the group situation. Then Marg and I went to stay with my other sister, Ibber. Spent the rest of the weekend there, being looked after by them. They were worried about me but understood the problems. We had all been there for each other over the years. Ibb and Marg took me to the station on the Monday morning and it felt like I was being evacuated from my family. They were worried about me, told me to ask them for any help, not to try and be strong all the time. I felt alone at King's Cross, but probably it has that effect on most people. Strange to come home and see the For Sale sign, but I didn't cry.

It was good to be back at the Sheep Pens with Ros, we caught up, as usual, with the news. She was sad about the house. She had listened to my worries and complaints for months and advised or said little, just heard me. Although she had often said couldn't we just sort our problems out, that we were a brilliant couple with a lot to throw away. Where would I live? Ian said I needed to stay in Cracoe to be near to Ange and that he would move out. Ros didn't want me to move away. I still didn't seem to be taking all this 'moving' seriously. Ian had asked about a cottage in Cracoe soon to be available – I thought I would keep George.

Not a lot of calendar stuff happening except Ros and Christine had written brilliant replies to *Ready Steady Cook*, they would be great on there, Christine loved cooking, it would be very amusing. Korean TV contacted us to ask if we would go on, how on earth did they know about the calendar and would it sell there? More interest from America, a programme called *60 Minutes*, from

CBS, wanted to make a news documentary for their show. We had never heard of it, but apparently it was massive in the US. Agnes, the producer contacted me to set up some dates. She said it would take at least ten days and their crew consisted of nine people. The programme goes out to about twenty million homes. I arranged for the crew to meet us in Cracoe, set up for them to come to our WI meeting at the village hall (another film crew for our members to ignore).

A few weeks later CBS were here and we met the crew at Angela's, then on to my house to decide where they would film me – decided on my kitchen. They planned a joint interview in the Dev with Moyra, Rita, Lynda, Ange, Leni and me. Morley Saefer was the correspondent, flown from US, just to interview us. He was older than we had expected. He and John, the producer, were like Waldorf and Statler from the Muppetts. They were obviously long-time friends, both looked like they had lived life to the full. Good sparky interview and they were pleased with the result.

The girls had planned a recce visit to Manorlands Hospice to look around before we opened a garden party there next week. I decided not to go. I needed a night at home to talk to Ian, after all, we were selling our house! I tried not to tell just 'anyone' what was happening – as Zen says 'the best explanation is no explanation' – fine with me! But I regretted not going, Ange called afterwards to say it had been wonderful, the matron was a lovely lady with the eyes of an angel. They were thrilled so many had gone. And I didn't achieve anything by staying at home, just went around in circles. Where would all our furniture go, for Heaven's sake? I hadn't thought of that before. Ian and I met them all in the pub afterwards for the other girls' interview with Morley. I told Ros she needed to shine, not be shouted down or overlooked, but to have her say with her charm full on. We had a drink with John and Morley. Agnes looked like she was out with her grandads – you must be able to work longer in America.

The next evening on my way home from work I saw CBS setting up. The village hall was full of stuff, all the lights on. Went home, changed, Ange picked me up and off to WI. Our president welcomed the camera crew, said we were used to it now. A local lady gave the talk on emancipated women's clothes. The competition was an old garment. My muff won first prize, fancy! Good supper, crew must have felt they were at their grandma's on a Sunday afternoon.

The CBS crew wanted to film my little practice Pilates group – Ros, Ange, Lynda, but Terry didn't want to come as the only man, because Christine and John were away, so we let him off. To make the whole atmosphere totally ethnic I lit two joss sticks and the burner Lizzi had bought me with the aroma of rosemary. Ian didn't like it, he obviously preferred dog and fags smell. (Like his reaction to the altar thing or puja as Preethi called it. Once, after staying with Preethi, I put a candle, a heart-shaped stone, the statue of a mother and child which Lizzi had bought me, white feathers and the pomegranate that Amanda had given me for abundance on the pine stool in my yoga room. A couple of days later Ian spotted it and asked what the hell it was. I think he thought it was to make him vanish. I explained about candlegazing, but he wouldn't accept that and thought it was more than that 'Trish'. Perhaps for spells.) Anyway, they arrived at 8.45 and the cameramen set up and filmed the group, which went well. Then they filmed my 'works of art' – my papier mâché Miss Nude Bather, Chippendale, Turkish Baths picture and the cat. I had made them in my craft phase, when I went to Margaret (from yoga's) art classes and they had won prizes at WI shows. If they were shown on *60 Minutes*, I could be exhibiting in New York. Lizzi would have to rush home and mix a bit of paste for papier mâché. CBS filmed Ange and me reading letters at her house. I had forgotten how many and how wonderful the letters are. There is a book in the letters. And then they packed up and went home. It had been fun filming and we would wait and see what kind of reaction they got to it in America.

A bizarre moment today talking to the chairman of WI, while having my legs waxed at Jackie's, she just gestured when I had to turn over. We talked about WI's portrayal in the film, they were anxious as to how WI would be depicted. Of course, the WI was not full of women in pearls and brogues, however if the general public didn't have the staid image of WI, the calendar would not have had the effect it did. That image has to be in the film.

Generally, the WI seemed to be embracing the calendar girls. Helen Carey (the national chairman) had invited us to model at the Triennial General Meeting at Wembley. All but two of the girls could attend, some on different days, but we could cover all the shows. We were in contact with a fashion consultant, who would organize the clothes for us, all from C&A. I filled her in with everyone's details again, no trouble. There would be 10,000 women attending each day, over the three days, I hoped we would have some of the US calendars to sell by then.

We did a pre-meeting interview with the *Daily Express* who were sponsoring the conference. We met at Moyra's at four-ish. There was a photographer there too. Good job I'd covered my spots up. Nice guy. The journalist was lovely and talked to Ange for a long time, all about the reasons for doing the calendar and the film. She seemed to have the heart of it after listening to Ange. Beryl filled her in on the WI stuff. I was very tetchy now about journalists talking to the 'Five' without getting Angela's viewpoint.

I travelled down to Wembley for the Fashion Show alone. Ange and Lynda followed the next day. I needed to start clocking up my supervised teaching hours, slowly but surely. I needed to be qualified to teach Pilates and earn a living, instead of all this messing around. Although the calendar was what I liked doing best, I couldn't earn a living from it. I arrived at King's Cross, then tube to Wembley Park but got on the wrong line, due to my great experience of tube travel (where were the limos when you needed them?). I ended up taking a taxi to the Arena and found the stand. We had a big dressing room and the four girls, Moyra, Lynn, Sandra and Rita were already there trying clothes on. Mine looked OK, I hoped they fit. It was a bit awkward on my own with four of the 'five' and I'd be glad when Lynda and Ange arrived.

The whole exhibition looked empty, but it was early on the first day. The stands looked interesting. At one stand I had 'om' tattooed on my ankle in henna, and talked on my mobile to Preethi while I was done. We arranged to meet tonight and have a meal with her and Amanda somewhere near her train station. I wondered how much trade they would do with tattoos for the WI. The stalls included reflexology, incontinence, Eros glide cream (called Stroke Ass). They were all there for their audience. There were constipation signs in the loos, made me chuckle.

Our first show was at 12.30. I looked out at the audience at say only about six ladies but it started to fill up after the announcement about the 'Ladies from Rylstone'. The first show went well, with a big audience and quite jolly. Afterwards we walked into the audience and they were all so complimentary about us and the calendar. We had our photos taken with lots of WI ladies.

Agnes from CBS arrived to talk to us all, they would film us modelling and interview some of the audience. I did an interview with Saga, while Moyra and Rita did the *Evening Standard*. I had two quick samosas for lunch, very spicy. It was all go – we did another couple of shows, plugging the calendar at each one. In a break between shows I found the LRF stand where they were selling calendars well. Sadly we'd only been able to get 400 though and tomorrow there would be 10,000 women there for the actual conference. We could sell so many. I was stopped all the time for congratulations and given such encouragement. What brilliant women. The atmosphere was wonderful.

Between shows we tried to look around the exhibition. The reflexology stand looked good, a treatment for £5 – booked in for the next day with Moyra and Sandra. We organized the timing so we could go and sing 'Jerusalem' with 10,000 women at the start of the conference before our first show. The guy selling the cream called 'Eros', not far from the incontinence stand, was doing good business!

Rumours were circulating that Tony Blair would be at the meeting tomorrow, although he was not on the schedule. We had our last show at 5 p.m. I was staying at Preethi's house, looking forward to seeing her mum and dad again after we had enjoyed such a brilliant night at the launch of her book. She met me outside, only a walk away to her house. In her room was a meditation candle and what looked like a bundle of sticks. She told me that it was a cleansing stick – I didn't think I'd be able to have one of those at home – a bit too spiritual and pyromaniacal for Ian!

We met Amanda at Victoria and decided on an Italian. Preethi had brought Amanda a signed copy of her book, although she had already read it and loved it, which I knew she would. Amanda brought us pomegranates for abundance. I was glad I'd introduced Preethi and Amanda, they got on really well, as I'd thought they would. It was a brilliant night, we talked about everything.

I woke up at 5 a.m. the next morning to hear Preethi's mum Indira singing at her altar, just faintly, but it sounded wonderful. I dozed for a while, then up. Preethi showed me how to douse and I asked 'it' interesting questions and got the answers I wanted. Yes to book! Then we candlegazed and meditated. I walked in the sunshine to the Arena and met up with the other girls. Angela, Lynda and Beryl were coming later that day, so we would have a new catwalk routine to learn. After our first show, we rushed over to the Arena for the official start of the meeting. It was fantastic to be there with 10,000 other WI members, singing 'Jerusalem' all together. Just as Mr Blair came to the podium we sneaked out to have our reflexology before the rehearsal. We were laid out on the most comfy beds with our feet in the air when Lynda, Ange and Beryl arrived from King's Cross. They'd had a good journey down, although Lynda was limping and wasn't sure she could strut her stuff on the catwalk. The show organizer's husband strapped a magnet to her ankle and amazingly enough she recovered quickly. We started with the new routine, which seemed complicated at first, but we were soon professional and Lynda was able to perform without the trace of a limp thanks to the magnet. The clothes looked good on everyone, well apart from a frock of Ange's, in which she looked like her mother. CBS and Yorkshire TV were filming us rehearsing and the real thing. Preethi watched the first show and chuckled, then left to look for a job. The show was timed for the first break in the meeting and we discovered that Mr Blair had been given the slow handclap. We should have stayed in! Apparently, he started off OK, then launched into what was interpreted as a political speech and a few ladies objected verbally, then quite a large part of the assembly began a slow handclap. Helen Carey asked for respect for the speaker, and he finished soon after. The ladies I spoke to were not making a big deal of it, they just said they had not come to listen to a party political broadcast, so they gave him his 'fourpennyworth'. I admired them so much and wish I had stopped in and heard it instead of having my feet done.

The audience were fantastic for the next show, buzzing with the onslaught on Blair and so wonderfully supportive of us. We posed for loads of photos with different ladies. It was brilliant talking to them all. Agnes's producer John was there too, watching it all happen. The crew were lovely. The media were everywhere now with the slow handclap, what a thing, more PR for the WI. Interviews with *Evening Standard* and *Express*. Next fashion show in the lunch break. Ros and Christine would have loved this, I wished they were here.

We sold out of calendars quickly. The way of this calendar has been 'nothing sells like a shortage'. We could have sold hundreds here. At the end of the day we met Preethi outside. Her mum was making Lynda, Ange and me a curry that night. As we pulled into the drive, Angela saw John's photo in Preethi's bedroom window, looking down on us. It was the first time we had been to an Indian family's house for a meal and they were so thrilled it was theirs.

Indira had made wonderful stuff, which I couldn't pronounce. We talked about their village in Southern India, which has no electricity or running water. All day was taken up with making a meal and getting water. What a culture shock for us that would be. Preethi said it was a special place, with a calmness and peace. We said goodbye to Preethi and persuaded her to come to the show the next day when Suzanne, Juliette and Nick from Harbour Pictures would be there. We took a taxi to the hotel where Ange, Lynda and I were staying. An ace guy picked us up, with lumpy dreadlocks, father of eight, aged from three to twenty-four. What a character, he told us the meaning of life on the way to the hotel.

We awoke for our last day at Wembley. It was a lovely morning. Over breakfast we read all the newspaper reports of Mr Blair's handbagging by the WI. What a time for WI, two major media happenings in fourteen months, both free and with a positive feeling.

It had been a successful trip for us, lots of publicity for the new version of the calendar, meeting the 'grass roots' WI members, hearing their support and admiration for the calendar, but we were still in two camps as calendar girls. Although we never talked about the problems in public, that was saved for our 'meetings', when Douglas acted as our chairman, poor man, and tried to keep us civilized! I am sure Douglas felt he could sort out our problems but it was too deep now. There was a big rift between us, both sides seeing only their own point of view. Everything had started so casually with no rules or regulations (apart from 'no front bottoms').

Another one of these meetings loomed up on us. What would it be like? Ange and I had a gin and tonic in the garden before tea and she said how she dreaded going. I told her not to. She didn't have to put herself through it. She felt it was unfair to opt out but I told her we could have a rota system, and I would escape the next one. She was so relieved.

Had three more gins (just joking) and went to the meeting. No wonder there was world unrest when eleven women with a bit of publicity were like this. The main issue this time was the recent realization of some of the girls that Terry owned the copyright on the photographs. It seemed to be incomprehensible to them that the photographer rather than the subject owned the copyright but even if they were of the Queen, he would own them. This led to criticism of the deal with workman. Some thought the royalties we were getting were paltry, in fact they were above the normal calendar royalties. They also criticized the agent's fee, but without him there would be no publisher, so no money at all. When we did the original calendar, all the money went to LRF, because we did all the work ourselves and took no money for it but we couldn't keep going like that. The US calendar was a business deal with all parties to make a profit, including the LRF here and the Leukaemia & Lymphoma Society of America. Terry very patiently explained that Workman owned the calendar now but that we would continue to work for them, promoting it. As had been the case since the start of the calendar, this was not a job, we weren't contracted to work, we were volunteers, each girl needed only do those events she wanted to be involved with, there was no remuneration for anyone. I had been criticized for saying that before, it was a no win situation for me. I tried to remain silent, like Lizzi had told me, but sometimes, it was difficult. More than anything I didn't want it all to end in bitterness, souring the positive image of the calendar. It was Terry's turn for criticism tonight. Thank God I stopped Ange from being there.

Exciting news, the script was ready for the first reading. Juliette had been writing away in the background, while all the 'trouble' had been going on and now she'd met her end of May deadline. The seven of us who'd signed releases were now able to read her draft. Juliette had been to stay in Cracoe a couple more times and had watched the 'action' at the TGM. She hadn't managed to attend our WI, but had visited a meeting local to her. The girls who hadn't signed talked to her, in fact on one visit she'd visited Moyra's house for tea, so it was all very civil, but we didn't mention to them that we were about to read a script. In any case, our reading was supposed to be confidential. Angela and Matthew were to read the script first at Matthew's house in Harrogate. That night we went to Lynda and Terry's for a drink or a few, it turned into more as usual. We sat out in the garden, as it was the only remotely warm night for ages, until the midgies started to bite. Lynda and Terry had felt worried all week about the script. I honestly had not, just felt it would be OK, because I trusted Juliette so much, and Suzanne and Nick. Matthew rang at 10 p.m. and said it was brilliant. What a relief. Matthew had been worried and imagined that Juliette had not asked or seen enough of us, but she obviously had. Angela and Georgina were still reading it. Nick and Suzanne had left them to read it alone while they went to buy a takeaway Chinese. Matthew wasn't sure of the effect they would have on the estate: Nick in his linen suit, like he had been to Henley and Suzanne in her leather gear. Then Ange finished it and she rang to say it was brilliant, funny, sad, so clever.

The next day was our turn to read the script. I collected Ros and Angela, then up for Terry. Beryl was poorly, but she was fine as long as Angela liked it. We collected Lynda from the gallery. It was Juliette's birthday, so we clubbed together for Georgina's sunflower picture for her and gave Suzanne a funny little angel. They stayed at Grants Hotel and had booked a room for us to read it in private. Angela went out with them and left us. We promised not to talk – tricky for me – it felt like exam conditions and we had paper and pencils for comments. The opening was brilliant, very clever. She had handled Ange and John so well. It was a bit disconcerting to read the part based on me, fact and fiction merging to create a new character. There were swear words from me, but also from my son, who was a bit naughty, not really Micky. The other main characters, all mixed in too, were Lynda, Ros and Beryl. Terry's part was just right, he was pleased, or it could have been relief. John features until halfway through and his death is beautifully written. I had finished quickly, so lay on the floor and relaxed. We chuckled a lot but couldn't speak and made lots of notes. When we were all finished, we discussed our points to change and they were very similar. We moved down into the Bistro. Nick looked nervous when he saw our notes but we had a good discussion over dinner over which bits needed changing. All in all we were thrilled with the story.

Then it was down to Covent Garden again for a teacher training day. I met Preethi there for coffee and saw the calendar in a bookshop, felt thrilling. She turned it to my page. Preethi is very wise, but then an unwise person could not have written *Gypsy Masala*. I caught her up with the Stewart marital situation. She asked me if Ian was a good person, aside from my criticisms, and he is. We had just got lost somewhere. She made me think, was I doing the right thing?

King's Cross again heading home and Ian rang to say I had passed my exams, fantastic news. Then I rang Carol and as I was telling her a white feather floated down in front of me. Thank you Angel. I was so relieved I had passed my exam, it was amazing what you could do in the midst of marital traumas and promotion of a calendar, although not doing a proper job of work frees you up a lot. You just never know where life is taking you. In yoga philosophy it teaches that we don't reach our prime until fifty-five years old – not the beginning of the end, just the beginning. Can't wait – only another four years. By coincidence it was George's birthday – was he 7, 8 or 9 – who knows? He is better being ageless, then he will stay like a puppy. Once an age is attached, there is a certain expectation of behaviour, ignore it and act ageless. Like women.

Back at home, we did a lot in the garden, tidying up for prospective buyers. Ian had done a lot of running repairs while I was in London, stuff that had been terrible for ages. We had some people looking around the house. I have always hated that. Ian told me that when he went to put the house on the market the estate agent told him so many women in their fifties were leaving their husbands, then said, that 'fucking calendar'. Lots of people would think that, I am sure. Ian also said something else, which made me feel really sad. We were discussing the future, in separate places, grandchildren and weddings etc. He said to tell Lizzi that he would not come to her wedding if she would prefer him not to, although he had always dreamed of the band playing at any do, especially a wedding, her or Micky had. It was terrible to hear him say that. I realized how ostracized he must have felt these last few years. He told me that he had contemplated suicide a couple of times because he was so lonely. To the extent that he had mentally outlined suicide notes to Lizzi and Micky. I felt dreadful.

The next week in the office (for a change), I just thought Ian was different. He seemed to have got a grip on his life, not depressed and moving ahead positively and without me. He looked good having lost weight, seemed like the brill Ian had returned. Suddenly, I started to cry and realized that wasn't what I wanted, to be on my own and him in a new life without me. I left the office and went to see Ros to talk it over with her. She was brilliant, told me to say what I felt and be calm! Ian came home and we talked and I said I didn't want to sell up and go our separate ways. He was a little gobsmacked at such a turn-around, but Aquarians are eccentric! Not funny really. Anyway he took the For Sale sign down immediately, rang the estate agent and took it off the market. We had lots of soul-searching all weekend. Ian had moved on and was making a life without me, which was what I thought I had wanted, but when it was actually happening, I didn't want it any more. We decided to try and stay together. This would be such a shock to Lizzi after all we had talked about, but I knew I didn't want to lose Ian, and I felt so happy I had said so, well sobbed so really. We went to see Ange, who was delighted. She thinks John has something to do with this. I must say the robin was outside the window chirruping loudly.

Well, I don't know who or what was guiding our destinies but I felt relieved and almost as if I'd been given a reprieve, a second chance. When I thought about what I had done and where I had been over the last eighteen months, it was not surprising that Ian and I had had our difficulties. When I read my diary, I realized I had never been at home, either physically or mentally. Although others might have 'blamed' the calendar for splitting us up, I could only be grateful for all the magnificent opportunities it had put my way and that, after a fantastic time, it was as if I'd finally realized what my true priorities were. I knew it was not going to be easy, but I thought that Ian and I had a good chance of making it. We talked so much about how we had felt over the last two years, longer really, because before the calendar we had major problems. Talking it all out, however nasty, was the only way.

One day Ian and I were at the Devonshire pub in Grassington, sat in the garden, for our lunch, having a deep discussion about 'life'. It was quite an intense moment and a robin arrived in the pub garden, on the ground first looking at us, then on the table near to us. John just lending a hand when we were floundering a bit. Ian told me again how often he had thought of committing suicide over the last two years, he had felt so alone. I felt dreadful listening to him say that, because I had been so closed to him, I had had no idea. I am learning what it feels like now though, the feeling of rejection. I have definitely had a taste of my own medicine. Although he agreed immediately to stay, it was not as cut and dried as that because he had moved on to another phase of his life, one which he hadn't expected to include me. As he said, I'd told him often enough that I didn't want him. So he had found another direction to go in, found someone else who cared about him, when as Micky had reminded me 'none of us cared enough'. I was surprised because this someone was not a person I ever thought Ian would be interested in though I knew of her interest in him. We had been involved in business in Skipton with her and her husband for a couple of years. But then he had never been this low before and if this had saved him from sinking to the depths it was a good thing.

Micky was relieved, he helped a lot in our tricky moments with his calm way, no drama or histrionics, just common sense. I would ring him if we were having a testing time and he would come over from Harrogate, where he was working now, and be there really, bring us back to 'normal'. We had a lot of nasty stuff to get over and leave behind us. Lizzi was not so thrilled, still worried I was doing the wrong thing, but she has to work through it in her own time. We talked about all their young years, all the family stuff we did. We loved them as little bairns, thoroughly enjoyed their growing up. Ian played a major role in their childhood, always there for everything they did. We just had to look through the photo albums to see the joyful times we'd had. Somewhere in the middle the kids had grown up and we had lost each other. It was wonderful to have Micky and Lizzi sorting us out now, the roles reversed. I can remember how I took care of my mam eventually after all her years of caring for me. What would she think? She used to say 'you reap as you sow', she was right, as usual. What goes around comes around.

I was so lucky to have such a lot of support, from old friends and from new ones that I'd made through the calendar. I was in touch regularly with Preethi. I emailed her regularly about the Stewart marital situation and she was always gentle and wise. I called her my counsellor, my Marjorie Proops, not that she would have ever heard of her.

We were OK, middling to good as I told Preethi. After so long living separate lives it took time to adjust to being 'together'. Lizzi came for the weekend before her twenty-fourth birthday. Twenty-four years ago, on 18 August, I was sat in our garden in Skipton, 14½ stones, in a stripy dress like a marquee, waiting for her to arrive. My mam, Marg, Ralph, Steve and Helen all waiting for Lizzi. From first being born, she seemed like she knew stuff. As a little girl, I always felt she knew more than me. She has been a joy. Hopefully she would find the atmosphere changed. We had to put the past behind us and move on. It was all right, she and Ian were OK together. Ian was a bit on eggshells. She had to come round in her own time, it was between the two of them now. We bought her a new car radio for her birthday, hers was stolen a few weeks ago. We all went to the Angel pub on Saturday night, Micky came across from Harrogate. Lynda, Terry, Angela, Ros and Chris came too. It felt good to be like a normal family again. Still feeling our way a bit, but the journey of a thousand miles begins with a single step. Or so Confucius thought.

A few other leavetakings coincided with my decision to stay put: such is life – change is good. Natalie and Chris, the landlords at the Dev throughout the calendar, had decided to move on. The village would miss them, they had helped so much with the calendar right from the very start, especially the launch, which they had helped make such a success. Since then we had taken journalists, TV crews and photographers there, lots had stayed in the pub. It had been a great venue. Lots of calendars had been sold from there and there were framed pictures of the twelve calendar photographs on the walls. Their leaving do at the pub was a great night, packed. The Blues Band played and they were good, loads of new songs. Ian sang well, it was lovely to feel part of the 'band' scene again. Carol and I danced a lot, now and then with Micky, I tried to not dance like an old person for him.

We'd also heard from Ellen Morgenstern at Workman, who was leaving to go to Disney. We would miss her but I felt sure that our paths would cross again, perhaps with the film. She told me they would only want two of us for the next tour, probably Ange and me. That would set the cat among the pigeons. I hoped though that Ros and Christine would be asked, although I understood why they wanted Ange and me, they already knew we could do it, but I would have loved Ros and Christine to have the experience of a 'US Tour'. I had not expected any of the Rylstone Five to be invited. They had talked to the press about the split just when the US calendar was to be launched. I think that as far as Workman were concerned they no longer represented the spirit of the calendar.

The next trip would be after the presidential elections in November, but before Thanksgiving. The *60 Minutes* programme was scheduled to go out before we arrived to twenty million people. They had hung on to it for ages, to try and tie in with a tour. Ellen also updated me on calendars and dosh: they had now printed 210,000 calendars, plus our 88,000. That meant we'd earned about $750,000 dollars overall for research into leukaemia. What a feat! That was incredible, nearly 300,000 calendars around the world. Roll on October 1st when, weird to think, I would grace that many walls! Ellen had been a fantastic publicist for the calendar, she was still, in her last few weeks at Workman, organizing the next tour. She had been a major factor in our US success.

I had kept in contact with Helen Carey, the national chairman of WI, who knew about the differences in the group. She would have heard all sorts of differing reports about the 'ructions' from Rylstone. We needed to explain the situation. I didn't want WI to feel that we were tarnishing their image. She was a friend of a friend of Angela's, who lived locally and had planned to visit them and to meet up with the six of us next month. We had met briefly at the TGM, where she handled the Blair incident so well, all the TV and press coverage had turned out so well for the WI, thanks to her.

We had a productive meeting bringing her up to date on all the calendar issues. Then Ange told her more about John, his work within the National Park, how he was known as Mr Sustainability, a man before his time. He would have liked Helen, she believes in sustainable development, too, and was doing so much for the WI, nationally.

Meanwhile things seemed to have quietened down with the calendar. Ian and I decided we needed a holiday so we booked one to Santorini. We enjoyed the holiday, it was a wonderful island, very romantic, but things were still not just right yet. I was not sure that Ian was convinced he had made the right decision in coming back. I was being patient, I knew he had a lot to forgive.

I was thrilled to receive another invite to Woman of the Year Lunch this time at the Café Royal. It seemed I was the only one apart from Leni, who'd not been able to attend last year, and was unable to attend again. I wondered who had nominated us. I invited Terry because for the first time men were invited to a reception to honour men who had furthered the cause of women in the workplace. Well he certainly had, working on the calendar. However disappointed the other girls were not to be invited to the lunch this year, they took it in good heart and decided to accompany me to London. Or at least what we had now come to think of as the 'film' girls did – Angela, Beryl, Ros, Christine and Lynda – came down with Terry and they went off to meet the crowd at Harbour Pictures and then off for drinks at the Groucho Club. They had a terrific time, not spotting stars as they'd expected but bumping into a man from Rylstone. He recognized the sunflowers and said his brother lived at Rylstone, then he recognized Terry, who had painted his dogs, then Lynda told him she had painted his mother. I remember the portrait, a bit like Hockney's mother. You never knew who you'd meet in showbizzy places.

The Woman of the Year Lunch was brilliant, a different format to last year. A celebration of women's work in the morning with a comedy spot from Maureen Lipman, talking about the women who influenced her life, her mum and aunties, in her Jewish family. I missed Ros spotting celebs.

The lunch was wonderful. The women on my table were two TV producers, one wanted to do a film of our story, but too late. An Indian lady, must have been seventy-five, because she came to study here in 1949, so stylish with wonderful skin. Always on the lookout for a tip, I asked her what she used and she said 'Elizabeth Arden', I'd be buying it. The food was good and the conversation really interesting. Someone asked me how the calendar had affected the men – different answer for different women, isn't it? I declined to elaborate!

Before we knew it, it was time to meet the men, who were all assembled downstairs. I rushed down and spotted Terry amidst loads of men chatting to a couple like long lost friends. Apparently, though, all the men had assembled, stood about, looking at each other, not talking until a very forceful lady had told them all to talk to each other like women and then they were fine. We met the other girls downstairs in the bar. What a day. Some of the women at WOYLA had been going for ten years, and I hoped I was on the list for ever now. I had met some brilliant women.

One night, while I was having my shiatsu, I got into some fairly spiritual stuff with Hélène. She told me that my energy was calming and very beautiful. She said that with the calendar we were on a path, a mission, and that we were being guided. She said Ange did not need to worry because John was taking care of her, guiding her and would not let anything harm her, she was surrounded by angels. She could see loads of angels around me. One day I would see an angel, she was sure. Hélène and I often spoke like this. I really liked that sort of thing, which was probably why I took Angela's thing with birds since John's death so matter-of-factly. I think some people worried that it might be a bit of an odd 'obsession', especially as before John's death, Angela had seemed outwardly anyway to be pretty conventional spiritual-wise, but to me it seemed a perfectly natural way of dealing with grief and loss.

We went to the LRF Open Day at Newcastle University Medical school. It was designed to show fund-raisers the advances that had been made and how the funds were used. It was a nostalgic trip for Ian and I; we had both worked at the RVI as radiographers in the seventies. Ian drove Chris, John, Ange and me there. I had arranged with Andrew Trehearne to have a local artist called Penny Ward there. She was in her eighties and had watched the progress of the calendar from the start. She had painted a beautiful sunflower picture and wanted to donate it to the charity. It was so beautiful that Ange wanted to keep it for herself but LRF were going to auction it. Penny was amazing, eighty-five and still painting, such a lady.

We were a bit late and hurried up to the lecture theatre where everyone else was and they clapped us in. Each speaker mentioned the calendar and when we went into the lab there was me on the wall. It was so interesting seeing the research. Such progress has been made especially in the transplant field.

Micky had his twenty-second birthday which set me musing. I was married at twenty-two, not that I wanted my two to think about marriage yet, there was so much else to do. It was a good time though. For five years until Lizzi was born we were very free, holidays, speedboat and water-skiing. Then Lizzi and Micky became our lives, I didn't work properly for twelve years, so I enjoyed every minute of them. Had wonderful friends, did everything for the kids and had a very free, happy time.

*

Angela had received a request from the Leukaemia Society of America via a lady called Marlene Burbash, to speak at the Dublin marathon in front of their team of runners and fund-raisers. The runners participate for adults or children with leukaemia, either survivors, undergoing treatment or in memory of someone. They did what was called 'team in training' groups, their training was all very organized. Six million dollars is raised from each marathon, there was one a month in cities like Boston, Chicago, New York, Dublin, Honolulu and now London.

Once again, the film girls came up trumps and we decided to go as a group, with husbands – Beryl and Terry, Christine and John, and Ian. Angela and I would be funded, but all the others paid for themselves. We felt it was important for us to be there, with half the royalties of the calendar going to the Society, and also the relationship we had built up in America.

In fact it was one of those events that made us proud to have done the calendar. Angela and I flew out the night before the others to do the *Late Show*, the one that used to be hosted by Gay Byrne. It was a windy night and we were on a little plane with propellers but we arrived safely. A car collected us from the airport. The hotel was lovely, one of the poshest I gather, rooms very nice. We settled in, unpacked, had a coffee and walked in to town, because we were told it was only a fifteen-minute walk. Forty minutes later we were still walking, the Irish must walk faster. Still it was good to walk around Dublin. We took a taxi back. We got dressed and ready for the *Late Show*, then met up with the organizers from the L&L Society and arranged a breakfast meeting for the next morning to discuss our schedule. A really nice driver turned up to collect us and we took our gin and tonics in the car with us. There was another guy in there who we thought was our escort, but he turned out to be another guest, an American correspondent on the show to talk about the forthcoming US elections. We went into make-up, it seemed ages since we'd done that, so nice and relaxing. The host was Paddy Malone, a really lovely guy. We were on first. He asked good questions and the audience were great. We didn't want to come off, but that is no change. After us the next guest was a lady – the oldest survivor of the *Titanic*, she was eighty-six. What an amazing woman. She was nine weeks old when her parents took her and her two-year-old brother to make a new life in America. They were in third class and would not have survived if her father had not woken up and got them on deck. They survived, but he drowned. Until she was eight she knew nothing about it, then her mother married again and she learnt a little, but no details. What a story her mother would have had, how horrific to be on that ship. Years later her mother died and an aunt showed her a photograph of her father. That was all she knew until they found the wreck of the *Titanic* in 1989 and she was discovered too. Since then she has been to America twelve times, opened 'Titanic' bars and a restaurant in Ireland and was in great demand. She was so bright and loving every minute. She introduced her escort 'Bruno' and was raring to go after the show but Ange and I were shattered and left before her.

The next morning we had breakfast with the L&L team. They were so appreciative that we'd come. We were to speak at the Pasta party, the pre-marathon do, to spur them on and give them lots of carbohydrates to help them run, on the Sunday night before the marathon on Monday. There would be 2,000 people there, 1,500 runners, our biggest presentation yet. We'd go to the start of the run on Monday and cheer the team off, then follow on round the course. Monday evening was the Victory Dinner, again for 2,000, and we would sign calendars. They'd bought

500 and were selling them for $20, so would make $10,000 if we sold them all.

We had a day to wander round Dublin and soak up the wonderful atmosphere. People kept recognizing Ange off the *Late Show*, I think it is her hair colour. Everyone was so pleasant and chilled, it was lovely. We were brought back down to earth with a jolt, though. Ros rang to say the article by Georgina Howell had appeared in the *Sunday Times*. Georgina Howell had actually stayed with Angela. It was entitled the 'War of the Poses' and there was a big split across all the calendar photos, it was worthy of the pun of the week in the *Sun*. Lots of inaccuracies, like the calendar had divided the village and insinuating we had been friends since childhood and had our babies together, none of us knew each other when we had babies and for some it was a very recent association. Roy the postman wasn't mentioned, he would be disappointed, he had waited for it to be printed and he had played such a major part, delivering all that mail, but then she saw everyone and their dog, too. Ange was hurt by it, especially as the journalist stayed with her, and assured her she would not write a negative article. I suppose a lot of readers wouldn't notice the inaccuracies, just take in the reasons and realize what we have achieved for leukaemia research. It was only that we knew lots of it was untrue especially about the film, where it said that 'the five' knew nothing about a film until Victoria Wood came along, what rubbish. It was a shame, perhaps after all the fantastic publicity we should have expected a backlash – that seems the way of the British press. We'd had such amazing support worldwide, especially in America where they admired the calendar with such enthusiasm. But now there was a feeling amongst some people that it should be over, that we had done enough, or that we must be sick of it, which was sad. There's nowt so queer as folk, as my mam used to say. She would have loved the calendar.

But thankfully, we were in Dublin where it was impossible to be down for long. It was easy to ignore the pettiness when we were getting such immense support from the Irish and Americans around us. We went down to the Dublin Society Hall, where the Pasta party was to be held, which was massive. There was a podium at the end of a huge auditorium. We were introduced to loads of people, all thrilled we were there and taking photos with us. We ate first, then came the speeches, all really moving, we were all in tears. Such sad stories, all affected by leukaemia. A fifteen-year-old boy called Aaron spoke about his treatment for leukaemia, how he felt, the chemo and now here for the marathon with his mum. He was a brilliant speaker, such a great lad. It confirmed the reasons we were doing it. There were two massive screens like at an Eric Clapton concert. I opened our talk as usual with the background of the calendar, figures and sales, a few anecdotes, the amount raised; then Beryl spoke about WI and our American tour and about how she hadn't thought much of Americans before the tour but that now she loved them! Then she took her kit off, and put her American T-shirt on, very discreetly, but nearly gave Greg, an organizer who as at the side of the stage, a heart attack. Christine next told them about her original photograph playing darts, 'not much to hide behind in a dart'; she had a sticky moment talking about her tea shot when she mentioned the cherries on the buns, tricky talking about 'buns' to Americans. Angela finished with the story of the sunflowers, how the calendar had helped her, what John would think about it all and how she hoped the money we were raising would find a cure for this dreadful disease. We had photographs taken, signed cards and talked to the runners and survivors. In the bar (our local now) afterwards, we met a lady from New York who was running the marathon the next day. She said she'd seen the article in the *Sunday Times* and we all went quiet, not wanting to comment really, but she said we had to move on, it was negative energy and she could see a positive energy all around Ange.

We woke up to horrendous weather for Marathon day. I couldn't bear to put shorts on let alone run 26 miles in them. We got a taxi to the Liffey, crossed the bridge and met the 'team in training' at the start. Everyone looked so cold but still cheerful. A brilliant Irish coach encouraged everyone, he'd spoken the night before and was great. Ange had her blue pashmina round her head, she looked like 'Mary' (mother of Jesus – Mary). We chickened out for a while and sheltered in O'Neills where the waitress recognized us and gave us free lattes, twice. After we warmed through we proceeded to the ten mile point, and cheered them on, honestly we thought they couldn't continue, with purple legs, drenched through. A lady we'd met called Tammy, from Seattle, who was the longest survivor of a bone marrow transplant and was now having treatment for breast cancer, had her chemo at the ten-mile point, then ran on. They all finished, in that terrible weather, what an achievement. We watched them come in, wrapped tinfoil around some and cheered them in. Chris hugged a frozen girl warm.

We went back to the hotel on the Team bus for a wash and brush up. We were worried about Mr January contracting trench foot, because his trainers were drenched. Beryl bought him new socks, but wouldn't let him change until he washed his feet. He steeped them (his feet) in Ange's room and said they felt a lot better.

The Victory Dinner was amazing. In the same hall, all set up again with balloons, a band and yummy food. Everyone looked so good after 26 miles. There were signs saying 'Rylstone Ladies' and a table set up for us to sign calendars. We sat down at 7 p.m. and didn't move from there until 10 o'clock. Such genuine admiration and support for us and they had just raised $4,000 each and run 26 miles! We signed all the calendars, all 500, had our photos taken with runners and their families, chatted, laughed, cried. It was wonderful that Chris was there, because she hadn't experienced anything like we had in the US.

Ian, Terry and John were amazed, especially when they were asked to sign calendars too! We didn't see the band, but Ian played harmonica with them in front of an audience of 2,000, lots of whom were standing in line waiting to have their calendars signed. We took $10,000 in three hours. Ian was a part of it all again and it felt really good. If only we could sell software like that.

The flight home was OK, no bumps, God was kind. We all met at Lynda's for tea and to catch up, I can't count all the wonderful people we have met through this calendar, all the friends we have made and will keep, I am sure. It was a very special trip for all of us.

We were only back a week and still buzzing a bit from Dublin and then we were off again to America for the November tour. This time it was to be Ange and me doing a 10-city, 14-day tour and Ros was coming out for the first week to New York and Philadelphia. It was very apt for Ros, because she is Ms November! Workman were printing another version of the calendar, a twelve-month from January 2001 to December 2001 because they were worried that people wouldn't want to buy a calendar that started in June 2000, now.

Our publicist, Kim, had been sending bigger and bigger schedules through, the last one being twenty-seven pages long. I couldn't imagine being in all those cities, 10 cities in 14 days, we could be Japanese. Still I was really looking forward to it, like last time except the difference was that then I couldn't wait to leave home, but now I knew I'd look forward to coming home.

Ian took us to the airport. It was sad leaving this time but I managed to buck up when we were upgraded! We travelled in Business Elite on Delta, fancy that! Ange did it, just asked if there were any available upgrades, she was looking when one of the other girls asked what the sunflower was for. They had both heard of the calendar and we talked a while, then as we left, she handed us the tickets and said there was a nice surprise for us. Nice! How many times have you walked through Business Class and hated them, well that was us! We were so excited. Also tried to get into the Business lounge, but we weren't cool enough and let the superior lady intimidate us. Sat in Butlin's with everyone else. When we boarded, it was heaven, they take your coats, Gentle Ben (as I called my fake 'fur') was hung up! Leather seats, which tip back flat, with no one's knees in your back or lying on you in front, a newspaper, your own TV screen and a goody bag in the seat pocket. People who were used to travelling Business didn't look at a thing, but we had the bags emptied, socks on, mask ready for bedtime, cream on and were already looking around for extra ones for our girls. Soon it was drinks, champagne, then dinner with a damask cloth and a rose on the trolley (reminds me of Victoria Wood), chose dinner from the menu – imagine. No little plastic trays for us, real china and glasses. It was bloody champion. We could have been legless, but held back and drank plenty of water, we didn't want to look too wrecked on tour. We took photos of each other in luxury. Ange said it was a cross between the Ritz and the Yorkshire Clinic. It would be hard to be in steerage again. We slept, chatted, watched TV and ate and drank. What a flight. A bit of a downer though coming off. We were so intent on pinching an extra goody bag, and in Ange's case two, that she left her camera on the seat. Didn't realize until we unpacked at the hotel. Perhaps God was telling her something?

The same driver met us at the airport as in April. He drove to the hotel, with Ange and I, so well-travelled by now, pointing places out to Ms November. The highlights of this tour were many. It was odd to be there during the bizarre election where they couldn't decide who'd won. The *60 Minutes* programme went out while we were there: we'd had an inkling that it would but we didn't know for sure, even until the night it was broadcast.

We were in Philadelphia and had seen in the TV paper that
60 Minutes was on at 7 p.m. We didn't know whether we would
be on, but needed to watch it. We were still driving at 6.55, we
couldn't find a hotel, so we drove into Allentown, Pennsylvania
and tried to find somewhere with a television. Kim ran into a
restaurant, no TV, Ange into a supermarket, felt as if she had just
landed from another planet, we were in black with sunflowers.
Someone in the street suggested Woody's Sports and Pizza Bar
downtown. Kim ran in and said could we watch *60 Minutes*, the
guy asked how long that was on! Told him she had three English
women in the car who had done a pin-up calendar and it would
be on the programme. He said OK, and we walked in while she
was showing him the calendar. He looked quizzically at us and
said 'a pin-up calendar?' She changed the channel on the TV,
and my God there was Morley, just introducing us. The piece
was brilliant, featured Ros a lot, she shone, must have known she
would be here! We watched and at the end thanked the staff,
signed a calendar for them and left. They still looked bemused.

Well after that the whole thing just went manic. We heard
that at one Barnes and Noble, they'd sold about 350 calendars
the whole week before *60 Minutes*, then 450 a day after it had
been broadcast. We did lots of radio, some television and loads
of signings in bookshops. These were often the most gratifying
events. Somewhere, could have been anywhere, we appeared for a
signing and there were already people queuing. Lots of banter in
the line, especially when Ange wondered how many photos she'd
signed of herself showing her bottom. Strange but I never thought
of our being nude or that I was signing a photo under my left
nipple. It seemed way above that somehow.

At a St Louis bookshop Marlene, who had organized Dublin,
drove nine hours to meet us, bringing her mum and sister. Her
sister's son has leukaemia and was waiting for a bone marrow
transplant, he is nineteen, showed us photos, he looked like
Micky. This is his last chance. What a terrible disease.

At a Borders Bookstore a very poorly lady called Georgie welcomed us. We did a presentation to a full room, signed 200 calendars. It was a wonderful atmosphere. There were people driving to other bookstores to buy a calendar, then bringing it back for us to sign. As we left, Georgie thanked us again, told Ange not to worry, she is surrounded by angels.

On to a Barnes and Noble signing. We signed all the stock in the café, with people constantly coming up and talking to us, all because of *60 Minutes*. Back through Macy's and on to Ruminator's bookstore. Hoards of people there, they clapped as we walked in. Signed prepaids, then upstairs to an amazing queue. The biggest yet, I think. A lady devised a great plan, to open the calendar at February, and put the cardboard in October to save time for us. She could have sorted the elections out. All down the line we could hear that instruction. A lady in line had a phone call from her Scottish mum, who wanted to talk to us, and passed us the phone. After signing 450 copies, we sat down for some soup before leaving for the airport to fly to Washington DC. Looking out of the window at the snow, we saw a fire engine pull up and I assumed there must be some problem because of the weather. They came rushing in. Ange laughed and said, they will have come for a calendar. They had! They hadn't been able to wait in line because they were on duty, so had bought them for us to sign.

It was a blur of signings, bookshops and TV studios. At one NBC interview, we met Sharon Glass from Cagney & Lacey (I think we'd worn better than she has). We thought we were headed to another studio, the Mall of America, which turned out actually to be in a mall, a settee right in the middle of the mall. We had a great interview with a big lady, with seats out front for the audience. I looked up and saw Santa Claus sat there. His own hair and beard, it was like *Miracle on 34th Street*.

We flew between cities and often on small planes. Ange hated that part. I only realized then that she wasn't scared of a bumpy flight in case we crashed, but of someone being sick on the plane. She has such a phobia of sick, yet she could and did do everything for John, growing from a person who hated the smell of hospitals. She hadn't ever been drunk enough, a night over a red plastic bucket would have dispensed her demons!

All week Kim had been trying to slot in a meeting with Leukaemia & Lymphoma Society of America, in Seattle. In nearly every city we met up with a representative from that chapter. We told Kim we definitely wanted to meet up, just a coffee would do in between media, and a meeting was arranged in the Bank of America building. We parked in the underground car park and took two lift journeys to the 76th floor where the ladies toilet is famous for the best view of the city. We discovered that rather than a quick coffee it was a proper lunch in the Columbian Club so we went for a tidy up in the loo. Used all the creams and lotions, hair stuff and felt much improved. There were about fifty people waiting to meet us. It's hard to explain how people from the Society feel about us, as if we have done a marvellous thing. Some of the people we knew from Dublin and we were intro- duced to the others. Aaron, who'd spoken at Dublin, was there with his mum and was thrilled we had come. We never expected this. We sat down and each person stood up in turn and explained their connection with the Society, then thanked us for being there. It was all very moving, there was such an enthusiasm amongst them, which came from the fact that they were doing something positive to make a difference and, like Ange, they looked to finding a cure with the money they raised. Lots of ideas were exchanged. I felt we had a strong connection with them. Ange and I gave a talk, just the background and the stage we were at now. We did one final TV interview, recorded because of developments in Florida. It was OK to get a President now, our tour was finished!

We had to fly from Seattle to New York for our final flight home. We arrived at the airport ready for Ange to work her charm for the flight to NY. Most of them had seen *60 Minutes* and we gave them one of our only two remaining calendars. We were waiting in the Starbuck's queue and a guy in a red jacket came and asked for Ange, she said I was waiting for a coffee, he said we could get one where he was taking us. He led us to the Executive lounge. We were upgraded! I emailed everyone from the exec lounge, it was heavenly in there, how will we travel normally again?

Gentle Ben was hung up again in First Class. Another wonderful, luxurious flight. Champagne to start the day/night, whichever it was. Recognized by all the crew, thank you *60 Minutes*. Kim said the calendar sales have been mega while we have toured.

At New York, Ange found the most official-looking guy and asked to be upgraded. He would see what he could do, she was amazing on a mission. Shopped a bit, feeling jaded now, God knew what time it was in English! Speaking of God, we had made a deal with him, if we got upgraded we would not take any extra bags, just our own. We met a lady from Keighley, who asked Ange if she would be pleased when it was all over, did we think we had done enough. Such a difference from the enthusiasm we had evoked in America. A gentleman in a red coat came to tell us we were upgraded. Champion. No stealing mind. Sank into those leather seats, food, drink and a bit of sleep. I worked out that our last meal, the lamb dinner, was at 4 a.m. Said goodbye to the crew. What a tour, I can't believe we have been to ten American cities in fourteen days. What a thrill.

12

We were exhausted, exhilarated and on a bit of a high when Ian picked us up at Manchester. It felt so different coming home this time. We were full of chat about the trip, it was lovely to see him. Tired as we were, we headed straight up to Lynda's for breakfast and to catch up on the calendar news.

It hadn't been quiet here calendar-wise, either. Before the US trip Ros had been contacted by Suzie Lamb, the producer of – wait for it – the Royal Variety Performance. Ros took the call at work, and was asked if we would like to appear on the show, singing with Richard Stilgoe and Peter Skellern. Very coolly, she said she would ask us all, and immediately began the ten calls. Everyone was surprised and thrilled, apart from Beryl initially. She told Ros she wasn't sure because she had wine tasting on that day. Ros was just thinking 'what!', when Beryl called her back and said an emphatic 'yes'. Ros had done all the organizing and liaising with the producer. They invited Terry to be in the audience, which was great because he hadn't done all the high-profile stuff, just all the hard work. Ros had discovered it wasn't easy organizing ten girls, all outfits, size details, travel, rehearsal, where was the telephone chain when you needed it. I faxed loads of info which Ros had collected e.g. bra sizes, below bust, above bust, waist, hips, leg length, and shoe size, to the producer.

While we were away, the available six girls, including Lynda went to London for a rehearsal. The morning of our return, Lynda described the routine and the outfits. After all those measurements the flesh coloured 'frock' was a shift gathered at the top with elastic, not a dart anywhere! The black shoes looked OK, with big black hats. Strapless flesh coloured bras, too. Yuk! They enjoyed a great day, the wardrobe lady, Liz Nichols, who Ros bonded with, took them shopping for the shoes and hats and the gold silk dressing gowns for us to wander about in. Lynda put the song on and performed for us, very funny, she should have been on the stage. The idea was for us to look nude, covered with large song sheets of 'Jerusalem' – naturally. We were to come on for the last verse 'Bring me my bow', either side of the Stilgoe/Skellern piano, then shimmy on 'desire', hip forward, hip back, curtsey to the Prince, raise arms on 'smear myself in home-made jam', the song sheet would be attached to us somehow and stay covering us up. The routine was not complicated. Lynda loved it.

It was to be just ten of us because Angela had decided to go to Australia for Christmas to stay with friends of hers and John's. She would be away on the day of the show. It was the best thing for her to escape Christmas here, she would have a wonderful time in the sun. I also thought the Royal Variety Show would be too hard for her to bear. After the differences of this year, to think we are all on stage because John had died, would be too much to accept. Lynda said they had all been OK together at the rehearsals, no nastiness.

The day before the performance Ange flew off to Oz. Ian and I took her to the airport, it was sad to leave her. She seemed very alone walking through the gate, after all the trips we had done together. I hoped she'd meet someone nice on the plane to chat to on the long journey.

The next morning we were off to London. A minibus collected us all to go to Leeds for the train. The trains were in chaos, no booked seats, just piled on and grabbed one, we were all quite near each other, chatting and friendly, excited about the show. Cars took us straight to the theatre from King's Cross. We went backstage at the Dominion, given our passes and led up to costume. All our 'outfits' were bagged up separately with our names on. I tried my 'frock' on, strange, could be hideous, looked a bugger, especially from behind, but a clever idea. It was copper piping round our waists, which hooked up on to the song sheets, which were quite large, covered our torsos, but looked nude. Big black hats. Worked well.

We stood around in our frocks and dressing-gowns until we were called to go on stage with Stilgo and Skellern. The stairs were tricky in high black slip-on shoes. We ran through the routine, shimmy, wink at the Prince, established our positions, curtsey. It seemed OK, all the team were helpful and it was good fun. Terry stayed in the audience and watched all the reheasals, he said we looked good.

Ros and me were sharing a room at the hotel, which was just around the corner from the theatre. She usually shared with Lynda, who always ran her bath, but Terry was with Lynda this time. I slept well, no snoring, and ate a big breakfast for energy. We spent all day at the theatre, rehearsing all day for the performance that night. Performing takes a lot of time. It was great watching the stars rehearse. We watched Shirley Bassey, among others. Our dress rehearsal was in the morning. We were up and down the stairs for make-up, but kept having to get out of our seats for real stars, it was hectic in there! We didn't have a dressing room as such, we were in the costume department, piled in with the cast of 'Notre Dame de Paris', who were all very fit, and limbered up a lot. In our many trips up and down steps, we passed the dressing rooms for Kylie's dancers, Ronan Keating, Shirley Bassey and West Life. We were made up early, later times for proper stars. Ours would have to last all day. We did a good rehearsal, then back for adjustments to our song sheets. Mine was perfect. Ate a sarnie, relaxed, then rushed back for our frocks for the finale. I had brought Lynda's boned lace dress, which I would have to be forced into. At the finale rehearsal, we were in the wings with Ben Elton, Kylie, Jane Horrocks and such like. We all walked on to 'Oh Come all ye faithful', fantastic, we were in the second row. Led on by Lynda, me last, but that's OK, I wasn't bitter. The song sheet routine was good but short, reminded me of my Auntie Nell's comment, when she said I had nice hands, big but nice.

There was a full dress rehearsal for all at 2.30. We were knackered with all that up and down stairs. Made-up again but had to get out of my chair for Rowan Atkinson. Our 'frocks' had little flesh coloured pouches for our mikes, but I declined to be miked up, then I could sing in the divine knowledge that I would be unheard. As I said to Richard Stilgoe, at least I *knew* I couldn't sing, some people don't!

We had an hour break so we went out to eat, all in the same restaurant, with loud music blaring. I had arranged to do a Radio York interview, then the Johnny Walker show, so I went into the toilet to escape the music. I told Johnny I was in the loo, then Chris and Beryl came in while I was speaking, so I introduced them. Chris spoke, but when they came out they only flushed their loos, they hadn't realized it was live!

Then it was back to the Dominion and more make-up. We watched Prince Charles's arrrival and the start of the show in the costume room. Soon we were in the wings, then we were on the stage. I wobbled on my shoes while looking at the audience, then I forgot to shimmy. Richard Stilgoe announced us saying we were the ones who had the original idea for *the* calendar, and I thought 'that was my idea' and felt really proud. It passed so quickly, then we rushed off and upstairs to change for the finale. The costume lady hadn't got a good word for anyone on the show. She said the children on the *King and I* would need trauma counselling. It was very amusing, a wonderful atmosphere.

The *Notre Dame de Paris* lads were still stretching and limbering up, they were so fit, great young lads, we talked a lot to Quasi. I asked him about their show, how often they performed and what a brilliant cast they seemed to be together. He said it was all show, that they hated each other really. 'Oh,' I said, 'so do we.' Downstairs again to wait in the wings with the *Blast* team, Russians acrobats and the Omagh choir, so international. Fantasic to stride on singing 'Oh come all ye faithful', it was goosepimple stuff.

Then we lined up for Charles, just chatting with the stars. West Life were naughty, irreverent to the future king. The tall one out of the group, gave me the red feather that the producer had worn in his back pocket the whole time, but then a girl came to make me give it back. No souvenir! Charles remembered us from Harrogate. Lynda was sure he squeezed her hand harder than anyone else's! Lionel Ritchie was smiling at me and when I walked along the line to tell Lynda, she said he had winked at her. We went over together to him and she thanked him for all the years of pleasure he had given her, he gave her a kiss! The Russians, French, Japanese, Americans and West Life all wanted photographs with Mr Bean, 'Ah Mister Bean', he has universal appeal. I prefer Black Adder. Afterwards we all went up to the Circle Bar for drinks and nibbles and were all given programmes – our photograph was in the 'Royal Variety Show' programme! We talked to lots of performers and met the Welsh national choir. They were lovely old men, they liked Beryl, must have sensed her singing ability, said they wanted to come and sing with us. Finally we walked back to the hotel. What a night. I couldn't remember going to sleep. So no change there. Ros and me giggled a lot, though.

Felt a bit fragile the next morning but we were able to take it slowly. Had a leisurely cuppa – water – no teabags left, we must have had them last night. We came around slowly. I ran Ros's bath, so she wouldn't miss Lynda too much. I was starving, had breakfast, then made a sarnie again, never know when we may need it. Moyra and Lynn had already gone to record a 'Handy Hints' type show for the BBC. Terry, Lynda, Chris, Beryl, Ros and I went off to Chelsea Harbour for lunch. They had never been, so it was lovely for all of us to meet up at Harbour Pictures' office.

We took a taxi back to the hotel to collect all our stuff, including song sheets, then, car to King's Cross. The train wasn't too crowded so we had no trouble getting song sheets on with frocks, cases and sarnies. Long journey with not much chat, we were all tired. When we eventually arrived at Leeds, the minibus was there to take us all home. It was a good swansong for the calendar, a fitting finale.

I had an email from Ange saying she'd arrived safely. She'd had a wonderful flight, best ever. She was recognized on the plane and taken to dinner at Raffles in Singapore. She said she felt like a celebrity.

Angela was fortunately going to miss the final calendar girl meeting. Where better to be than Oz? I wouldn't have let her come to the meeting anyway. For the original eleven, the calendar was coming to an end. We had decided this would be the final meeting. The US calendar had sold out and since the five had never been happy with Workman 'owning' it anyway it seemed a good time to end it. We heard from Kim with the figures, they were amazing. Workman had sold 210,000 calendars (added to our 88,000). There were only a few left in this country, mostly at WH Smith's in Harrogate. It was fitting for the Royal Variety Show to be our last engagement as a team.

Nonetheless I felt the usual dread, waiting for the usual tense atmosphere, but overcame my trepidation and took lots of calendars to be signed, in case we weren't all together again. Others had done the same, we signed calendars and Christmas cards for each other in quite a jolly way! The meeting went well. I tried to take Lizzi's advice (she'd had a running commentary about our troubles) and say very little. Beryl only had to touch my arm once to stop me. Douglas Osborne from LRF, who'd been chairing our recent meetings as an outside and neutral party, wound it all up, congratulating us on the success and achievement. A few sticky bits, the 'five' wanted all contracts and copyrights to be held by LRF. By this they meant the Workman contract and the film contract, which as it stood was held by all seven of us who'd signed a release individually. But Douglas, while trying as always to be helpful, pointed out the impracticality of that.

It was also suggested that way back in the beginning we had made an agreement for each girl to have her outtakes back. We'd actually made no formal agreements on anything, way back, just blindly plunged into the whole thing, but whatever, there was no security in having them in ten pairs of hands. However, Lynda intervened here to explain how hurtful the suspicion and criticism of Terry had been, but said she agreed that the girls who wanted their photos destroyed should have their wish. Ultimately, Terry had sole ownership of those photos, but he agreed to burn the relevant copies. That option was accepted. I didn't want mine burnt, there is something a little macabre in burning images. Lynda would organize the witnessed burning, so there was proof to prevent any more solicitor's letters disputing the facts.

We toasted the calendar with champagne. All signed more calendars for each other and Christmas cards to send out to sponsors. Douglas left. The meeting wasn't as hostile as some had been but I was still glad that Ange was away for it.

There was a pub quiz after the meeting, so the usual quizzers went through to it. Now these meetings and main media are over it might be easier to be civil with each other, but it would never go back to how it had been before. We had all been challenged with this calendar and found wanting, all of us! Surely though an experience to be proud of, we had made a mark, done something good out of a tragedy. It was Roy's (the postie's) quiz. He always does a good one, with a music round which Ian likes especially. Guess what, we won, me, Terry, Lynda and Ian. Lynda and me tend to make the numbers up. A good result, Ian and Terry have won for four weeks, they would be hated soon.

To put it all in perspective, it was today that Marlene's (from L & L Society of America) nephew has his bone marrow transplant. He is Micky's age, and this was his only chance. They live in Cincinnati and drove nine hours to meet Ange and me in St Louis on our US tour. This was the reason why we did the whole thing and we must never forget that, while we were drinking champagne and bitching on.

What had worried me most about the split with the girls was that it might damage the image of the calendar. That was the reason we never replied in the press, just tried to keep our dignity. As Douglas said, you couldn't air your differences in the national press. Who knows, maybe it had spiced it up a bit in some people's minds but what came next was in a different league entirely. It really shook me.

A couple of weeks before Christmas Terry and I were doing an update of the year for the *Craven Herald*, outlining all we had done, any regrets (we said no), any downside to the calendar (again no), would we miss it (I said yes, Terry not really), just generally talked about this last year. I was full of joie de vivre, because Terry had brought me my Christmas tree. I was looking forward to decorating my tree after Terry left. Ten minutes later the doorbell rang and two men stood there. The one who spoke was young, longish hair, overcoat, quite cityish, the other was smaller but in the shadows. Asked if I was Mrs Stewart and said they were from the *Sunday People*, there to talk about our marital problems. I just felt horror. He said he had talked to several people that afternoon, knew the whole story, but would like my side before it went in the paper on Sunday. I told him I would be interested to read it and shut the door.

My first reaction, sitting on the stairs was how dreadful life must have been for Paula Yates, who had died so recently, with scum reporting her life to the world. This was nothing on that scale I know. My second thought was what an awful way for the calendar to end, with crap in a paper like the *Sunday People*, after the tremendous success. Fortunately we didn't know anyone who read it. Then I rang Ian who made a few calls and discovered they had already been to Skipton trying to find us and asking questions. I didn't want to make it into a drama, so didn't tell anyone else. Unfortunately it was also WI Christmas dinner at the pub, and I couldn't *not* go. I went over early in case the 'reporter' was there, but no sign. Then I discovered that the paper had been in contact earlier in the week with Moyra, wanting to do a piece on the men behind the WI calendar. As if! Not wanting to say too much, I suggested we avoid such a lowlife paper.

Fortunately everyone knew about Ian and I splitting up in the summer, and that he had seen someone else for a while. While we were at the WI dinner, Ian discussed it with Terry who said it would be fish 'n' chip paper next week. When we met up in the pub afterwards, he warned Moyra to tell her group to be careful who they spoke to. I was worried that they would try and find Lizzi and Micky which may have seemed paranoid, but unless this sort of thing happens to you, you can't imagine the panic you feel. I did find a feather, so maybe my angel would take care of it.

A bizarre thought, the next night while sitting in an Indian restaurant in Halifax – the week before I'd been on stage at the Royal Variety Show; perhaps next Sunday I would be in the *Sunday People*. When we arrived home from Halifax, there was a letter pushed through the door. It was from Adam Moss of the *Sunday People* and as I read it, I felt my flesh crawl. It claimed that a third party had given information about Ian and I, and that they were planning to run the story. They thought we should cooperate because they did not want 'to cause any more distress by questioning your friends and family'. They thought they might make a feature of how our marriage had survived this trauma. It concluded: 'I believe it would be best for everyone concerned if you were to cooperate. At least then, you would have some control over what goes into print.'

I couldn't believe it, on *Sunday People* paper, he must have written it after I closed the door on them and put it through, but thankfully, I didn't look until tonight. What kind of person writes that, it was threatening really. It made us want to retaliate, but then we'd sink to their level, and to be honest who reads the *Sunday People*? The main sadness for me was who told the paper and why. Had someone really rung up, or had they made it up to get me to answer? I couldn't think it was a calendar girl. I still can't.

I warned Lizzi and Micky not to read it. I didn't want them to have that image forever. It will make Ian out to be a bastard, which he wasn't. We must stay strong together, now we all realized what we nearly lost, and I didn't want some scummy newspaper or the evil person who instigated this, to win.

I tried to look on the 'bright side' and carry on as normal but it was difficult. On a day when there were no reporters I just thought well who are they talking to now? We went for dinner at Terry and Lynda's. They had been brill through all this, so encouraging, Ros, too as always talks such sense, was so lovely and caring. It would have been so much harder without their support. As with the whole calendar. Thank God Ange was away.

It hung over us like a cloud, not knowing if or when it would be in the paper. I felt sure they would tie it in with the TV screening of the Royal Variety Show but thank God it wasn't. Terry looked first thing and rang us with the all-clear. Beryl, Terry, Chris, John, Ros, Chris, Lynda, Terry all came to our house to watch the Royal Variety Show. I had said nothing to Beryl and Christine, I knew they would be mortified. Ian cooked Indian for us all. Lynda arrived regally, just like the Queen with a tiara on, fur coat and very much lipstick. It was fantastic watching it, remembering standing in the wings, with the copper piping around our waists. How long was the camera on Lynda? Of course I didn't mind being last on and hardly seen! Nor did Christine! We loved watching it over and over again. In fact the whole show was good. Ros heard (from her source) it was the most enjoyable one for Prince Charles.

Another day, another scum reporter. A grey-haired old guy in a navy suit with a briefcase – must have had the lowdown on me in there – turned up at my door. Perhaps they sent an older man to try and get the story where two youngsters had failed. I so wanted to push him down the steps. He was small, I could have easily. He sat outside in his BMW and I quelled the desperate urge to go to the dustbin and push a couple of topstones on his car. I just closed and locked the door. He returned two hours later, this time with his mac on, it was foul weather I am pleased to say for him to snoop around in.

I spent a horrible knotted up night, but I couldn't let this upset me so tried to let it go. Ian felt dreadful. Next Sunday they said it would be in, but who knows. Another Sunday to wait for. It would be Christmas Eve, how festive. Just had to remember this was nowt to what Princess Diana suffered permanently, everything written about, crap photos, trying to demoralize her, spoil her life. She couldn't trust the people she confided in, luckily we could. What a lowlife career in the gutter press. Perhaps they spend their afterlife in hell up to their necks in other journalists. If it was in, there must be a reason, why at this stage would the calendar be soured?

Marg and Ralph arrived on the 21st for their pre-Christmas visit. They were staying until Christmas Eve. We ate in, then went across to the pub to see Ros. I hadn't told them about the 'issues'. I didn't want to worry Marg if there was no need. I felt it wouldn't be in, but Ian and Andrew at LRF (who I'd told) thought it would be. Thank God Ange was in Oz. We hadn't told her anything, no point. She was swimming, sunbathing and going out to dinner a lot, sounded wonderful and I wished I was there. We emailed a lot, it was tricky trying not to mention it, when we had always discussed everything.

Hell it was nearly Christmas Day, where had the week gone? I worked in Halifax to finish the year off and was late home to Marg. My heart sank when she told me that a guy had been on the phone eight times to speak to Ian. She had been so nice to him, joking with him, thought he must be a friend, when he asked for 'Ian' (why would she think otherwise?), then gave him Ian's mobile (old one, but she didn't know). I was just about to tell her about all the crap, when the phone rang again and I answered. The guy asked for Ian, I asked why, he said it was personal and even though I was family he didn't want to say. I realized he obviously thought I was Marg, we sounded so alike, so I let him. He was very reluctant to tell me, but I insisted I wouldn't pass on the message unless he gave me more details. He said he was Chris Tate, the editor of the *Sunday People* and it was imperative that either Mr or Mrs Stewart ring him immediately, which was how they panic you into a reaction. I said I would pass the message on and if they wanted to speak to him, they would ring. Then we told Marg and Ralph it all. Fortunately they knew the truth about Ian and me but were horrified, and couldn't believe it really. Ralph suggested we give our side of the story, but I still thought we were right to say nothing. My mam would think my life was even more like a penny novel now. She said I lived in chaos, but seemed to enjoy it. I had always liked a bit of something going on, but this was too much!

The next night we were singing carols in the Dev at Grassington. Beryl and Terry spotted us trying to get to the bar and asked us to sit with them. Beryl knew now and was disgusted with the papers and worried for us. That was the thing, really, it wasn't for me, but all the people who would be really upset for us, and didn't know the truth. It was good to sing carols, drink mulled wine, eat mince pies and forget the crap. The collection was for the heart fund for Sally Slater, the little girl who had the heart transplant, she had done so well. Two brilliant fund-raising ventures from one area. Surely nothing would happen to spoil the positive effect of the calendar?

Ian was convinced it would be in. We had such an interesting conversation when we got home. Made me chuckle. Our relationship had improved so much in the last few weeks, so much closer than we had been for years – nothing like a little shake up to make you realise what you are losing! We were talking about how awful the last few years had been, how alone Ian had felt, even before the calendar. One thing I hadn't realized had petrified him: I used to play Gabrielle's 'I will rise again' in the car, so it was always on when he drove the car, he thought that's what I was doing without him. He also said he thought I had turned 'gay', because of all my women friends, and how distant I was from him. It made me laugh but he was serious. And I have never ever owned a pair of denim dungarees!

Amanda was coming up again for Christmas – we hadn't scared her off with the tense atmosphere of last year. A different kind of drama for her this year. She was flying up on Sunday, Christmas Eve, and we were going to collect her from Leeds airport. She texted me from Heathrow to say 'it' was in. She said the article was crap but that I looked good! The headline read 'Strip calendar: jilted Miss October gets the pip'. Ian thought 'Hunt for Miss October' would have been better. It was tucked away in the middle, cobbled together with small photos. It said I was a shapely blonde, living in a whitewashed cottage. I didn't want to see it. It made Ian out to be weak, just looking for something to do while I jetted off round the world, making money for charity. I was determined not to let it get to us, it was nothing to us. Let us keep our dignity, and worry only about the people who do matter to us. Lynda and Terry said it wouldn't harm the calendar and was good publicity for the film.

We collected Amanda and went straight to church to pray for the editor of the *Sunday People* to slip on the ice and break his legs, only joking. It was a lovely service. Ange's parents, Frank and Joyce, both did readings, good stuff in the sermon, especially for a person vilified that very day in the gutter press. We told Rachel the gruesome news, totally shocked her, but like everyone she feels for us. Milky coffee and mince pies afterwards. I love chapel coffee, always makes me feel safe, especially today with all those nasty reporters. What I did feel though, was that lots of people would think I had got my just deserts, that it served me right. After all the good press, TV and accolades that I had it coming. I wondered whether I didn't feel a bit that way myself. I never felt I had the right to object or try and stop any of the crap, I felt it came with the territory, that we had been lucky with all the wonderful coverage and this was to be expected now.

Lizzi cheered me up with this Christmas thought: Do you know what would have happened if it had been three wise women instead of three wise men? They would have asked for directions, arrived on time, helped deliver the baby, cleaned the stable, made a casserole, brought practical gifts and there would be Peace on Earth.

We rang Ian's dad to tell him not to read his copy of the *Sunday People*. Unfortunately too late. They have known nothing of our difficulties, so it was tricky to explain after an article like that. They had so enjoyed the calendar, proud of their connection and the achievement, what a way to sour the success. I hoped it wasn't the talk of their 'club', the Blyth Spartans. Their only concern was for us and Lizzi and Micky. Our poor bairns, fancy seeing your parents in the *Sunday People*, not that they would read it. Could be worse though, I suppose, it could have been the *News of the World*!

We had Christmas Eve night drinks at Terry and Lynda's, their granddaughter Helena was so lovely, laughing at the wiggling Santa. Lynda showed us her nativity scene in the inglenook

fireplace. Unfortunately she had lost baby Jesus, so now he was a
bean, yes she had actually painted a bean, with a little face, in
swaddling clothes. May sound strange, but it looked good, cute
even and like baby Jesus. This could be a new Christmas line for
the Logans. Reminded me of when Lizzi and me made all that
papier mâché stuff, boxes and dolls, and Lynda put them in her
gallery, but told people they were made by local children because
they were so crap. We talked about the piece in the paper, trying
to dismiss it. Matthew would send a bill to the *People* for using
my photograph. He would make them donate some dosh to LRF,
so you see some good will come out of evil. It was evil, too, and
terrible to think someone wanted to harm us. If in fact it was
true that someone had rung the paper, or had they made that up
to get a reaction from me. Also there was the posibility of idle
gossip to a journalist when asked if the calendar had caused any
marital rifts, well actually Tricia and Ian . . . I would prefer to
believe the latter, instead of wondering 'who' all the time.

   We had to just call in at the Dev later that night, to face the
public. Amanda is a positive presence to appear with. People
looked a bit uneasy as we walked to the bar, it went rather quiet.
Moyra, Sandra and Rita were at the bar, but said nothing. David
(Red Leader) commiserated with Ian, and a couple from across
the road said how sorry they were, that they hadn't read it, but
they had obviously been given the full story verbally. Everyone
else had obviously read the paper and they seemed more embarrassed than us. Sales must have increased in Cracoe and Hetton
alone! I felt a bit threatened, then pulled myself together. There
aren't many folk who have nothing to hide, especially from the
Sunday People. What a risk if it had been someone I knew. I
wondered if we would ever know. A heartwarming moment,
when Ben (Micky's friend) said, leaning on the bar beside me,
that he thought I was really brave to have come in, he admired
me for it – made me want to cry – but I didn't!

   Well it had happened and the worst was over, or so we

thought. But then, on Christmas Day a reporter from the *Daily Mail* tried to get to us. Yes, actually on Christmas Day. Mr Wallace rang us from their detached whitewashed cottage at the fell gate, obviously the reporter was looking for the 'shapely blonde in the whitewashed cottage' as reported, and mistakenly thought the description was true. You would think *they'd* know not to believe what they read in the press. We knew he was on the way and I persuaded Ian not to open the door, he so wanted to hit him. Thank God Micky wasn't here, because between them they would have done and felt a lot better. He was a puny little specimen of a boy. Ian said if this had happened in his grandma's mining village of Cambois, everyone would have rallied round and got rid of them. But just a young lad on a job on a Christmas morning. A very different kind of Christmas morning.

No reporters on Boxing Day, felt a bit cheated. Just joking. It was hard to believe another New Year's Eve was nearly here. Last year we were all together at the new village hall, well me and Ian weren't exactly all together, but thank you God we were now. What a difference a year makes! We had a wonderful walk showing Amanda the delights of Malham, thought about John, with all these people eroding his paths. He would have hated it. It is such a popular place with the limestone pavements and the Tarn. The Park have relaid all the walkways, it looked well cared for, that bit would make John happy. We had only managed the Sheep Pens once this week, a complete breath and two corkscrews.

The next day Amanda and I met Carol at Bolton Abbey teashop for coffee and to give her birthday presents. Another glorious day, it restored my soul in spite of snooping reporters. Gregorian chants in church. Bought little prayer cards, this is where I found 'Footsteps', which was read at John's funeral. Ian went to the Dev, put a few people straight about the article over a pint! Then went to collect Lizzi from the airport. She had been in Ireland for Christmas, flew back for a few days on her own, then Adrian was joining her in Cracoe for New Year, while we were away in the Lakes. George would have them to look after him. In a strange way it had been a lovely Christmas, a bonding experience!

The next morning we went to work, leaving Lizzi in bed. She rang us at 2 p.m. She had not been long up, still in her Ralph Lauren pyjamas, with mascara all over her face. A guy from the *Daily Mail* came to the door (so this is 'door-stepping'), Neil Sears, with the usual sidekick photographer, whom she recognized from the launch, perhaps he was with the *Yorkshire Post* then. He asked for us in connection with the article in the *Sunday People*. She told him we wouldn't speak to him, and started to close the door, at which point he asked her age. She told him that was of no relevance to him, and just as the door closed he asked if she was eighteen. Feeling flattered she locked the door, then realized because of the state of her and her spots, he probably thought she had teenage acne. It's all a learning curve, she handled it well. However the reason he asked was because he needed to know if she was over eighteen to be able to take a photo of her. The bastards, that was all they were, what if there had been a crap photo of Lizzi, alongside the 'other' woman? How would Lizzi have coped with that? Surely there could be no interest for the same old rubbish to be in another paper. *Sunday People* readers were one thing, but *Daily Mail* were another kettle of fish. Micky could deal with it, not read it, or listen to anyone talk about it. The effect would be greater for Lizzi, who was working hard at rebuilding her relationship with Ian. To see another, or even to know there would be another despicable article was too much to take.

We went to Keswick, in the Lake District for New Year to stay with friends of Lynda's and Terry's. On New Year's Eve Lynda and I were the cabaret at midnight, 'tasteful mind, nothing crude'. We just slipped into our Royal Variety show outfits and did our turn to the WI song. Seemed to go down well, Ian said it did, so must have been OK. Obviously no *Sunday People* readers there, nothing scummy mentioned. It was wonderful to be away from the phone and papers. We met some great people, Ian was on form telling jokes, someone asked if he was a stand-up comedian. The next day Terry's friend challenged the group to top his contribution to the party, 'nude' dancing girls, a stand-up comedian and a stunt man (Terry fell spectacularly into the Christmas tree).

Bad news when we arrived home, a *Daily Mail* phone call from Neil Sears, Ian told him he was wasting his time. Ian was sure it would be in now, I didn't think so. If no one else spoke to them, there was nothing new. I asked my angel not to let it. This morning I found a feather and showed Ian, but he said he was sick of sunflowers, feathers, angels and robins. Then he went to put the milk bottles out and there on the step was a robin, hopping up and down. Made him laugh. Thank you John.

Back to work, hard to get up early and walk George. Ros and I didn't quite make it to the Sheep Pens, well to the first gate. We haven't done it much lately. Roll on spring, it was so dark in the mornings, Ros and I needed torches.

We had an email from Ange, wishing us all Happy New Year. She was in Adelaide, she spent a very hot new year there, telling our jokes one every half-hour over dinner. She'd been to the tennis, got great tickets and saw the Prime Minister in the members' box. Typical of Ange, she'd decided to go up to him and had a nice chat. He said, 'Don't I recognize you?' Ange blushed, thinking he's seen me in the buff. Then he said 'Didn't you used to play tennis for Britain?' They were off to Blackpoint at the weekend, a 'shack' on the beach. She was very excited about reading the second draft of the script. Suzanne told me it was nearly ready and they would come up to us and send a copy to Ange in Oz. We decided to wait until she came back, it seemed silly to read it separately.

I did a talk on Pilates at WI. It had seemed like a good idea last January when I proposed it. Needed to swot up, it was so long since I'd done any! Not a good thing for a trainee teacher to admit, but I did *think* about it a lot. I felt quite nervous, but didn't have any Triple A. I tried to look thin and like it was doing me good, I wore black lycra and breathed in a lot. Chris was my model and she looked good. Supper was yummy. No more contact from the *Daily Mail*.

Ros and I got to the second gate next morning, still pitch black. We were building up after the festivities. Ian and I were looking after Sky while Lynda and Terry were in Brighton, and she was difficult to see in the dark. I got back and was just sorting through my desk when Ros rang to say it was in the *Mail*, horror. I rang Ian straight away, he bought a copy and read it out. Not a lot different from the *Creople*, with a few extra pathetic one liners. He rang the pub and asked them to remove their copy from the bar, so everyone wasn't reading it in there. Then I rang Lizzi. I was so sorry because whereas no one she knew would read the *Sunday People*, lots read the *Mail*. I wondered if anyone would comment to her. I felt sick. I rang Marg, Ibb, Lynda and Terry, Andrew Trehearne, Diana and left Micky a message on his mobile. It was a very cobbled together piece, nothing new, but awful headlines, 'WI cash in on nudes'. It sounded like we were taking money. A laughing photograph of me. I had never had a full page to myself before, why now?

In a strange way it was a relief, because we didn't have to wonder if or when it would appear. I felt so miserable and could have cried, but I had so many lovely phone calls that I thought 'pull yourself together' and I did. Lynda and Terry phoned from Brighton, so sorry, but Lynda said I must be famous, because in there were Princess Diana, Madonna, Catherine Zeta Jones, David Frost (looking big on a beach) and me. It was Lizzi and Micky I was most concerned for, but they were both ace, so I was fine. I hoped no one in her office saw it, but at least her photo wasn't in. (She'd have been doubly worried since she'd worn the pyjama top they would have got on camera into the office as a blouse. Everyone would have known if he had got a shot of her.)

The night after the article appeared we braved the pub and went to the quiz. You have to do it. Guess what else we got that day, a letter from the *News of the World*, could we go any lower? This time they offered us money to 'set the record straight once and for all' and added: 'We would treat it with sensitivity, knowing how stressful the emotional situation must have been.' It had been delivered by hand. Of course the *News of World* is known for its sensitivity. Ian made sure he was overheard in the pub saying we had been offered £50,000 for our story. He also warned the other calendar girls that it might not stop with us and to be careful: papers looking for dirt usually found it.

I still thought our best policy was to say nothing. However if they were paying they might get a good story from someone else. People would always sink to their own level, and there wasn't much lower than selling your story to the *News of the World*, just taking the money for spewing out personal issues, especially when there were family and children to read it. No good would come from this kind of money. Do you know, though, it is an ill wind. Lynda bought the *Daily Mail* because of the article on me, she never buys it, but in it there was a vegetarian diet, which she did and lost 6lb.

Fortunately I had my yoga day here with Barbara, and the usual gang. Only Barbara knew about the papers. Jill, her daughter had seen it, and she was mortified, told me I needn't mention it if it upset me. But they knew about Ian and me anyway, so I just filled them in on how those kind of papers got their stories. We had a lovely day and I felt recharged by them, as usual. All they cared about was that we as a family were OK, and that was all that mattered. I always had a tale to tell them, especially since the calendar, but this beat all. They had been there for me throughout, with a blow by blow account each month. This even surpassed the female condom episode. I kept them at the forefront of innovation. When Marg's friend worked for the Terence Higgins Trust, she gave us one of the first female condoms, it looked like a small freezer bag. I showed it to all the yoga girls and they were absorbed, what a conversation we had, and they were totally ahead of the frame when news filtered through to the rest of the country!

The next morning, Fred (who lives opposite our house) rang us, because he had noticed there had been a black Saab parked in the pub car park for over an hour with a guy in it, very interested in our house, with a clipboard, so he took the registration. Ian looked out and the guy immediately picked up what he thought looked like a camera. We rang Rob, the pub landlord, who told him to move out of the car park, and saw that he had a telephoto lens, laptop and his mobile phone, all set to send our photos down the line for tomorrow's paper. He drove off, then Richard from the pub saw him at the corner and rang us. We were just about to walk George and Ian said we should stay in. Instead we put hats and sunglasses on and in disguise went out. Ian looked like Noel Gallagher. By now I was finding it all very amusing. I didn't want some creep to be paid for a different photo of us, if we looked like anybody or nobody all covered up, there was no point printing it. After that we got the coal in wearing hats and sunglasses. When our friends Margaret and Ian came for the weekend, we all went out dressed like that. I thought we should all wear masks, especially answering the door.

Nothing in the *Screws of the World* yesterday, but I think Ian Botham saved us, poor guy with a big story on him. He and his family have raised millions for LRF. That counts for nothing. We now know how much of that article will be implied. Still in hats and sunglasses to get the milk in! I had kept the dining-room curtains closed all day, it was pathetic. Told Andrew at LRF this morning. He thinks that if this had to happen to anyone it's a good job it's me, because I can deal with it. I suppose that is a compliment. He also told me that they had made a breakthrough in the treatment of leukaemia, what wonderful news, the press and TV were at their offices. This was what Ange meant when she said we may raise a million and it may be the million that they need to find a cure. Our money will have helped this research, and that was why we are doing it, not to be dragged into the gutter by the press. As Oscar Wilde said, we are all in the gutter, but some of us are looking up. Where are those journalists looking? Ange emailed to say she'd been swimming with seven dolphins today, perhaps she saw Flipper. I will swim with dolphins one day.

The day that Ange came home, we took Frank to the airport to meet her, he was very emotional when she walked out. She looked wonderful, tanned and healthy and relaxed. The plane had landed at Bombay and was full of people fresh from a dip in the Ganges. Ange looked the same colour. Ian had a sneaky look in the *News of the World*, nothing in, but such a load of crap about lots of other folk. How do people believe that, they must never get out. Chatted all the way back, but didn't tell Ange the dirt, I would have to do that later when she came for tea. Two days before she was up to her ankles in sand, now she was in snow. There was about 4 inches this morning.

It was awful telling Ange, she was horrified, so sorry it had happened to us, and she hadn't been here to help us. It was extremely depressing having to say it all, Ian was upset, it seemed worse somehow. He thought that it was the end now, but I felt they would hang on to it until there was talk of the film in the press. I had to realize that each time I am mentioned this crap will probably be in.

Terry got £1,000 cheque for LRF for my photo in the *Mail*, some good comes out of evil, waiting for the *Sunday People* now – who would be next?

Ian got a call from Neil Sears again, answering an alleged call from him. What! A bogus call, pretending to be Ian, leaving his mobile number, which was a new number, hardly anyone had it. And a bogus email to the *News of the World* saying 'I am Ian Stewart, the husband of Miss October, I wish to sell my story, please ring', and his new mobile number again. Ian rang both, explained the situation and left a password which he would use if he did ever want to speak to them. It was like MI5. Well, we had to change our home phone numbers – who'd have thought it? The nightmare continued. Silence was still the best reaction.

Though I did try to complain to the Press Complaints Commission. I would never have thought to complain, but we had been harassed by reporters and our privacy invaded. Terry put me on to them because there had been quite a bit about a party the PCC (as I now know them) were holding that evening which Prince William and Prince Charles were due to attend. It seemed worth a try. But the guy from the Press Complaints was not in the least impressed with my sense of humour, I tried very hard. Told him I should have been invited to their 'do' along with Charles and William, but he just told me to complain directly to the editors, then if it still persisted to call him back. No editors were available because they were all getting ready for the bloody 'do'. I spoke to PAs, who told me I had to put it in writing, so I faxed and posted it, outlining the sequence of events. Nothing happened. Hopefully, everyone else who mattered would ignore it as well. Perhaps this would stop it, but I was not sure of anything any more.

The following week I heard from Workman that they wanted to produce a 2002 version of the calendar, using the same pictures. They had advance orders of 50,000. LRF were thrilled, but the five girls refused, via their solicitor. They wanted the calendar to end and their lives to return to normal. So for five of the naked ladies the calendar had come to an end. Who knows, maybe they are right to want it to end, but I can't see things that way. For no effort we could have raised a lot more money for research, we never know who of us will need it, without fund-raising there will be no cure found.

A fitting epitaph? The outtakes were burnt. Lynn witnessed the burning at Terry and Lynda's, on behalf of Moyra, Sandra, Leni, Rita and herself. She signed the form to say they had been destroyed by burning, a little pagan ritual. I kept emailing Lynda amusing messages about silver bullets all day (very childish) 'Firecracker'; I called her and told her to wear a string of garlic.

Despite their desire for it all to end, the calendar girls were still in demand, especially in America where we had been invited to Seattle to the Annual Meeting of Leukaemia & Lymphoma's big charity lunch the following May. Six of us dearly wanted to go and now that there were no calendars we needed something to take to sell. We thought of a photo of the six of us, made into a postcard, following on from our calendar shots, but as a group, perhaps we'd call it 'six of the best', but then Mr September came up with the brainwave 'Baker's half dozen'. We did it around Lynda's kitchen table in one hurried evening. Just slipped out of the dressing-gowns again, Chris across the table holding a cup of tea (not wringing her hands together this time), Beryl with her president's bell, Angela with 'Jerusalem' song sheet, Ros still knitting that scarf, Lynda with her palette and me eating one of my apples.

So for the rest of us, Baker's half-dozen, we get on with our lives and continue to enjoy what bounty the calendar brings us. We have a full 2001 schedule of talks and presentations, which we love and miss each other when we have nothing planned for a while. There is no question that though the calendar's main intention of raising funds for cancer research has been abundantly realized, it has also brought us as individuals countless blessings (and in some cases challenges). For Ian and I the challenges have turned into blessings. What doesn't kill you makes you stronger.

I think we all look forward to the film with anticipation. Another exciting experience awaiting us. I hope that above all Angela is happy with its portrayal of the painful events of her life. It's not over yet.